The Human Rights Enterprise

Political Sociology series

William T. Armaline, Davita Silfen Glasberg, and Bandana
Purkayastha, *The Human Rights Enterprise: Political Sociology,
State Power, and Social Movements*

Daniel Béland, *What is Social Policy? Understanding the
Welfare State*

Cedric de Leon, *Party & Society: Reconstructing a Sociology of
Democratic Party Politics*

Nina Eliasoph, *The Politics of Volunteering*

Hank Johnston, *States & Social Movements*

Richard Lachmann, *States and Power*

Siniša Malešević, *Nation-States and Nationalisms: Organization,
Ideology and Solidarity*

Andrew J. Perrin, *American Democracy: From Tocqueville to
Town Halls to Twitter*

John Stone and Polly Rizova, *Racial Conflict in Global Society*

The Human Rights Enterprise

Political Sociology, State Power, and Social Movements

William T. Armaline,
Davita Silfen Glasberg,
and Bandana Purkayastha

polity

First published in 2015 by Polity Press

Polity Press
65 Bridge Street
Cambridge CB2 1UR, UK

Polity Press
350 Main Street
Malden, MA 02148, USA

ISBN-13: 978-0-7456-6370-8
ISBN-13: 978-0-7456-6371-5 (pb)

A catalogue record for this book is available from the British Library.

Typeset in 11 on 13 pt Sabon by
Servis Filmsetting Ltd, Stockport, Cheshire
Printed and bound in Great Britain by Clays Ltd, St Ives plc

The publisher has used its best endeavours to ensure that the URLs for external websites referred to in this book are correct and active at the time of going to press. However, the publisher has no responsibility for the websites and can make no guarantee that a site will remain live or that the content is or will remain appropriate.

Every effort has been made to trace all copyright holders, but if any have been inadvertently overlooked the publisher will be pleased to include any necessary credits in any subsequent reprint or edition.

For further information on Polity, visit our website: politybooks.com

Contents

Acknowledgments

We would first like to thank all of the thinkers, teachers, artists, revolutionaries, students, activists, journalists, whistleblowers, agitators, and organizers – famous and nameless – who gave their lives and freedom so others could have a shot at a decent world.

This book is our attempt to place a critical sociology of human rights and sociological concepts ("human rights enterprise," "human rights praxis") in the canon of human rights scholarship. More importantly, this book is meant to inform a human rights praxis that might directly confront oppression and threats to collective human survival.

Very special thanks are owed to Roseanne Njiru and Erika Del Villar for their work copy-editing and compiling the index. If our work meets the critical standards of an academic readership, it's because of their tireless efforts to clean and finalize our manuscript. Similarly, we're indebted to our many reviewers for their guidance and constructive criticism. Scholarship should be tempered – worked and reworked for strength and aesthetic. This is never done alone.

On that note, we would like to express our endless gratitude to our editor Jonathan Skerrett and production editor India Darsley at Polity Press, and to copy-editor Helen Gray, for the editing, stewardship, promotion, and production of this book. We are fortunate to have met such fine, talented, and hard-working professionals in this process. Additional gratitude is owed to

Acknowledgments

our friends and colleagues at San José State University and the University of Connecticut for their continued support.

We would also like to acknowledge our friendship and mutual support over several years working together on two books, journal articles, and several conference presentations. We have each become better teachers and scholars from our friendship, and highly recommend that others in academe take advantage of opportunities to do the same.

Davita would like to thank her ever-growing family: her children Morgan, Gillian and Scott, Irwin's children Alan and Julie, Terri and Rich, Aaron, and Liana, as well as her grandson Scottie and Irwin's grandchildren Jarrod, Sammie, Eli, and Jonah. They continue to inspire her, teach her so much about humility and humanity and all that truly matters in this life, and enrich her existence beyond measure.

Bandana would like to thank her family and friends across India, France, the USA, South Africa, England, and Australia, but especially Indra and Aheli Purkayastha who have to live through endless nights and weekends of work, and who continue to cheer every book and every achievement as they take on all the work left undone. A special acknowledgment of the memory of all the family members on whose shoulders she stands today.

Finally, William would like to thank his wife Nicole Steward and dog Chomsky for reminding him of everything worth living for. He would also like to thank Blake, Asa, and Donaisha for their laughter and joy.

1

The Human Rights Enterprise and a Critical Sociology of Human Rights

Introduction

As teachers, we share the experience of students asking about the "point" of human rights in the United States, since no one seems to know or talk about them, and since they carry little weight in US courts. While we disagree with the notion that formal international human rights are irrelevant, we owe our students and readers the courtesy of honest reflection. The United States is far from internalizing and employing international human rights practice, and has a contradictory relationship to human rights as a body of international law.

This book goes into production as a leaked Senate Intelligence Committee report now details the extent and highly illegal nature of the CIA's use of "harsh interrogation techniques" – torture – at Guantánamo Bay and other secret "black sites" across the world, following the September 11, 2001, attacks in New York City. The Guantánamo Bay detention facility is in itself a direct challenge to the civil and political human rights to due process[1] and protection from arbitrary arrest and detention.[2] Of the 154 people still imprisoned at Guantánamo Bay from 22 different countries, 76 of them have long since been cleared for release by the US government, and 45 of them are being held even though the US government admitted that it lacked the necessary evidence to bring formal charges of any kind. In total, the US has imprisoned 779 people there – *at least 21 have been children, the youngest of whom was only 13 years old* (ACLU 2014). Techniques of torture used on suspects and detainees at Guantánamo and other detention/rendition sites "included waterboarding, which produces a sensation of drowning, stress positions, sleep deprivation for up to 11 days at a time, confinement in a cramped box, slaps and slamming detainees into walls" (Watkins, Landay, and Taylor 2014). The international community has repeatedly condemned CIA torture programs as a violation of international law (UDHR, Article 5; ICCPR, Article 7), but up until this point the US Justice department, CIA, and Department of Defense have argued vehemently that the interrogation techniques were legal, and did not amount to torture ("cruel and unusual punishment") as defined by the 8th Amendment of the US Constitution. Previous arguments by the Justice Department's Office of Legal Counsel stated that methods like waterboarding were not torture because those carrying out the interrogations "didn't have the specific intent of inflicting severe pain or suffering" (Watkins, Landay, and Taylor 2014).

However, the newly leaked report punches holes in these already questionable legal claims. It includes evidence that "The CIA used interrogation methods that weren't approved by the Justice Department of CIA headquarters. The agency impeded effective White House oversight and decision-making regarding the program. The CIA actively evaded or impeded congressional oversight of the program. The agency hindered oversight of the program by its own inspector general's office" (Watkins, Landay, and Taylor 2014). In addition, the report calls into question the thesis of former Bush administration officials and award-winning film *Zero Dark Thirty* – what comedian Bill Maher rightfully called a "despicable product placement for torture" – that techniques like waterboarding were somehow effective in the pursuit and prosecution of Bin Laden and other al-Qaeda leaders. Indeed, the defenders of US torture programs in pursuit of the disastrous "war on terror" in the Middle East and North Africa cannot argue their efficacy, even on the now tired basis of "national security" and "keeping people safe." These programs, and the efforts of Bush and Obama administration officials to passionately defend their legality and legitimacy, at the same time refusing to even consider criminal indictments of program architects, embody the completely contradictory and hypocritical stance of the US government with regard to the "rule of law," international law in particular. They also demonstrate a central flaw in how we go about "doing" human rights in the world – where state governments are assumed to reasonably represent the interests of their people (rather than, say, the interests of capital or the elite), and states are structurally positioned as the guarantors of human rights practice in the world.

Further, the international legal system designed to facilitate universal human rights through the actions of member states currently struggles to keep pace with threats to collective human survival, let alone rights practice (Chomsky 2007a; Schellnhuber 2012; Parenti 2011; IPCC 2013). Beyond such blunt responses, it's difficult to engage the common questions of our students in our professional roles since sociologists in the US have yet to engage fully with academic or applied work explicitly dedicated to human rights.

With all that in view, we have two goals for this book. We first aim to identify the potential contribution of (political) sociology to the studying and realizing of human rights, and to define a "critical sociology of human rights" as a maturing, relatively new[3] concentration. Second, we'll demonstrate the utility of political sociology to interpret, critique, and re-envision contemporary *human rights praxis*. Human rights praxis refers to the process through which theory, scholarship, and/or cultural practice inform social action to realize human rights, and, in turn, how the empirical history of human rights struggles can and should inform scholarship. We hope our work provides a provocative and convincing argument on how to inform and participate in human rights struggles, while demonstrating in some detail how sociologists make significant contributions to contemporary human rights scholarship.

Political sociology is a strong and vibrant specialty in the broader discipline of sociology and social science. Political sociology evolved through investigations of power, particularly in describing the relationship between the state,[4] the economy, and society.

This specific body of political sociological literature is referred to as critical state theory, the subject of chapter 2. Simply speaking, political sociologists are concerned with understanding how power works in, through, and between human societies. Specifically, political sociologists tend to examine various forms of domination and resistance, measures of inequality, and the ways that ruling relationships between people and between societies are affected by social movements, as is demonstrated by social movement theory, the subject of chapter 3. Political sociologists have a great deal to offer human rights scholarship in that: (1) as sociologists Freeman (2009, 2011) and Woodiwiss (2005) suggest, laws and (human) rights are ultimately expressions and embodiments of state institutionalized *power*, which is a central concept for political sociologists; (2) international human rights law is a product of treaties and agreements between *states*, and conceptualizing the state is a primary goal of political sociologists; and (3) efforts to *define and realize*[5] human rights have often taken the form of social movements. Indeed, the history of human rights can and should be seen as a history of social struggle over very real matters of power, resources, and political voice.[6] These realizations should have significant implications for how one goes about doing intellectual and applied human rights work, and should place certain demands on previously dominant approaches.

Dominant approaches

Traditionally dominant human rights scholarship from the fields of law and political science has tended to focus primarily on: (1) formal legal approaches to defining and realizing human rights in our world (international law and international relations); (2) the various legal and philosophical traditions that provide the foundation for what we now understand as international human rights and humanitarian law (political theories); and (3) the relationships between state policy and politics at the national and international levels (international relations and comparative politics).[7] In other words, the story of human rights is often focused on the story of the United Nations (UN), and the origins and evolution of human rights as a legal concept and body of international law.

From a legal standpoint, human rights are defined and articulated by *human rights instruments*, formal agreements between participating UN member states that *sign* (agree in principal with) and *ratify* (enter legally binding agreement with) the instrument. The most basic, original, legally fundamental set of human rights can be found in the cluster of instruments called the International Bill of Human Rights (IBHR), consisting of the original Universal Declaration of Human Rights (UDHR), and its binding Covenants, the International Covenant on Civil and Political Rights (ICCPR) and International Covenant on Economic, Social, and Cultural Rights (ICESCR). International human rights are further articulated through "single issue" instruments such as the International Convention on the Elimination of all forms of Racial Discrimination (ICERD), and the Convention on the Elimination of all forms of Discrimination Against Women (CEDAW). Many but not all of these instruments are legally binding as international treaties. The international obligations of most states under multinational or bilateral treaties are found in and articulated by the Vienna Convention on the Law of Treaties established in 1969 (Goodhart 2009). Specifically, states that sign and ratify binding human rights instruments are bound to *respect* (not directly violate the treaty), *protect* (prevent others, such as private corporations, from violating the rights defined in the treaty through the rule of law), and *fulfill* (create an environment in which people can reasonably enjoy their rights) the rights defined in the instrument (Donnelly 2003, 2010). These instruments ultimately codify human rights as legal obligations of member states, subject to the ability, will, and resources of states and state actors (governments) to fulfill these international legal obligations.

The United Nations and human rights instruments evolved out of the observation that states could not always be trusted to ensure the rights of their citizens, as made clear in the acts of genocide and nuclear destruction that characterized World War II (Lauren 2011; Ishay 2008). These same states granted themselves the authority and responsibility of designing and implementing human rights and humanitarian law through the newly minted United Nations. One might note the seemingly obvious contradictions of such an expectation, while noting the repeated inability since the inception of the UN to persuade states – powerful ones in particular – to meaningfully ratify key human rights instruments in full, let alone abide by their stated legal obligations. Scholars have for some time pointed out the simultaneous near universal acceptance of fundamental human rights and the legitimacy of international bodies of law, and the equally common tendency for these same states to excuse non-compliance with international law due to *state sovereignty* (Donnelly 2003; Ishay 2008; Stammers 1999).[8]

Powerful states like the US often undermine the binding nature of ratified instruments through inserting "fine print" or *reservations* – most commonly, the claim that instruments are "not self executing" (Hertel and Libal 2011; Blau and Frezzo 2012; Armaline, Glasberg, and Purkayastha 2011). In so doing, the global hegemon takes great care to define its role as a chief architect of legal instruments, without any of the pesky responsibilities or obligations outlined in those instruments (Chomsky 2007a, 2007b).

Absent straightforward enforcement mechanisms that are more common at national and regional levels (such as the European Union), international human rights instruments are often bolstered by oversight organizations whose purpose is to monitor and, to whatever extent possible, encourage the implementation of human rights by member states. These oversight committees are typically established through *optional protocols* – additional agreements that can supplement instruments with a variety of tools or provisions meant to facilitate compliance. Common examples would include the United Nations Human Rights Committee, established by the First Optional Protocol (114 member states) to oversee compliance with the International Covenant on Civil and Political Rights (ICCPR), or the Committee on the Elimination of Racial Discrimination (CERD) established to oversee compliance with the International Convention on the Elimination of All Forms of Racial Discrimination (ICERD).

The collectivity of these international legislative bodies,

oversight organizations, and the growing number of officially partnered *non-governmental organizations* (NGOs) vested with the task of ensuring human rights, are called *human rights regimes*. These regimes can be found at various levels: global (UN), regional (such as the Council of Europe/European Convention on Human Rights (ECHR)), or local (such as "human rights cities"[9]). The assumption of human rights regimes is that they have the authority and ability to hold states – or the appropriate level of state government – to the letter and intent of human rights instruments. Although theoretically the establishment of international human rights instruments and human rights regimes would seem to introduce a powerful agreement among nations as to the meaning of human rights and their obligation to ensure them, in practice this is simply not the case. For instance, research suggests that the ratification of human rights instruments does not seem to have a "normative" effect on human rights practices within the member state, particularly for less democratic states (Hathaway 2002). This is not to suggest that ratification is meaningless. It's to suggest that ratification isn't the end of the story – we cannot assume that legal rights in theory translate to practice. Indeed, we live in a world that is incredibly far from reflecting universal human rights practice with any consistency. We will return to this point full force in coming chapters, controversial for some dominant scholars but seemingly obvious to everyday people struggling under neoliberal capitalism, war, state surveillance, incarceration, foreign refugee status, and impending ecological collapse.

Without delving too deeply into the large and well-represented body of literature in political science and legal studies concerning human rights instruments and human rights regimes, it can be said that "legal scholars and political scientists have dominated the study of human rights and, as a result, these studies focus on the courts and governments, almost as if the state alone were responsible for human rights innovations" (Clement 2011: 128). This is not to suggest that formal, legal approaches to defining and realizing human rights are somehow unimportant, illegitimate, or completely ineffective; nor that scholarship on the legal aspects of human rights work has no place. In fact, we join others (Blau and Frezzo 2012; Hertel and Libal 2011) in urging powerful and resistant states like the US to ratify and internalize any number of international and regional instruments, such as the American Convention on Human Rights (ACHR). To be fair, for traditional scholarship out of law and political science, the focus on states and legal regimes is as much a feature of disciplinary necessity as of intellectual choice.

As Foucault (1977) suggested of disciplines such as criminology in relation to modern forms of punishment and social control, scholarly disciplines often form and evolve in many ways to reify uncritically the very institutions, policies, and practices under investigation. In this sense, traditional disciplines are at a loss to explain the central problems and contradictions that continue to plague efforts to achieve universal human rights practice via international law and the duties of states. Unlike political sociologists, the fields of law and political science tend to treat the state and its legitimate authority as somehow assumed and unquestionable, where the state and its legal authority are social facts that elude critical reflection or thorough conceptualization in real (particularly political economic) contexts. Further, these often-positivistic analyses of human rights work begin and end with the creation of legal rights and mechanisms.

A similar critique was levied by anthropologists representing the *ethnographic turn* since the late 1990s, who suggested that human rights scholarship failed to analyze whether or not – let alone why – any number of human rights instruments and legal mechanisms had any effect on the ground, in the lives of actual people. In this vein, they (Wilson 1997, 2001, 2006; Cowan, Dembour, and Wilson 2001; Goodale 2006) investigate the "social life of rights," insisting that the success or failure of any international or national law meant to facilitate human rights practice would ultimately depend on how real people in real socio-cultural contexts come to interpret and then interact with state mechanisms and state policy. Similarly, sociologists since the 1990s have entered the human rights stage motivated by the gap between legal discourse and social realities, particularly exacerbated and brought to light during the height of social conflict over neoliberal economic globalization.

Toward a critical sociology of human rights

Sociological analyses of human rights offer a welcome and much-needed addition to a body of scholarship long dominated by other fields. This should come as no surprise given the legacy of scholarship for the explicit purpose of social justice and social change that defines even classic critical sociology (e.g., Karl Marx, W. E. B. Du Bois) as a body of intellectual and political work (Feagin and Vera 2001). Sociological work explicitly dedicated to the concept of human rights seems to have most recently emerged when social problems such as skyrocketing global wealth disparities and disastrous neoliberal development plans came to the forefront in conflicts over economic globalization in the 1990s. This body of literature illustrated the usefulness of classic sociological theory and method for the analysis of human rights as a concept, legal regime, and broader body of social movements (Turner 1993, 2006; Waters 1996; Stammers 1999). Sociologists and some critical anthropologists immediately set themselves apart from dominant human rights approaches with their *social constructivist* approach (Waters 1996; Morris 2006) while questioning the notion that rights practices could be achieved through responsibly acting governments rather than the social movements so often needed to keep them in check (Stammers 1999). This would seem readily apparent from the anti-globalization movement at the time that openly targeted corporate and state power represented by new, powerful, non-democratic, unaccountable international decision-making bodies like the World Trade Organization (WTO). At the height of the anti-globalization movement, well-documented, high-profile street battles and sustained civil disobedience erupted in cities like Seattle to resist the unchecked power yielded by solidarity between corporations and powerful military states (McNally 2006; Klein 2000, 2010). Contemporary forms of public demonstration, resistance, and organized disobedience, as well as the police and military strategies to confront them, have all arguably been shaped by this period of political conflict.

Critical sociologists, also informed by the anti-capitalist and anti-war movements of the past 20 years, go further to conceptualize human rights as a contested terrain and product of social struggle (Clement 2008, 2011; Armaline and Glasberg 2009; Armaline, Glasberg, and Purkayastha 2011). They work from an historical observation: the struggles that ultimately define and realize human rights are often against or in spite of the states charged with the protection of rights in the first place. Further, human rights struggles are increasingly shaped by and targeted toward systems of privilege and oppression and their social and ecological effects – neoliberal economic globalization (capitalism) in particular. This recent body of critical sociological work should be seen as a precursor to what follows here, as it built the beginnings of a consistent critique of human rights as a legal project and shed light on the implications of critical sociological inquiry – how human rights can and should be "done." That said, there is still no easily identifiable, theoretically consistent *sociology of human rights* that offers both a fundamental critique of dominant approaches to human rights, and uniquely sociological concepts with clear applications for public intellectuals in the field of human rights.

We aim to join others in changing that here. Drawing from recent scholarship (see, for example, Stammers 1999; Sjoberg, Gill, and Williams 2001; Blau and Frezzo 2012; Freeman 2011; Blau and Moncada 2005; Brunsma, Smith, and Gran 2012; Clement 2011; Armaline and Glasberg 2009; Armaline, Glasberg, and Purkayastha 2011), we will generally define the critical sociology of human rights as an approach with at least five unique characteristics: (a) law and legal discourse is seen as socially constructed and understood as an expression and source of institutionalized power; (b) the state and other formal bodies of institutionalized authority, such as the United Nations or International Monetary Fund, are approached critically and are fully conceptualized in appropriate structural context(s); (c) civil, political, economic, social, and cultural rights are seen as inextricably linked (rather than exclusive categories of rights from which states can successfully pick and choose), particularly at the level of human rights practice or implementation; (d) sociologists, if public intellectuals, are presumably concerned with formal human rights regimes and international law – or human rights scholarship for that matter – to the extent that they tend to inhibit or facilitate *human rights practice*,[10] however substantively defined;[11] and (e) sociologists share the historical perspective that human rights as a concept and practice are ultimately the product of social movements and social struggle.

Why we need a critical sociology of human rights

If we apply political sociology to analyze the relative success or failure of human rights as an intellectual and legal pursuit (Are human rights working? Why or why not?), a fundamental critique of dominant human rights scholarship and formal, legal human rights regimes emerges. We see that often states – especially powerful states like the US, Russia, or China – cannot or will not meet their international legal obligations as defined by human rights instruments (Armaline and Glasberg 2009; Clement 2008, 2011; Blau and Frezzo 2012). This is largely because of conflicts over state sovereignty, "national" (read: dominant) interests, and the lack of necessary resources and/or political will to meet such obligations.

Political sociology helps us to understand the relative failure of states to realize universal human rights practice in real political economic contexts. State theory and empirical research on the connections between state and capital suggest that states, particularly within the context of neoliberal global capitalism, are far more constrained by the wishes of capitalists and the shifting structural necessities of the capitalist system than by the material and political needs of the vast majority of people. Seen in context, human rights are "one of the few countersystems available for critically evaluating, for example, the neo-liberal political and economic model, which has attained almost total global dominance" (Sjoberg, Gill, and Williams 2001). The instrumental and structural limitations placed on states by capital directly confront the expectations and model put forth by formal human rights regimes and traditionally dominant human rights scholarship. States are defined as the primary responsible mechanisms and "duty-bearing" parties for achieving universal human rights practice. For these instruments to work, state governments must choose human rights practice over the accumulation of capital for the corporate owning class, wherever these interests conflict. Unfortunately for proponents of classic Western liberal theory, such rights protection is far from the norm. What deeper understanding of states and modern institutions of rule can be gleaned from what seem to be such obvious, but often overlooked, observations? *What if states commonly cannot or will not provide the most fundamental dignities to their people?*

Moreover, the question of whether and how well states recognize and enforce human rights is not simply one of motivations and intentions of political leaders: these leaders function in an institutional setting where non-governmental actors from powerful institutions (particularly economic actors like corporations and financial institutions) affect the state's ability to do so. For example, even a well-meaning state will be hard-pressed to provide for human rights to food, shelter, healthcare, education, and adequate employment in the face of corporate decisions to export jobs or international aid regime impositions of structural adjustment programs (SAPs) as the conditions upon which aid is secured. Such was the case when Mexico was forced, in 1981, to accept a structural adjustment program imposed by the International Monetary Fund (IMF) at the expense of the state's ability to provide for a wide range of social welfare expenditures. This loss of domestic policymaking power in the face of powerful non-governmental actors has been repeated around the globe as a feature of neoliberal capitalism and "development."

Further, the state itself is not a separate, independent entity when it comes to other social institutions; it enables and supports various institutions (education, for example) that in turn confine and affect the state's range of discretion. Perhaps most importantly,

the capitalist political economy affects the state, even as it is structured, made possible, enhanced, and encouraged by the state. For
example, as we will see in chapter 2, the US Congress deregulated
the US banking industry in the 1980s. This empowered financial
institutions to engage in highly risky and at times illegal practices
that ultimately undermined the national and international economies, while enriching the banks and their leaders. In so doing,
the state's ability to address increasing hunger, homelessness,
and unemployment were consequently and willfully constrained.
Similarly, corporate interests in the military-industrial complex[12]
escalate fears of international terrorism that in turn coerce state
policymaking to engage in unjustified and illegal wars (e.g., the
second US invasion of Iraq) and to compromise the right to
privacy,[13] among a myriad of other constitutional and human
rights, in the name of national security.

Finally, states do not exist in a vacuum, disconnected and iso-
lated from the rest of the world. This is why political sociologists
speak of *political economy*, to demonstrate the inextricable link
between states and capitalism, and between owners and rulers – if
and when they aren't the same people (Parenti 2010). How do
global capitalism and neoliberal approaches to global economic
development, for example, affect states' ability to implement
human rights, particularly in the contemporary political economic
climate of global recession and state austerity? *Global economic
restructuring*[14] refers to the reorganization of international economic policies and practices since the 1970s, including public and
private relations and processes of production and finance capital,
by existing economic and political elites. That is, powerful corporate actors such as major corporations and commercial banks,
along with key state actors, strongly influence international policies and practices to ensure that these policies and practices remain
consistent with their interests. This reorganization continues to
have enormous effects on the political, economic, social, and
cultural relations within and among societies, and shapes human
rights as a terrain of struggle. While human rights instruments and
human rights regimes focus on states and their compliance with
international human rights standards, what happens when private

economic relationships and practices create obstacles? How do human rights regimes exert authority over powerful private economic actors to seek compliance with the standards enumerated in human rights instruments?

We will explore the questions posed so far through what we call the *human rights enterprise*: the process through which human rights are defined and realized, including but not limited to the legal instruments and regimes often authored by international elites. The human rights enterprise includes both legal, statist approaches to defining and achieving human rights through agreements among duty-bearing states, and social movement approaches that manifest as social struggles over power, resources, and political voice. The human rights enterprise offers a way to conceptualize human rights as a terrain of social struggle, rather than a static, contingent legal construct. In an examination of human rights as a terrain of social struggle, the contradictory role of states becomes more clear: while states are the primary duty bearers under international law, social movements most responsible for realizing human rights – from the civil rights movement to modern anti-globalization, anti-war, environmental, and anti-capitalist movements – almost always form against or in spite of the states (and often partnered private interests) charged with rights protection. The role of states in the broader human rights enterprise is further complicated by their tendency to appropriate and apply international law and the legal discourse of human rights to legitimate self-interested policies and practices (Peck 2011).

An analysis of the contemporary human rights enterprise makes clear that human rights are often developed and forced into practice through the struggles of grassroots organizations and non-elites from below – not so much from the compassionate actions of states to respect their international agreements. Efforts to achieve human rights practice should be understood as struggles over power and resource that are often waged against or in spite of states and other powerful interests. Finally, the specific history of struggles to achieve rights practice suggests that grassroots organizing and direct action, including forms of open resistance and disobedience, typically involving networks of non-governmental (NGO), social movement (SMO), and community organizations, are the most commonly successful approaches (see also Clement 2008, 2011) to realizing human rights in any lasting, meaningful way.

Why focus on the US?

The US is the sole global hegemon and military superpower, while also perhaps one of the worst actors when it comes to direct and indirect involvement in the violation of human rights instruments and the undermining of international law, as illustrated through the sizeable literature on *American exceptionalism* (Hertel and Libal 2011; Ignatieff 2009) and the chapters to follow. The United States, with little criticism (if not support) from some of the most dominant US-based human rights NGOs (Peck 2011), at times coopt human rights discourse to pursue more narrow interests – the Iraq War is the most glaring contemporary example. Scholars have for some time criticized the Western dominance of human rights law and discourse since their inception (Ishay 2008). As a related point, it seems necessary to mention how a powerful Western nation like the US can simultaneously fail in its own human rights obligations while employing human rights discourse to achieve unrelated ends – both undermining the success of the human rights enterprise and illustrating the questionable role of states in that process. Human rights discourse is appealing for such purposes in that:

> [For] the United States, which is more forthright than today's Europe in proclaiming its national interest, the ideology of Human Rights serves to endow foreign interventions with a crusading purpose that can appeal to European allies and above all to their domestic opinion, as well as to the English-speaking world in general (Canada and Australia in particular). It is the tribute vice pays to virtue, to echo LaRochefoucauld. (Johnstone 2014)

With all of that in mind, this work focuses on the United States for several reasons. Since the sphere of economic and military influence of the US is so deep and vast, arguably without historical precedent, and since the US is also home to many of the most powerful corporations on earth, US domestic and foreign policy has massive effects on the human rights prospects of everyone else. Further, unlike students and public intellectuals elsewhere, those of us in the United States arguably have the greatest capacity to resist and affect the actions of the US government and related business interests (see also Chomsky 2007a,b). In this sense we advocate that human rights scholars and activists in the US focus inward, to accompany and inform resistance against the most powerful corporations and military state the world has ever known. Such a position should also be seen as in line with the traditions of public intellectualism and liberation sociology (Feagin and Vera 2001), where one openly studies society in order to engage, change, inform, and improve it. Though the human rights enterprise and other concepts offered here can be employed to any number of global contexts, we apply them to the United States in order to reiterate the importance of this reflection and focus inward.

What is to follow

In addition to the academic task of conceptualizing a critical sociology of human rights, this book is intended to address what we see as the most pressing questions facing the broad efforts to define and realize human rights practice in the lives of people and in the lasting structure of our communities. What are the fundamental problems with dominant approaches to defining and realizing human rights through the formal, legal agreements between nation-states and international legal regimes? What can we as scholars learn from the history of struggles to define and realize human rights in order to ensure mutual human survival and the protection of basic human dignity in the world? How can critical sociology and concepts like the human rights enterprise contribute to our understanding of human rights and their realization?

The following chapters provide the scholarly tools for unpacking these important questions. Chapter 2 examines the question of power and the state using state theory, with a specific emphasis on global economic restructuring and the global recession of the twenty-first century. We will trace the history of US state policy relative to finance capital that set the table for the crisis in 2008, and examine its global reach. We will also explore questions fundamental to political sociologists and any critical sociology of human rights. What is "the state"? How is the state defined in international law (human rights instruments)? What is the role (including and beyond stated "duties") of the state according to the formal international human rights regime in the effort to realize human rights practice? What does critical state theory suggest about states' likelihood to successfully play their intended role, given (for example) the context of global neoliberal capitalism? Do theoretical concepts of the state and empirical studies of actual human rights struggles suggest that states are positioned to facilitate the achievement of human rights practice as expected?

Critical state theory and political sociological work on the process of global economic restructuring suggest that states may not be the appropriate mechanisms to protect and provide for human rights in the face of other interests. If we are critical of states' willingness or ability to meet international obligations, how can we explain or interpret the relative success of many human rights campaigns?

In chapter 3, we apply sociological research on social movements to suggest how we might interpret the collective local and global efforts, employing formal and/or informal means, to define and realize human rights in people's everyday lives. That is, social movement theory will help us understand how people challenge states and powerful economic actors to define and achieve fundamental human dignity, however articulated. We explore this issue through an analysis of anti-racist struggle in the US, focusing specifically on the civil rights movement. Our discussion of resistance to white supremacy threads through struggles for political, civil, economic, cultural, and social rights, and examines the intersections of struggles within nation-states with those in the international arena. We also document how the fact of rights won in one era does not ensure their permanence in future eras. Without persistent resistance, rights protections can regress as dominant interests leverage control over the state and public policy discourse, as is arguably demonstrated by current threats to voting rights established in the Civil Rights Acts of the 1960s.

Chapter 4 examines the very meaning of human rights in the context of contemporary definitions of corporations as citizens with rights. A great deal of scholarship demonstrates the historical processes through which corporations became the most powerful mechanisms in modern global capitalism, primarily through gaining the rights of people with few of the responsibilities ("limited liability") (Bakan 2004). Private corporate interests and their legal obligations to maximize profit for shareholders often pose significant threats to human rights practice. As we will suggest, the boundaries of rights, seen through a political sociological lens, include conversations about to whom/what such rights do *not* apply. These are not entirely new questions. Political scientists and sociologists have for some time documented debates over, for example, the boundaries of the right to "property" and right to political participation (Ishay 2008). The boundaries of the rights of corporations, particularly given the increasing mobility of capital post-globalization, take on new significance as the world struggles with a global recession arguably caused by corporations and large financial institutions. When we apply a political sociological lens, what happens to our interpretation of "rights" and how and to whom they apply? Where are the boundaries of "human rights"? How do rights translate into tangible power relationships and social experience? Under US law, as in some other nations to varying degrees, corporations enjoy many of the rights (often identical to human rights, such as rights to expression or "free speech") of people. What are some of the implications of this in terms of tangible power relationships and social experiences? How important are these boundaries for the realization of human rights?

Finally, in chapter 5, we explore some contemporary implications of a critical sociology of human rights and political sociological analyses for human rights struggles. How would a critical sociology of human rights guide our efforts to realize human rights in current contexts? First, we take seriously the contemporary threats to even the oldest and most central civil and political rights concepts in an age of mass surveillance and seemingly perpetual conditions of war. Second, we take stock of some global priorities, recognizing that threats to collective human survival – wealth disparity, nuclear proliferation, and ecological collapse most notably – should enjoy the primacy of our efforts. Finally, we illustrate and endorse some strategies for engaging in human rights praxis to address the significant challenges of our day. We join many others in suggesting that current contexts provide excellent opportunities for public intellectualism and the radical "accompaniment" of existing struggles (Lynd 2010). Current debates over US military actions and massive surveillance powers, movements against the drug war and mass incarceration in the US, global debates over climate change, and global resistance to the growing wealth inequality clearly revealed since the "Great Recession" began in 2008, present abundant options to create a more just and sustainable world.

2

Power and the State

Global Economic Restructuring and the Global Recession

Covering the elusive "jobs recovery" since 2008, the *Hartford Courant* ran a story on Mark and Diane, a married couple in their late fifties, who were employed full time when Mark lost his traveling sales job in 2012 (Lee 2013). Neither of them worried too much: although he didn't receive unemployment benefits because the state defined him as an independent contractor, their health coverage came from her bank management job. Two months later, Diane lost her job after 20 years with the bank. More than six months later both were still looking for work with no luck. Diane received $546 each week in unemployment benefits, but health insurance for both of them cost $1,000 each month in addition to $600 out of pocket for medications. If they found full-time employment they would still need to work full time into their seventies to compensate for lost finances. By then, Diane will have accumulated a pension from her years at the bank, but they had to use some of Mark's 401(k) savings to survive, and it's shrunk to about $30,000. They were facing foreclosure on their home if the picture did not improve soon.

What is going on here? This is not the story of a couple that made frivolous or selfish financial decisions and got themselves in a bind. These are folks that did all the "right" things to remain financially solvent, prepare for a decent retirement, and enjoy the American dream of homeownership. Through little fault of their own, the bottom fell out of their existence, leaving them to struggle for food, shelter, healthcare, and a decent existence in

20

Getting started – human rights and the state

In order to explore the relationship of the state and human rights, we need to be clear about what we mean when we say "the state." The *state* refers to the manner in which political positions are organized and how these positions structure and institutionalize power and political relations in society. This is not the same thing as *government*, which refers to the people who occupy these positions within the state to develop and administer state policy and practices. This difference is important: individuals in government frequently change, as might specific policies; but the structure of political and power relations (such as electoral processes, policy-making processes, and the organization of relations between the government and corporations, labor, consumers, and others) remains, regardless of who occupies positions in the state. To illustrate, ratified human rights instruments may be in place, but their implementation ultimately depends on the agency of individuals in all branches of government to employ human rights practice and make them work.

The UDHR defined a wide range of rights to which it declared all humans were entitled. It did not explicitly assign the state with the responsibility of enforcing human rights, but that responsibility is implied: the success of the UDHR, like all international human rights instruments, depends upon the state's willingness to protect human rights even when doing so may conflict with other state interests and policies, such as those governing finance, trade, and the social construction of "national security." So, for example, state interests in "national security" cannot trump the non-derogable human right to freedom from torture. In short, the state must adopt a "rights first" approach to policy and practice. Moreover, beyond states' willingness to enforce and prioritize human rights, the success of human rights instruments also depends on whether states have the ability, infrastructure, and resources necessary to develop rights-protective policies.

Although the role of the state is only implied in the UDHR, it is more explicit for those party to the International Covenant on

Economic, Social, and Cultural Rights (ICESCR) in, for instance, the 1997 Maastricht Guidelines. The guidelines detail expectations on states to provide for positive rights such as the rights to work, healthcare, or housing (Felice 1999). Success for the ICESCR as a human rights instrument depends heavily on the voluntary actions and policies of states to abide by their agreements (McCorquodale and Fairbrother 1999; Koskenniemi 1991). A contradiction arises in that the institutions and their incumbents who required such an international instrument were the same ones entrusted to oversee implementation and monitoring of human rights.

Indeed, many repressive or powerful states simply ignore, discredit, or only selectively recognize international law and standards when they conflict with dominant national priorities and agendas. There are no consequences delineated in these human rights instruments should the state not abide by the international agreement; nor is there any institution endowed with the power to impose consequences. International human rights instruments presume, first, that the state is capable and governments are willing to abide by their international human rights agreements, and, second, that the state is the only institution of power affecting human rights. This is not the case. Take, for example, the G. W. Bush or Obama administration's dismissal of United Nations objections to the pre-emptive war in Iraq, military interventions in Libya or Syria, the treatment of prisoners at Guantánamo Bay and other rendition sites, and the repeated refusal to conform to global environmental standards enumerated in agreements like the Kyoto Protocol. Since sanctions against powerful states are non-existent or ineffective, watchdog efforts by UN bodies and partnered NGOs are limited in their ability to intervene when state policies or practices violate human rights.

Additionally, human rights instruments tend to be framed around the relationship between the state and individuals. The state is charged with ensuring human rights and refraining from violating the rights of others through policy or practice. But what about protecting human rights from the threats of private interests, such as *transnational* or *multinational corporations* (TNC or MNC)? The 1999 Global Compact (from the 1999 World Economic Forum), for example, was designed to set minimum standards and guidelines for private corporations to prevent human rights violations. Unfortunately, the Compact called for voluntary participation without threat of liability or sanction (Monshipouri, Welch, and Kennedy 2003), thus severely limiting its efficacy. And the Compact did not have any power to ensure that states would pursue enforcement if it contradicted national policy or practice. In the US, for example, publicly traded TNCs are structurally and often legally required to prioritize the interests of their shareholders and thus to place the *maximization of profit above all other concerns* (Bakan 2004) – we will return to this in chapter 4. Although human rights instruments assign states the responsibility of insuring and protecting rights, corporations must by law protect the rights of shareholders even when in violation of human rights and environmental standards. As such, the rights of shareholders often trump the rights of stakeholders to human rights. In order to enforce international human rights instruments, then, states must be able to sanction some of the most powerful collective actors (TNCs) in the modern world for practices directed by those very states and their most powerful members (significant shareholders). Formal human rights regimes do not adequately address this antagonism. Moreover, the current incarnation of global economic restructuring further complicates the ability of states to fulfill these expectations.

This discussion boils down to several questions. What are the relationships and structure of power between the state and society, and how do these relationships facilitate or hamper the implementation and enforcement of human rights? Is it possible for the state to consistently secure human rights, or is it constrained against doing so? If it is constrained, what are the forces of constraint or fundamental inadequacies at work? In order to explore these questions, we need to examine critical sociological theories of the state. Several competing models dominate this literature, and most focus on the relationships between elites (the wealthy and powerful), the state, and the political economy (capitalism).

Sociological theories of the state

Instrumentalism/business dominance theory: "capture" or domination?

The earliest sociological theory of the state since World War II featuring the role of economic interests is *instrumentalism*. In this model, based on a somewhat orthodox Marxist approach, the state exists in a capitalist society, and as such is subject to capitalists' interests. Capitalists gain their power and wealth from ownership of the means of production, and then leverage that power and wealth to control the state as their instrument. Instrumentalists illustrate cases where capitalists (also represented by corporations and banks) control or virtually capture the state by taking over or inhabiting key positions of the state apparatus in order to secure legislation and judicial decisions supporting their interests (Weinstein 1968; Miliband 1969, 1983; Domhoff 1970). Perhaps the most obvious example of state capture is when capitalists exercise the "revolving door" in Washington, referring to the ease with which politicians step in and out of public service and private industry – typically lobbying – in order to serve their own and other capitalists' interests. And instrumentalists make a pretty strong point here. Members of the owning class are often elected to public governing offices: Governor David Rockefeller of Virginia, Governor Nelson Rockefeller of New York, President John Fitzgerald Kennedy, Senator Ted Kennedy of Massachusetts, Representative Joseph P. Kennedy of Massachusetts, Governor DuPont of Delaware, Presidents George Herbert Walker Bush and George W. Bush, and Vice President Dick Cheney just to name a few. All these men were officers of major corporations or scions of significant industrial capitalist families.

An instrumentalist theory of the state can explain a great deal and is particularly useful in, for instance, examining the role of current or former bank executives in the highest economic posts of federal government. Still, no single theory is complete, as we will find in the following sections. Instead, each theory of the state adds a bit more to the complicated arrangements between economy, power, and institutions of authority and governance. Critics of instrumentalism argue convincingly that few capitalists have ever actually captured the state outright, and that competing capitalist interests can prevent direct capture of the state apparatus. More revisionary instrumentalists argue that capitalists might actually be more effective in securing policies consistent with their interests if they *didn't* sit in the command positions of the state because such blatant abuses of power would quickly lose legitimacy. These theorists offer a more subtle perspective of business dominance rather than outright capture of the state. In this view, capitalists do not own the state or capture its key positions. Instead, they dominate the state by sitting on important non-elected advisory groups like the Council on Foreign Relations (whose membership is heavily corporate and whose charge it is to advise the President on foreign-policy matters), heading regulatory agencies, making significant financial contributions in support of political campaigns, and heavily lobbying key legislators in support of corporate interests (Useem 1984; Domhoff 1990, 2005; Prechel 1990, 2000; Akard 1992, 2005; Lugar 2000; Burris 1992; Benoit 2007; Clawson, Neustadtl, and Weller 1998).

Indeed, a business dominance framework certainly can be seen in the revolving doors between government and the likes of Goldman Sachs, arguably the largest multinational investment banking firm that deals in securities, investment management, and global finance; it is a central figure in marketing and dealing in US Treasury funds. Many of its top-level personnel have served in major state positions. Robert Rubin, for example, was the US Secretary of the Treasury during the Clinton administration, as was Henry Paulson during the George W. Bush administration. Mark Patterson, Goldman Sachs lobbyist, became Treasury Secretary Timothy Geithner's Chief of Staff in the Obama administration. Former Goldman Sachs director Stephen Friedman became Chairman of the Federal Reserve Bank in New York in 2008. Others served in key international state positions. Mario

Monti, for example, was the Prime Minister of Italy, and Mario Draghi was the Governor of the European Central Bank.

Goldman Sachs, one of the most powerful banks deeply involved in the fraud and theft that caused the 2008 economic meltdown (Ferguson 2012), benefited handsomely from the subsequent $10 billion preferred stock investment by the US Treasury under the federal Troubled Asset Relief Program (TARP) to bail out major banks (a state bailout that banks and investment firms strenuously pressed for, aided by Henry Paulson's pleas to Congress for its absolute necessity). The Securities and Exchange Commission later charged the firm in 2010 of securities fraud, resulting from its failure to disclose to investors that Abacus Mortgage security was designed to fail in the firm's attempt to profit from the housing-market debacle. The company settled the case with a payment of $550 million, a mere fine for a company worth nearly $3 billion at the time (Ferguson 2012; Taibbi 2011; also see company profile at <http://topics.nytimes.com/top/news/business/companies/goldman_sachs_group_inc/index.html>).

Business dominance analysts would point to the revolving door of the US Treasury Department personnel as key to Goldman Sachs's windfall of federal funds and its relatively mild rebuke by the federal government for its fraudulent behavior. For example, Secretary of the Treasury Henry Paulson began working at Goldman Sachs in 1974, ultimately becoming its Chief Operating Officer and Chief Executive Officer; he was still with the firm in 2006, when its fraudulent mortgage securities practices were reaching toxic heights. Those practices, among several other practices that severely damaged the economy, were facilitated by federal deregulations of the industry that Paulson himself had helped steward through Congress in the 1990s and early 2000s (Ferguson 2012; Taibbi 2011). Among the deregulations he helped push while at Goldman Sachs were repeal of the Glass-Steagall Act that had kept the financial industry well under control since the Great Depression, relaxation of mortgage disclosure regulations, and continuation of the Federal Reserve's failure to enforce regulations governing mortgage banks. Treasury Secretary Paulson continued to aggressively press to minimize the power of the Securities and Exchange Commission (SEC) by reducing or eliminating its funding. The SEC is an agency that could oversee, regulate, investigate, and sanction the practices of powerful firms like Goldman Sachs. Business dominance theorists would not be surprised at all to know that the US Justice Department ultimately dropped all investigations of Goldman Sachs in 2012. For business dominance analysts, the circulation of personnel between the private industry and the state, the "kid gloves" handling of Goldman Sachs by the Justice Department, and the subsequent economic free fall, frames the loss of homeowners' rights to their housing and property and the general population's right to jobs and a living wage.

While this analysis may be somewhat compelling, it is limited. For example, business dominance theories imply but do not necessarily prove that corporate leaders always share a clear, conscious, and unified understanding of capital accumulation interests and the policies necessary to secure pro-corporate policy. In addition, both the instrumentalist and business dominance perspectives share an individualistic emphasis: if the individuals who occupy the commanding seats of government power or key influential organizations were to change, the state would presumably legislate to protect non-capitalist interests (and perhaps human rights that are not consistent with corporate interests). If, for example, labor rights activists were to be elected to Congress and the White House, or to take control of the Council on Foreign Relations and the regulatory agencies, and to become the largest, most important campaign finance contributors, state policy would favor labor interests instead of capital accumulation interests. Perhaps unfortunately, this does not seem to be supported by empirical history. What prevents successful capture of the state from below?

The business dominance and instrumentalist analyses offer a view from above, focusing on political and organizational elites, and ignoring the role of non-elites and resistance in policymaking. They imply that non-elites accept without resistance what capital accumulation interests and actors force the state to do, even if it is not in non-elites' interests. Yet history tells us that resistance from the bottom up has frequently been significant in facilitating the production of policy that business interests found abhorrent, such as the right of workers to collectively bargain (first granted in the US to workers in private industry in 1935 under the National Labor Relations Act, and later extended to cover all federal workers in 1962), or the Community Reinvestment Act of 1977 that forced banks to negotiate with community activists to reinvest in underserved communities.

Capitalist state structuralism

In contrast to the instrumentalist and business dominance view of the state as an actor in a capitalist society, and therefore the state as simply an actor within that society, *capitalist state structuralists* see a *capitalist state*. That is, the very structure of the state itself is woven into a capitalist political economy, in part because the modern state did not develop in a vacuum – it developed in conjunction with a global capitalist economic system. The state is bound to and ultimately shaped by the capitalist system. In contrast to instrumentalists, capitalist state structuralists argue that individuals are powerless to institute policies and practices that contradict capital accumulation: state policies must be forged by the position of the state within the larger capitalist economy. Because of the imperatives of the capitalist political economy, state managers have no choice but to create and implement policies that protect the conditions of capital accumulation and to thwart the conditions that threaten accumulation. State managers who do not follow these imperatives risk plunging the economy into severe crises, which in turn would create political legitimacy crises that all but ensure jeopardizing the future of state managers' positions as political leaders (Poulantzas 1969, 1978; Mandel 1975; Wright 1978; Valocchi 1989; Block 1987; Glasberg 1989; Glasberg and Skidmore 1997). As such, legislators may agree that the implementation of a living wage makes sense from a human rights perspective, but they often argue that it is not practical or feasible because it would impose an undue burden on businesses by reducing profit and making them less competitive, particularly on the global market where labor is much cheaper.

Capitalist state structuralists emphasize that because the state is the structural unification of contradictory class relationships between labor and capital, direct control by class-based organizations is unnecessary. Pro-accumulation and pro-capitalist state economic intervention is not the result of the participation of corporate actors in the policy-formation process; policy instead results from the contradictory relations of power *embedded* within state structures themselves. It is an expression of the state's underlying, pro-capitalist structural bias. It is a capitalist state, and as such cannot do otherwise. This implies that the state can embrace and enforce human rights only to the extent that these are consistent with or do not threaten capital accumulation interests. If this is the case, it is difficult to envision which fundamental rights (IBHR) would be within the ability of the state to actually enforce; all would seem to challenge – in one way or another – capitalist and corporate interests in securing increasing profits.

Capitalist state structuralists and business dominance theorists agree as to *what* the state does: it legislates to secure the conditions of capital accumulation and in the interests of capitalists (which suggests that the state either cannot be trusted to protect human rights, since it is captured or dominated by corporate interests, or is unable to protect human rights because these are not consistent with capital accumulation interests). But these theorists disagree in their explanations of *why* the state does so. Instrumentalists and business dominance theorists argue that the state produces policy consistent with accumulation interests because political leaders are either capitalists themselves or they are dominated by capitalist interests. In contrast, capitalist state structuralists argue that the state legislates in capitalist interests because state managers simply have no choice: they must restrict their legislative actions to policies that will not threaten capital accumulation. But both perspectives imply a similar outcome relative to human rights: the state will be unlikely or unable to enforce human rights in a capitalist political economy. For instrumentalists and business dominance theorists, this is because the elites are simply not motivated to do so because they are enriched and empowered specifically by denying the rights of others; for capitalist state structuralists, it is because human rights are not consistent with the imperative of capitalist expansion.

As a significant limitation, capitalist state structuralists and instrumentalists/business dominance theorists share a view that discounts the significance of resistance in policymaking processes and in political practice, although with a subtle but important difference. Instrumentalist and business dominance analyses emphasize corporate elites and their role in the state while excluding altogether an examination of resistance from below; capitalist state structuralists argue that although such resistance might occasionally occur it is insignificant, highly mechanistic, and often lacking class consciousness. The state's role is to preserve the unity and overall goals of capitalists by mitigating the potentially divisive structural contradictions and antagonisms within that class and to arbitrate antagonisms between capitalists and labor. Capitalist state structuralists would not be at all surprised, for example, by the stunning bailout of the very financial institutions that plunged the economy into the Great Recession: the state had no choice but to bail them out because failure to do so would ensure their collapse and thereby cause the recession to devolve into a deep and perhaps intractable economic Depression. And the state further ensured the power of these institutions to profoundly affect the health of the economy by allowing them to grow ever larger through mergers and takeovers (Taibbi 2013).

The state institutionalizes labor/capital conflicts and thus minimizes potentially destructive antagonisms between them with legislation granting labor the right to collective bargaining. The Taylor Law in the United States outlaws the labor strategy of striking by workers of "essential services," such as police, firefighters, sanitation workers, air-traffic controllers, teachers, and so on. Under the Taylor Law, striking workers lose two or more days' pay for every day they remain on strike; they may even lose their jobs altogether. Anti-strike legislation like the Taylor Law weakens labor power by legislating against their most effective strategic mechanisms, thereby mitigating if not altogether squashing labor resistance from below.

Capitalist state structuralists would not be surprised by the federal TARP program in 2008, which invested nearly $5 billion to bailout large commercial and investment banks in an effort to stem the hemorrhage of the subprime mortgage crisis which ignited an economic meltdown. A capitalist state structuralist analysis would argue that the state had no choice but to invest such a huge infusion of money in the banks even as it was sharply cutting investments in anti-poverty programs. Banks are the mainsprings in the capitalist political economy, and a crisis in the banking industry could cause a catastrophe for the overall economy and for the state. Were the state to ignore the mortgage and foreclosure crisis and the consequent widespread and deep economic recession, it would plunge the US, and the global economy, into a severe economic Depression that would rival that of the 1930s. The state maintained that exact position, even though banks that had accepted billions of dollars in bailouts clearly invested very little of these funds in preventing mortgage foreclosures while providing huge bonuses for executives and dividends for shareholders. The working class and middle class lost their grip on their right to housing, secure employment, and food, while the banking industry solidified its grip on the state and the economy.

While capitalist state structuralism more clearly links the state and its policymaking ability to the structure of the political economy, it does not explain how it is possible for the state to occasionally produce policy and practices that are antithetical to capital accumulation interests. If the state is constrained to secure the requirements of capital accumulation, how is it possible that capitalists do not always gain their objectives? For example, how do we explain workers' rights legislation (such as worker safety and health policy, minimum wage policy, the right to collective bargaining, etc.)? How do we explain the Community Reinvestment Act that requires banks to reinvest in underserved communities where they do business? This is an analytical problem shared by the instrumentalist/business dominance perspective: if capitalists capture or dominate the state, as instrumentalists and business dominance theorists assert, how is it possible that they sometimes fail to thwart policy and practices that contradict their interests? How is it possible for capitalist states like the US to ratify international human rights instruments that run counter to private capital accumulation interests?

Just as importantly, capitalist state structuralism and instrumentalism/business dominance perspectives share a narrow emphasis on the internal national structure of the state, thereby tearing the state out of its global context and rendering invisible the external or international forces that might affect the state. Yet there is ample evidence that external or international forces may be quite significant. For example, when Mexico stood on the precipice of bankruptcy in 1982, an organized private banking community primarily from the United States refused to renegotiate its credit until the International Monetary Fund imposed some very strict austerity conditions on the country. These conditions included the devaluation of Mexico's currency, the privatization of key industries that had previously been owned by the Mexican state (such as oil), and sharp curtailing of social welfare expenditures in favor of devoting substantial proportions of the national budget to paying their debt to private banks in the United States (Glasberg 1989). Mexican state managers had no choice but to accept these conditions. Faced with the alternative of complete economic meltdown, they effectively lost control of their own domestic policymaking to the forces of the international aid regime outside their state structure. The capitalist state structuralist model does not provide a theoretical mechanism for exploring this.

But even this story remains fixated on political and economic elites, and still leaves out the role of resistance from the bottom up: although it was clear that human rights were trumped by private profit-making in Mexico (as elsewhere around the globe, then and now), what was happening among non-elites? Neither of the theoretical perspectives so far makes room for such an analysis.

Class dialectic perspective: "bringing class back in"

Instrumentalist/business dominance and capitalist state structuralist analyses ignore or discount the role of resistance in state policy and practices. In contrast, the *class dialectic perspective* introduces the role of labor as well as the state and capitalists in the production of policy. In this model, far from being absent or highly mechanized and devoid of consciousness, organized and deliberate resistance from below can in fact exert substantial pressure on the state to address their needs, even if these contradict capital accumulation interests (Zeitlin, Ewen, and Ratcliff 1974; Zeitlin and Ratcliff 1975; Whitt 1979, 1982; Esping-Anderson, Friedland, and Wright 1986; Levine 1988; Eckstein 1997; Jackson 2008). Resistance from below is most effective when it is organized, mobilized into social movements, and able to create mass disruptions (for example, with labor strikes; international boycotts; and cross-border mass actions) (Jenkins and Brents 1989; Quadagno and Meyer 1989; Quadagno 1992). When the state cannot legally and institutionally mediate top-down and bottom-up conflicts it may resort to its monopoly on the use of force to repress non-elite unrest and mass disruption (Lenin 1976). But the state resorts to the use of force and violence as a last resort, when its usual *hegemonic*, institutional mechanisms to coopt or otherwise mediate non-elite resistance become ineffective (Witte 1972; Schmitter 1974; Galbraith 1985; Levine 1988; Swenson 2002).

This analysis might help explain what the previously discussed models could not. How is it possible that capitalists and capital accumulation interests do not gain their objectives each and every time if they are either so powerful or if their interests are embedded in the state structure itself? How do we explain the existence of human rights instruments, policies, or practices that contradict capital accumulation objectives if capitalist interests are so powerful? The class dialectic model suggests that this is possible because capitalist and capital accumulation interests are in fact *not* impervious to non-elite resistance; they are subject to organized struggles from below, and so is the state.

Does that mean that when labor and/or human rights interests are reflected in policy that capital accumulation interests necessarily lose? Not at all. The state commonly produces policies and engages in practices that benefit labor and other human rights interests, while simultaneously supporting and legitimating the broader political economy and therefore wider capital accumulation interests (Quadagno 1992). State policy in this model mediates and institutionalizes labor and capital conflicts into forms such as competitive trade unions representing highly limited classes of workers (instead of the wider industrial unions that represent all workers in a single, large union) that are more amenable to capitalist interests. To illustrate, the existence of many competitive unions representing workers in a single industry offers far more opportunities to divide and conquer workers in a struggle against capital than a single, unified union, representing all workers regardless of trade skill or industry.

Similarly, labor laws in the United States provide for the right to collective bargaining and the formation of labor unions, but impose restrictions such as no-strike clauses and binding arbitration in contentious labor contract negotiations. And although a federal minimum wage law sets a floor below which wages may not go, there is no guarantee that this will be a living wage; since minimum wages are not tied to inflation, the minimum wage is typically far below poverty levels. To gain sufficient wages above the legal minimum to approximate a living wage, workers must negotiate contractually with employers. And to get federal support to raise the minimum wage, workers must struggle against the dominating influences of corporations and small businesses alike, which typically rise above the usual rift that divides their interests (small business versus major corporate interests) to coalesce and apply their considerable resources to influence policymakers. As a perfect example of this, a progressive coalition of students, professors, and community stakeholders in San Jose, California, succeeded in raising the minimum wage to $10.00/hour within city limits in 2012. The campaign involved several years of grassroots organizing, lobbying area businesses and politicians, and repeated forms of public demonstration, direct action, and civil disobedience in order to succeed – and now the movement is considered a model for local and national expansion (Thompson 2012).

Class dialectic analysts would point, as well, to the demonstrations in Wisconsin by more than 70,000 state workers in 2011 in protest of massive cuts in state employment by the Governor, Scott Walker, and his demands that state workers pay more for their health insurance and pensions; these increases in worker contributions would have essentially resulted in a 7 percent cut in state workers' income. More importantly, workers were protesting his avowed goal of breaking the backs of public workers' unions by crushing their right to collective bargaining and restricting negotiations to basic wages only (Davey and Greenhouse 2011). State workers had already agreed to pension and healthcare concessions in recognition that the state budget was indeed in trouble; but their concessions were not enough for the Governor, who was adamant in his insistence on squashing public worker unions. State workers received widespread support from workers around the US and the world: resources poured in to feed protestors who had taken over the capitol building, and to help keep the area clean and organized. The Governor also received strong support from Governors in Ohio, Indiana, and others, who were seeking to similarly break public unions and the right to collective bargaining. Police refusals to remove protestors from the capitol building would not surprise class dialectic analysts either: police are state employees, too, and this was their fight as much as it was for teachers, firefighters, sanitation workers, and the like. But despite weeks of protests, the legislature passed a measure to restrict collective bargaining and the Governor then rescinded planned layoffs of over 1,500 state jobs. Clearly, the goal was less one of balancing the state budget and more of seizing an opportunity to turn back workers' rights. And although a groundswell prompted a recall election to remove Governor Walker, he managed to remain in office, thanks in no small part to over $100 million of campaign financing that poured into the state, largely from private conservative sources outside Wisconsin that overwhelmed the process.

The protests in Wisconsin were echoed in the spread of Occupy Wall Street, another development that is consistent with a class dialectic perspective. Here, protestors were angered by the widening gap between wealth and poverty, often with the willing help of the state. The deepening economic crisis and the subsequent loss of homes, jobs, and healthcare benefits were the price of making policy consistent with capital accumulation interests and two protracted wars in Iraq and Afghanistan (both of which benefited private defense contractors such as Halliburton while admittedly doing little to enhance security against terrorism). Protestors initially received support from police, who refused to arrest peaceful demonstrators; months later, however, demonstrators were forcibly and often violently removed from several occupied encampments around the country as local businesses began to complain that growing tent communities were a blight and threatening to their business. While the OWS movement became more quiescent during the winter months of 2011, it re-emerged in the spring. It did not succeed in gaining state policy to address wealth inequality, but it has succeeded in opening nation- and worldwide conversations concerning inequality and the relationship between the state and private capital interests, something class dialectic analysts would see as part of the ongoing struggle.

While the class dialectic model does introduce the role of an organized resistance from below to an analysis of the relationship of the state and society, it shares the implication of other models that the state is an object and an arena of struggle between accumulation and non-accumulation interests. But might the state also be an actor itself, with its own interests? The contradictions and antagonisms created by the state's role as implementer, enforcer, and protector of human rights become strong here: What happens when the state's own interests conflict with human rights interests?

State-centered structuralism: "Bringing the state back in"

In contrast to both business dominance and capitalist state structuralist theories, which characterize the state as an institutional target for takeover or influence by powerful economic actors, *state-centered structuralists* argue that the state itself is a powerful actor, and is the site of bureaucratic political power. For these analysts, the state is neither a capitalist state nor subject to capitalists' manipulations and control. The state has its own institutional interests separate from the demands of external groups or economic pressures, and thus state managers can independently produce policy whether it suits various interests other than itself or not. State policy is shaped not by the class backgrounds of its personnel or by the compelling structure of the capitalist political economy, but by the imperatives of *bureaucracies*. The state, as a bureaucratic and political structure, is an institutional separate entity from the economy. As such, state policy and practices are shaped not by influential or dominating elites or by the inexorable demands of maintaining a robust capitalist political economy; policy and practice are shaped by past policy precedents, political and party interests, and state managers' interest in expanding their administrative domain and autonomy. The state is not affected by the mechanisms of intraclass unity, emphasized by business dominance theory, or by the "capitalist nature" of state structures, asserted by capitalist state structuralists (Skocpol and Ikenberry 1983; Skocpol 1985, 1992; Amenta and Skocpol 1988; Hooks 1990, 1991; Amenta and Parikh 1991; Amenta and Halfmann 2000; Chorev 2007). And, as insulated from pressures from above as the state is in this model, the state is also impervious to pressures from below. From this perspective, the state answers to no one but itself and its own bureaucratic interest in institutional expansion and survival.

Here, the state is characterized as neutral relative to competing interests, transcending the pressure and influence such interests might exert, regardless of the resources these interests might control and regardless of the structure of the political economy. However, this characterization of the state as a class-neutral or class-transcendent institution raises questions concerning the past backgrounds, allegiances, and interests of state managers themselves. Who are the state managers, and what are their class backgrounds? How do they shed their past class allegiances and interests when they become state managers? Is it possible for state managers to fully divorce themselves in any meaningful way from their class backgrounds and experiences?

In this scenario, what would impel or encourage the state to implement and secure human rights? The state-centered model does open a space for analyzing state policy that is not governed by capitalist interests or the compulsion to secure the conditions supporting capital accumulation. Here, policies such as reproductive and civil rights, LGBTQ (lesbian, gay, bisexual, transgender, and queer) rights, children's rights, the rights of people with disabilities, environmental rights, and the like (if not indigenous rights, which may more clearly contradict the state's interests) may be understood as the product of party politics or the interest of some bureaucratic agencies to expand their administrative sphere. So, too, would Wisconsin Governor Scott Walker's attempt to subvert or eliminate state workers' right to collective bargaining as a way to expand the state's range of discretion and power over labor and budgets. Less clear in the state-centered model, however, are the conditions under which it would become in the bureaucratic interest of the state to do so. According to this model, it would seem that it is always in the state's interest to expand its administrative domain, a position that is vague at best, and non-falsifiable.

Further, is it realistic or even plausible for state managers to ignore altogether the imperatives of the political economy to remain vital? If state managers are guided only or even primarily by their political party and bureaucratic interests, is it reasonable for them to discount the effects of their decisions on economic stability? Might their policy decisions based on bureaucratic and party interests undermine the very administrative domain they presumably seek to expand, if these decisions in fact risk plunging the economy into recession or worse? Once again, we are confronted with the dilemma posed for a state that is vested with the responsibility to implement and enforce human rights, while at the same time pursuing its own administrative and bureaucratic imperatives: how does the state reconcile these contradictory roles?

Although state-centered theory does open a space in which it becomes possible to understand human rights policy and practice, the perspective shares a focus on elites with instrumentalist and business dominance theorists. Where instrumentalist and business dominance theorists focus on *economic* and *corporate* elites, state-centered structuralists focus on *political* elites among state managers, implying that the two groups of elites are separate and distinct. This focus ignores an important factor in the concept of the human rights enterprise: what is the role of resistance from below?

Anarchist theory and direct action from below

Anarchist theory,[1] as opposed to the previous theories, begins and is infused with the assertion that the state is illegitimate, regardless of the mode of production defining the structure of any given society (i.e., capitalism, socialism, communism, etc.). Put simply, anarchism refers to a form of socialism (public control of the means of production) that does not include a hierarchical state (Guerin 1970). Anarchism assumes that societies can be bound through voluntary (often democratic) associations rather than at the threat of coercion by the state and other hierarchical social systems – racism, patriarchy, heterosexism, and so forth (Guerin 1970; Shannon and Asimakopoulos 2012; Amster et al. 2009). The previous theories of the state presented here, and heavily influential in political sociology, analyze and critique the capitalist state (as in capitalist state structuralism) or the state in capitalist society (as in instrumentalism/business dominance theory). Anarchists, increasingly influential on political scholarship (Amster et al. 2009; Shannon and Asimakopoulos 2012) and absolutely influential on contemporary social justice movements, go beyond political economy to critique the state *as such*. To anarchist theorists, the state is an institution based on hierarchy, coercion, and control, and is therefore illegitimate regardless of the character of the people who fill its positions (Guerin 1970). Thus, anarchists differ from other analysts on the nature of the state, apart from some left-wing Marxists (see, for example, Pannekoek 2003, or Flank 2007), in their emphasis on its post-revolutionary form – or what social alternatives to capitalism and the state might look like.

Marx argued for what he called "the dictatorship of the proletariat," envisioning a state controlled and run by workers after the working class had carried out a successful global revolution. According to Marxist theory, the state exists to manage divergent class interests (and especially to manage the affairs of the capitalist class as a whole). Once the workers took over the state (or abolished the existing state and replaced it with their own "workers' state") and social classes were eventually abolished, the state would "wither away" because its purpose as manager of class antagonisms would no longer exist. One might ask, in the absence of the state, what mechanisms would ensure public access to resources (social and economic rights), as promised by state socialism, and individual access to freedoms and political voice (civil, political, and cultural rights) that would differentiate communism from the temporary dictatorship of the proletariat or modern bureaucratic dictatorships?

In contrast to orthodox Marxists, anarchists argue that the state will never simply wither away, and question the assumption that any centralized power structure would gradually allow itself to simply disappear (a critique with which state-centered structuralists might agree, although for different reasons). Instead, anarchists predicted that such models of *state socialism* would end as bureaucratic dictatorships, as arguably seen in the former Soviet Union, China, and at the hands of many other so-called "communist" countries born in the twentieth century. The implication for human rights in this prediction is foreshadowed in the observation by the anarchist Mikhail Bakunin (1964: 269) that "freedom without Socialism is privilege and injustice, and . . . Socialism without freedom is slavery and brutality." Anarchists commonly eschew electoral strategies for bringing about social changes, preferring instead to engage in direct action. Direct action involves strategies to lay bare a social problem or to pursue alternative practices or social arrangements. Although anarchists are often portrayed in popular media as nihilistic, taking violent and destructive action, direct actions are not necessarily empty of meaning or violent. Any refusal to engage in business as usual, or action taken to disrupt business as usual, can be a non-violent form of direct action, including collecting unused or discarded food from catering halls, restaurants, and supermarkets to distribute to the hungry, exercise of squatters' rights on abandoned property, refusal to pay taxes, labor strikes, and public graffiti. Such acts, furthermore, are generally taken for a very real purpose: civil disobedience and non-compliance are intended to expose serious social problems, and frequently to articulate viable, effective alternatives. Anarchists argue that the process of exerting pressure on elites from below, to meet the needs of the masses, empowers people and facilitates an assimilation of collective self-management, as opposed to a reliance on rule from above (as is the case in statist, class societies) (Graeber 2009).

Anarchists do not offer a comprehensive sociological theory of the state (for a beginning, see Harrison 1983, or Price 2007), but we can identify points of agreement between anarchist theory and the theories and perspectives we previously discussed. For example, anarchists share an observation with capitalist state structuralists that the capitalist state functions to serve the interests of capital accumulation (Berkman 2003). Similarly, anarchists share with proponents of the class dialectic perspective the view of direct action by non-elites as an influence on state policy. Like state-centered structuralists, anarchists note that the state has interests of its own – regardless of whether or not it is a capitalist or socialist state. The unique contribution that anarchists bring to the table in this discussion is a theory of the post-revolutionary state: since the state has interests of its own, the working class must abolish it as an institutional form in order to achieve an egalitarian future, rather than take it over or replace it with a "workers' state."

While classical anarchism focused on the state and capitalism as central locations of power, as do most critical sociological theories of the state, many anarchists increasingly argue against domination more generally (see, e.g., Gordon 2008). In contemporary anarchist theorizing, social class is often described as closely intertwined and intersecting with other modes of domination, such as patriarchy, white supremacy, and heteronormativity. While the working class was seen as *the* agent of revolutionary social change by many past anarchists, and in class dialectic theory, most contemporary anarchists argue for a more intersectional approach (see, for example, Shannon and Rogue 2009). However, anarchists (and many Marxists, feminists, critical race theorists, and queer theorists) are just beginning to theorize about the multiple layers of oppression that exist in contemporary society and how they interact (and, ultimately, how to dismantle and replace these structures of oppression).

It is important to note the role of anarchist or left/socialist theory in contemporary human rights and social justice movements (Shannon and Nocella 2012; Amster, DeLeon, Fernandez, Nocella, and Shannon 2009; Greaber 2009), a point to which we return in chapter 5. Theoretically, anarchist approaches to the state help to explain the empirical observation that human rights often emerge from below in social movements and everyday practice, rather than being granted and provided for by the state as might be expected. Further, "critical" (Marxist – such as instrumentalism or capitalist state structuralism) and anarchist theories of the state recognize the state's hegemonic and coercive roles in the service of power, and can easily address why social movements for things like food, shelter, political voice, and equal protection under the law (all fundamental human rights found in the IBHR) are often met with coercion rather than support from the state.

State theory, social movements, and human rights

The competing power structure models we have just reviewed each provide insights into the relationship between the state and the economy, but, over decades of debate, there has not been a resolution as to which offers a more powerful model. Moreover, few analysts have explored the intersection of state theory and social movement literatures. One notable exception is the work of Glasberg and Shannon (2011). They offer a framework of a multidimensional analysis of the state, oppression, and resistance that explores the resonance between elites, non-elites, social structures of power, and the process of social movements. However, even here the analysis is not one of human rights itself; the focus is on the dynamics of *state projects* (Jessop 1990), defined as:

> set[s] of state policies and/or agencies unified around a particular issue or oppression. Policy is not random; more recent policies build on, are shaped by, or challenge prior policies ... State projects thus involve dynamic and ongoing claims processes in which social constructions (such as gender, race, class, and sexuality) may be reinforced or challenged and altered. (Glasberg and Shannon 2011: 75)

While human rights certainly could be construed as a state project, the model does not incorporate a sociology of human rights, and still implies that human rights remain a state-endorsed, state-facilitated endeavor (even in the face of persistent empirical evidence to the contrary).

Sociological theories of the state offer a variety of models to explain and illustrate the relationship between the state and society, in real political economic context, with implications for our understanding of human rights. In particular, we can understand human rights as a state project, an ongoing process involving not just the state and other powerful institutional actors in the crafting of policy, but also actors from below engaged in resistance and everyday practice that define human rights in action. That state project is not simply a national relationship, bound by artificial political borders wherein the state imposes its laws on its citizens; rather, the human rights state project is a *global* state project.

Political sociological work on the process of global economic restructuring, sometimes referred to as "economic globalization" or "globalization from above," suggests that states may not be the appropriate mechanisms to protect and provide for human rights in the face of other interests (see Armaline and Glasberg 2009; Armaline, Glasberg, and Purkayastha 2011). If states' willingness or ability to meet international obligations are in question, how can we explain or interpret the relative success of many human rights campaigns? This previous work and the following chapter illustrate that struggles to achieve human rights practice are often against or in spite of states and powerful private interests; these struggles can also be formal (legal) and/or informal in nature (see Chomsky 2004, 2007b, 2010; Bakan 2004; Dangl 2007; Shiva 2000, 2001, 2008; Monshipouri, Welch, and Kennedy 2003).

We recognize that state theories are largely class-centered models, in that not all state policy and practice is predicated on class relations. There are, for example, state projects centered on gendering, racialization, heteronormativity, and social constructions of age, none of which can be explained using class-based models. In short, we cannot simply "add and stir" non-class state projects into existing models; we must reconceptualize state theory to embrace a model based on the intersectionality of the wide range of institutional organizing principles that dominate society (e.g., Glasberg and Shannon 2011). For our purposes here, however, we are retaining a class-based perspective: the state's relation to international law is infused and tinged with the structure of the political economy, such that state decisions concerning compliance are filtered through lenses defining social constructions of economic impacts. The potential for actualizing human rights practice is consequently bound to the state's perspectives of its position in the global economy and the factors that will affect that position. We therefore retain a class-based perspective here for the purposes of exploring the recent incarnation of global economic restructuring and its effect on human rights, even as we recognize that state projects are not limited to class.

When we apply critical sociological theories of the state, the limitations of states to fulfill their international legal obligations and successfully facilitate human rights practice in the context of neoliberal global capitalism come into focus. To bring the relationship between state, society, and political economy further into focus, one can examine the implications of global economic restructuring (GER) and the deep and protracted global recession of the twenty-first century for the relative success or failure of the global human rights regime that depends on the actions of states.

Neoliberal economic globalization "from above": the human rights implications of global economic restructuring in greater detail

It makes little sense to examine economic crises in the twenty-first century as an individual national phenomenon. Global economic restructuring has reshaped national and international economies, reorganized the relations of production, and inextricably tied the fortunes of one state to another. Global economic restructuring, dominated by major TNCs that transcend national boundaries and often forms of law, is the product of several interlocking factors, including the precedents set by national and international efforts to address shortages and access problems associated with oil and other material resources during the 1970s; the increasing dominance of large transnational corporations as the normative corporate form; the acceleration of the dominance of transnational private financial institutions and "postnational finance capitalism" that includes the International Monetary Fund and World Bank (Parrenas 2001); and the emergence of transnational trade organizations such as the World Trade Organization (Robinson 2001; Sassen 1994, 1996; Naples and Desai 2002) that increasingly dominate the development of international trade and production relations.

One defining feature of global economic restructuring and the postcolonial global economy is deepening international debt of poor and wealthy nations alike (Schaeffer 2003) and the consequent challenge of many states to secure fundamental human rights for their populations. For instance, indebted states are commonly forced by the requirements of structural adjustment programs to redeploy limited financial resources to meeting debt obligations rather than meeting the human rights needs of their domestic public. States that stand on the brink of bankruptcy have little choice but to comply, even at the cost of diminishing human rights practice (Amin 1997; Bond 2003; Bond and Manyanya 2004; Desai 2002; Cooke and Kabeer 2010; Rowbotham and Mitter 1993; Moghadam 2005; Mkandawire and Soludo 2003).

So how did global restructuring shape and frame the global economic crisis of the twenty-first century? How could such a huge and far-reaching crisis happen, and what did it mean for human rights?

Global economic crisis in the twenty-first century

Prior to the stock-market crash at the end of 2008, the US economy was looking pretty strong: the Dow Jones Industrial Average hit a high of 13,338 at the start of the year, when the unemployment rate was 4.6. But seemingly out of the blue, the bubble burst, sending the market tumbling to terrifying lows – the Dow was down to 7,449 by the end of November; the unemployment rate soared to levels unseen since the 1930s (reaching a national rate of 9.6 by 2010, and double digit rates in many metropolitan areas), and banks were collapsing under the crushing weight of monstrous levels of housing foreclosures (Market Watch 2008; Dow Jones Report 2008; US Census Statistical Abstracts 2008). The US stock market suffered the single largest absolute loss in wealth in its history, at an astonishing rate of 33.8 percent. Only twice in the nation's history has there been a larger percentage loss in the Dow Jones Industrial Average (37.7 percent loss in 1907, and 52.7 percent loss in 1931) (Market Watch 2008).

The popular press, and even some politicians, began whispering: were we heading into (or already in the throes of) another Great Depression? The US was clearly not the only economy on the planet caught in this death spiral: most if not all of the biggest and erstwhile most robust economies in the industrial and post-industrial world were experiencing the same nightmare, and worse. The total loss in global equities values hit over $30 trillion in 2008 alone (Market Watch 2008). Why is this story of concern to human rights advocates? How is this global situation related to Mark and Diane's personal financial catastrophe? How did this happen?

Bank (de)regulation

Prior to the Great Depression of the 1930s, there was very little if any federal oversight and regulation of the banking industry. Financial institutions were free to engage in business as they saw fit, wildly speculating in their investments, and often overexposing their assets in the process. The casino mentality that dominated the industry ultimately sparked the benchmark economic debacle of the stock-market crash, panicked runs on banks, and a deep economic Depression that sent shock waves far and wide.

In an attempt to gain better control over the practices of an industry so central to the national economy, Congress passed the Banking Act of 1933, commonly referred to as the Glass-

Steagall Act. This bill established the Federal Deposit Insurance Corporation, insuring the savings accounts of individual depositors up to $100,000, so that even in the event of a bank collapse individuals would not lose their life savings. On a broader, perhaps more important level, the bill restricted the activities that different classes of banks could engage in, establishing different market niches for each class of bank. That way, large commercial banks would not overrun smaller mortgage or savings and loan institutions because they could not compete in the same market niche; and no single bank could so dominate the industry, or the economy, to the detriment of all. For example, no individual financial institution could lend more than 10 percent of its available assets to a single borrower, thus limiting the bank's risk and exposure to the fate of that one borrower (Federal Reserve Bank of New York 1933).

Not surprisingly, from the very start the industry railed against the restrictions the bill introduced. Despite the language of the regulations, the truth is that the defined market niches were more liberally interpreted by federal banking regulators over time, allowing large commercial banks to expand their range of discretionary business and increasingly etching away at the industry's much-hated fetters imposed by the Glass-Steagall Act. Yet banks continued to balk at being regulated.

It wasn't until 1978 that a real opportunity presented itself to the financial institutions to hold as a bargaining chip to Congress in their pursuit of the repeal of Glass-Steagall to deregulate the banking industry. And, notably, it was an opportunity borne of a crisis generated in no small part by the banks themselves, stewarded by state policies; the opportunity did not just happen or materialize out of thin air.

The original auto bailout: Chrysler Corporation

By 1978, Chrysler Corporation was in grave trouble. The once-upon-a-time auto-making giant was hemorrhaging revenue, profits, and market share, its stock value was plummeting, and it owed a tremendous amount to its lenders. When it turned once again to its lenders for debt relief and further support, the financial institutions collectively refused to lend the firm so much as another dime. The grim future facing the firm – and its hundreds of thousands of workers – was bankruptcy.

At the time of this crossroads, Chrysler's lending consortium was composed of a total of over 325 financial institutions (Glasberg 1989). This was because the Glass-Steagall Act's restriction against any single bank lending more than 10 percent of its available assets to any one borrower forced banks to form lending structures, or consortia, in order to collectively provide for the huge borrowing needs of major corporations and governments, since no bank by itself had anywhere near the amount needed. These lending consortia technically violated the legal restriction against bank collusion, but the 10 percent restriction necessitated their existence. When banks joined together in a lending consortium, each provided the amount they legally could, essentially "chipping in" the share they could afford. That spread the exposure and risk of each individual bank, enabled major corporations and governments to access the finance capital they needed to do business, and ensured the safety and security of depositors. Thus, lending consortia were not included in the Glass-Steagall definition of collusion. But the existence of lending consortia structurally empowered the industry, particularly the largest commercial banks, in a way that violated the spirit if not the letter of Glass-Steagall: it gave the banks the ability to wield the power of pulling their collective purse strings, which they did to great effect in their pursuit of repeal of the Glass-Steagall Act when Chrysler stood on the brink of bankruptcy.

Congressional leaders pleaded with Chrysler's banks to bailout the auto-maker with more loans and the purchase of Chrysler's stock, in order to prevent the economic shock waves certain to reverberate wide and deep throughout the economy; a Chrysler bankruptcy had the all-too-real potential to thrust the nation into a very deep recession, or worse. Consider what the bankruptcy of a major firm in a central industry means: not only would a major employer itself go out of business, so too would much of its supplier industries, including rubber, steel, aluminum, glass, textiles, and electronics; whole towns, where these firms were essentially the only major employer, would themselves head into severe economic recessions or Depressions, prompting massive unemployment and bankruptcy of smaller local shops and deep cuts in municipal services, including education, police, fire departments, sanitation and public works, elder care, and the like. And the massive widespread unemployment would serve to inflame economic woes nationally because disposable income and consumers' ability to spend would dramatically decline. Few members of Congress would have constituents who would be safe from the effects of such an economic catastrophe. Banks sensed a crucial moment and seized the opportunity: they adamantly refused to budge, leaving Congress terrified at the grim prospects they faced and ready to negotiate with banks (US Congress, House 1979). What would it take to get the banks to agree to keep Chrysler afloat?

Needless to say, the banks were not at a loss as to the price they wanted: they would agree to swap Chrysler's debt for equity by buying its stock in exchange for a promise from Congress that they would deregulate the banking industry. Congressional leaders were furious at this bold quid pro quo demanded by the banks, and many viewed it as extortion. Banks appeared unmoved and unconcerned by the public relations problem of appearing to callously hold the national economy hostage; they remained focused on the goal of repealing the Glass-Steagall Act. Finally, after many heated exchanges, Congress and the banks agreed to the deal: Chrysler was pulled back from the brink of financial collapse, workers' jobs were presumably saved, and Congressional members avoided having to answer to an angry constituency as to why they allowed jobs to be destroyed (US Congress, House 1979). More importantly, financial institutions had succeeded in gaining an elusive but much-sought goal: by 1982 most of the hated regulatory restrictions had been removed or substantially relaxed, allowing banks to significantly expand their range of business; this set the stage for a free-for-all in the industry where there were no protections for smaller banks from the excesses of, and domination by, the larger ones.

Much of the debate in Congress over deregulating the banking industry was framed in the larger state project of economic intervention. The 1970s and 1980s were a time of retrenchment in which several industries were deregulated, including telephones, trucking, and railroads. The concept that prompted this round of deregulation was laissez-faire (neoliberal) economics: once the federal government was out of the way, industries could operate in an environment of free-market competition in which the invisible hand of the market disciplined the firms. Uncompetitive firms would fail and disappear, and more efficiently run, profitable firms would prevail. Size never figured in this equation (except in Congress's definition of major corporations as "too big to fail"); Congressional leaders never considered that larger corporate entities would pose severe barriers to entry into the industries by smaller, independent firms. Nor was there any discussion of why the banking industry was uniquely different from any of the industries previously deregulated.

Financial institutions are the sole organizations with the role of absorbing all excess finance capital not presently in use (and sitting in savings accounts or pension and trust funds), and invest it by determining its allocation: banks alone get to decide who receives this capital and who does not. The problem is that this arrangement is organized around the distribution of a unique resource – *finance capital*. Unlike any other, finance capital is the sole resource necessary to purchase all other resources required to do any other activity, whether it concerns business or governance. Moreover, unlike any other resource, there are no alternatives to finance capital: those who need it must somehow access it or be completely unable to do business or to govern, which itself poses significant challenges to states' ability to enforce human rights. And unlike any other resource, finance capital is distributed not by a single provider but by a collective of hundreds, and sometimes thousands, of providers, working together and organizing their decision-making for the benefit of the providing group even if that is detrimental to the user. Finance capital is also the sole resource that is only borrowed rather than purchased once and used; as such, finance capital forms a relationship between provider and user that is long-term and poses long-term and far-reaching consequences for the borrower. That unique quality of finance capital places its controllers in an incredible position of power relative not only to other industries, but to the state as well (Glasberg 1989).

Unfortunately, when Congress deliberated whether or not to deregulate the banking industry, they failed to grasp an understanding of finance capital as a unique resource and an extraordinarily powerful base for its providers, making it unlike any of the other industries previously deregulated. Instead, much of the debate centered on the idea that they had already deregulated so many other industries they saw no defensible reason not to also deregulate banks, especially after having made the promise to do so in exchange for saving the economy from the disaster of a Chrysler bankruptcy (Glasberg and Skidmore 1997). The sun was beginning to rise for the banking industry, even as truly ominous storm clouds were gathering for human rights. What effect did bank deregulation have, and how did it affect human rights?

Corporate welfare, bank deregulation, and the savings and loan crisis and bailout

Bank deregulation unleashed a torrent of previously forbidden activities in the banking industry. Without the controls of Glass-Steagall, large commercial banks were now free to compete with smaller savings and loan institutions, investment banks, and insurance companies for business. Previously established market niches no longer defined which markets each would serve, allowing the larger, better-endowed banks to encroach on the markets of these other financial institutions with greater resources in competition for business. And all financial institutions could now engage in riskier investments in an attempt to amplify the assets at their disposal in this unequal battle for market share and for financial assets.

Savings and loan institutions, for example, could now invest in junk bonds, high-yield but extremely high-risk investments that previously were not allowed. Banks could now invest heavily in speculative investments of home and commercial constructions that did not necessarily have buyers, though banks assumed they would when construction was completed. Savings and loan institutions, in particular, were overexposed in this market: under Glass-Steagall, their market niche was to provide low-rate mortgages to American middle-class homebuyers, which meant their returns on investments would be meager and occur over an extended period of time (usually 30 years), and they were restricted in the interest they could pay on customers' savings accounts. Bank deregulation meant they could now offer much greater interest rates on customers' savings accounts in order to attract them away from the larger commercial banks, to generate more cash on hand to invest in the speculative real-estate market. But that meant they were paying out higher rates in the short term than they were getting paid on old mortgages in the long term, creating a severe cash gap (US Congress, House 1990).

It wasn't very long before this cash gap became compounded by the overheated real-estate market, which was by now so saturated there were not enough buyers, and homes and commercial space remained empty and on the market. It also didn't take long before the junk-bond binging became so out of control that whole banks began to go bankrupt. By 1984, junk bonds accounted for nearly 22 percent of the bond market (US Congress: House, 1989); by 1989, 183 savings and loan institutions owned $14.4 billion in junk bonds, 91 percent of which were concentrated in 30 thrift institutions in California, Florida, New York, Texas, and Missouri (*New York Times* 1989). And so was born the savings and loan crisis of the 1980s, when thousands of these institutions went bankrupt.

The collapse of the savings and loan industry sent Congress back to the drawing board to take unprecedented action: they bailed out the industry as a whole. Bailing out major corporations was nothing new to Congress. They had already bailed out over 450 major corporations since World War II, including Lockheed and Chrysler, because, unlike small businesses, major corporations were "too big to fail." The likes of Chrysler Corp. and Lockheed were so huge as employers and as economic actors that the national economy could not afford to allow the invisible hand of the market to discipline them and let them go bankrupt.

But Congress had never before bailed out an entire industry; and they had never before bailed out any corporate entity with a blank check. Every corporate bailout before this had been defined by a specific amount, but the savings and loan bailout was achieved with no such defined limit: the ultimate cost of the bailout was initially estimated to be $500 billion over more than 40 years, with subsequent estimates of the total cost somewhere closer to $1 trillion before it was over (Hays and Hornick 1990: 50). And now the definition of "too big to fail" was expanded to mean not only how many people were employed and how much the firm contributed to the economy, but whether a company was "too centrally important an actor" to be allowed to fail (Glasberg and Skidmore 1997). Congressional leaders believed they had no choice but to bailout banks because these institutions collectively held the resources we all need: families in need of mortgages and student loans, corporations in need of major investments and loans, and governments in desperate need of deficit financing. Without banks we would all be doomed to massive economic Depression. No other firm or industry can claim such central importance to our common interest. Never was the existence of corporate welfare, the state subsidization of private profit-making, made more apparent.

Notably, the corporate welfare of the savings and loan bailout was not accompanied by any attempt of Congress to rein back in the excesses that they had unleashed with bank deregulation. Instead, the bailout allowed larger commercial banks to buy the assets of the failed savings and loan banks while the US absorbed the losses, thereby accomplishing the same acceleration, already under way in all other industries, of increasing concentration of assets of productive capacity in fewer and fewer hands. But, in this case, the process was achieved with Congress's extension of corporate welfare to the savings and loan industry, underwriting the risks of private profit-making for the benefit of private beneficiaries at the expense of smaller, less powerful members of society.

While the machinations of corporations and banks might seem far removed from human rights for individuals, they were, in fact, central to the gathering of elements that set in motion Mark and Diane's, and millions of others', personal crises. It is hardly merely coincidental that this latest incarnation of corporate welfare was undertaken during precisely the same historical "mean season" (Block et al. 1987) in which social welfare programs of the War on Poverty collectively came under severe attack. The culmination of that attack was codified in "welfare reform" of the Personal Responsibility and Work Opportunity Reconciliation Act of 1996 that harshly cut how much money and the amount of time over a lifetime that anyone could collect benefits, on the erroneous assumption that welfare recipients (and their children) were lazy, refused to work, and made a conscious lifestyle of living off the public dole. The assumption was that a loss of benefits would "motivate" otherwise indolent recipients to finally get a job (an assumption that ignored the fact that more than two fifths of the recipients did have jobs; they simply had jobs that paid so poorly they remained below the poverty line). And it ignored the fact that a significant proportion of the poor were children, not able-bodied adults; children were hardly in any position to secure employment. The policy sent millions into deeper poverty, hunger, and homelessness. Welfare reform hit poverty-stricken people of color, particularly single mothers and their children, hardest, as dwindling job opportunities were more readily accessible to white applicants (Neubeck and Cazenave 2001; Neubeck 2006). The increase in corporate welfare came at the expense of social welfare; private profits, particularly of financial institutions, trumped the human rights of the poor, the working class, people of color, single mothers, and children.

Resistance was not absent during the 1970s and 1980s, however. One key piece of legislation that community activists were able to achieve was the Community Reinvestment Act (CRA) of 1977, a piece of legislation that actually empowered community organizations in their struggle against the banks. CRA enabled community organizations to stop banks from expanding their business with new branches or new business ventures without opening their books to these organizations for scrutiny. If the banks' books demonstrated a failure to invest in the communities in which they already had branches (a practice referred to as disinvestment, or redlining), they would not be allowed to expand. At that point, banks would have to enter into negotiations with the community organizations to develop agreements to reinvest in the local, underserved communities. The use of CRA challenges to bank expansions worked (Bostic and Robinson 2005; Immergluck 2004; Schwartz 1998, 2000; Squires 1992, 2003; Shlay 1999), bringing over $35 billion in reinvestment to previously underserved communities by the time Congress took the unprecedented step of bailing out the savings and loan industry.

Financial institutions were not surprisingly furious at this new, effective weapon of the previously weak, and sought to find ways of circumventing the provisions of CRA. The strategy they developed set the stage for the housing foreclosure crisis that sent the economy reeling by 2008.

The wolf is at the gate: predatory lending

The challenge banks faced was how to at least appear on the books to be a "good economic citizen" in the communities where they currently did business, if not actually acting as such. That required some ability to show that they were in fact reinvesting in previously underserved communities so that community activists could not hold up their desired expansions. The cynical strategy they adopted has now come to be understood as predatory lending. Banks aggressively sought to place mortgages in poverty-stricken communities with subprime lending, adopting practices that stretched the bounds of acceptable practice, and often stepping firmly over the line into strictly illegal practices, all of which served to violate the rights of those seeking a small piece of the American dream of homeownership.

While observers now often use the term "predatory lending," the concept has not been clearly defined. In general, predatory lending involves practices of extending credit that injures the borrower, usually by depleting or dispossessing the owner of equity the borrower has previously amassed in homeownership (Goldstein 1999; Bradley 2000). These practices may involve one or more of several techniques of subprime lending. Prime-rate lending is credit extended only to the lowest-risk borrowers. Subprime lending is credit extended at rates higher than the prime rate. Not all subprime lending is predatory: indeed, almost everyone who borrows money accesses credit at interest rates above the prime rate. Subprime lending extends credit to borrowers with risk factors such as poor credit ratings, and as such carries higher interest rates to offset the higher risk such loans pose. Its purpose is to "reward consumers trying to get out of debt and improve their credit by allowing them to build equity in their homes and to transition into prime loans as their credit improves" (Bradley 2000: 160).

The key to subprime lending is that the higher interest rates charged are justified by the level of risk posed by the loan, is applied to all borrowers without discrimination, and carries terms and conditions similar to those applied to prime lending. In contrast, predatory lending is a subcategory of subprime lending, in that it harms rather than helps the borrower with interest rates well beyond the risk posed, is differentially applied to borrowers based on social characteristics (such as class, race, or age), carries terms far more punitive than those applied to prime lending, and is structured in ways that in general attack and erode the equity position of the borrower, rather than helping to build it.

Not all predatory lending is illegal. Predatory lending that is not specifically illegal includes such practices as shifting and bundling unsecured consumer debt (such as credit card debt) into mortgages; application of extraordinarily high annual interest rates, points, and closing costs, well beyond that justified by the risk; single-premium credit insurance; balloon payments on adjustable rate mortgages; mandatory arbitration clauses; repeated refinancing, frequently resulting from high-pressure sales tactics; application of daily interest on late payments; highly aggressive, often abusive collection tactics; pre-payment penalties; failure to report good repayment track record on borrowers' credit reports; and failure to provide clear and accurate loan balance information.

Lender practices that are illegal but still common include: failure to disclose loan terms; failure to provide a Good Faith Estimate; failure to itemize all charges; kickback and referral fees to mortgage brokers, real-estate agents, and contractors; balloon payments on loans with less than five years' maturity; requirements of advance payments; interest rates that rise after default; knowingly structuring loan payments the borrower cannot afford; falsifying loan applications, including forging signatures on loan documents; charging fees significantly higher than the market rate; requiring credit insurance; and changing loan terms at closing (see Bradley 2000).

Subprime lending increased dramatically, especially in the 1990s and into the next century: the number of financial institutions specializing in such lending rose during the years of 1973 to 1999 from 104,000 to 997,000 (US Department of Housing and Urban Development 2000). Furthermore, between 1994 and 2003, the total dollar value of subprime loans rose from $35 billion to $332 billion (Lord 2005). Between just 1994 and 1998, the total dollar value of subprime loans in the US rose more than 500 percent (1999 Home Equity Lending Directory, pp. 1–2). In Connecticut alone, that figure increased by over 42 percent; notably, the increase was by more than 85 percent in neighborhoods where more than half the population included people of color (Collins 2000). Case studies in major metropolitan areas around the country indicate similar patterns in their findings. For example, one study in Philadelphia found that while conventional lending increased by 61 percent between 1992 and 1998, subprime lending exploded by 4,800 percent in two particularly economically poor census tracts. A measure of the damaging effects of these loans can be seen in the fact that foreclosures in these two tracts jumped by 93 percent since 1990 (ACORN 2000).

Subprime lending appears to be related at least in part to social characteristics. In Atlanta, for example, subprime lending in 1997 in low-income neighborhoods was 30 percent higher than elsewhere in the city, and communities of color received 250 percent more subprime loans than all of Atlanta (Gruenstein and Herbert 2000). In Ohio, subprime lenders provided more than two thirds of the refinance loans in census tracts largely populated by people of color (NCRC 2007). In North Carolina, the most recent data from the Housing Mortgage Disclosure Act indicated that subprime lending was concentrated in counties with high populations of African Americans. African Americans received 10 percent of conventional loans, but 20 percent of subprime loans (Bradley 2000). Noted McNally (2010: 1124), "by 1998 . . . subprime mortgages comprised one-third of all home loans made to African Americans and a fifth to those made to Latinos," and those figures continued to rise steadily into the next century. Krivo and Kaufman (2004) found that both groups were given mortgage loans with significantly higher interest rates than those given to whites, and are 1.5 to 2.5 times more likely to pay interest of 9 percent or more. Most notably, these borrowers were not steered into subprime mortgages because they represented a high risk: nearly two thirds of these borrowers "qualified for traditional mortgages" (McNally 2010: 124).

Why would banks place mortgages that clearly will not be viable at some point in the future? And why target populations that are unlikely to be able to sustain the mortgage payments in the long run, or deliberately structure loans with a high probability of future failure? Part of the answer lies in the change in the industry, prompted by federal bank deregulation policy, from one dominated by a conventional mainstream lender to an industry with a wide array of financial players, with some of these financial service providers not being subject to CRA regulation (Temkin, Johnson, and Levy 2002); many of these specialize in offering subprime credit, originating a higher percentage of loans and higher percentage of subprime loans in low-income communities (Cochrane, Surette, and Zorn 2004; US Department of Housing and Urban Development 2000). These new sources of credit, ungoverned by CRA legislation, operate under the radar of CRA protections for the community. And they easily become handservants to the cynical abuses of those institutions that are subject to CRA challenges: when larger banks aggressively secure unfair mortgages in previously underserved communities, they immediately sell them off to the secondary market of these smaller investment banks; as such, the originating bank now looks like it is acting in good faith to serve the community in which it currently does business, while avoiding the inevitable foreclosure when the mortgage can no longer be paid. Originating banks have targeted the poor and people of color because these are the citizens who have previously been ignored in the market for homeownership, and are thus far more vulnerable to the aggressive offer of an opportunity to access homeownership.

For most of those targeted by predatory lending, it is the only chance to own their own home. For banks, it is the chance to circumvent the CRA restrictions, even if it does mean the violation of others' human rights, and even if it means reproducing racialized inequality (Beeman, Glasberg, and Casey 2010). But while this arrangement helped banks avoid the restrictions of CRA, and at least temporarily put previously ignored people into their own homes, the dream of homeownership was short-lived: the predator was at the gate, and the foreclosure crisis soon loomed over the homeowners (particularly homeowners of color, who as a group were just beginning to finally join the American dream in ever-larger numbers), the communities in which they lived, and the wider economy. By 2010, banks were estimated to have repossessed more than 800,000 homes (Associated Press 2011); overall, 2.7 million of the 42.2 million Americans who took out mortgages between 2004 and 2008 lost their homes to foreclosure (Berlin 2012). Notably, more than 56 percent of African-American homeowners have lost their foothold in the American dream to foreclosure (McNally 2010: 126). And former Bank of America employees have alleged that the bank "deliberately denied eligible home owners loan modifications . . . to shepherd homeowners into foreclosure . . . [which] yielded the bank more profits than the government-sponsored Home Affordable Modification Package," and offered cash bonuses and gift cards as incentives to employees who hastened foreclosures (Conlin and Rudegeair 2013).

It is important to note that this was not simply a crisis of individuals overextending themselves into mortgages they could not possibly afford; it was a crisis triggered by zealously calculated and predatory violations of people's rights as a strategy to circumvent the provisions of CRA that empowered communities, in order for banks to continue to amass private profit. It was not simply a crisis created by rogue individual bankers; it was a crisis borne out of the standard practices of the industry in its pursuit of profits alongside a drive to subvert CRA and the empowered community activist organizations. Sadly, standard operating banking and finance practices designed to subvert state policies and safeguards continue to plague the economy, both in the US and around the world. Witness the 2012 admission by James Dimon, JP Morgan Chase's President and Chief Executive Officer (and member of the Board of Directors of the New York Federal Reserve), that the firm's dubious practice of hedge investments and trading had resulted in an eye-popping $2 billion loss.

This latest revelation illustrates that the same practices that ignited the Great Recession continue unabated, and are being preserved and protected by the same owning class who continue to block (and to fund and support politicians who block) any real regulation and oversight. Indeed, far from being the enemy of private capital accumulation, the Obama administration and the Justice Department have not aggressively pursued criminal charges and indictments against predatory lenders or hedge-fund managers. And despite the creation of the Consumer Financial Protection Bureau and a promise to "clean up Wall Street" and create a "fair playing field," there has been an absence of all due haste to re-regulate the banking and finance industry. Wall Street and the banking and finance industry remain free from federal regulation and criminal liability, at the cost of economic human rights for working people affected by the fallout.

The foreclosure crisis was thus not simply a blip on the economic radar, restricted to the single industry of banking or housing; it was a severe crisis in a central element of the overall economy and therefore positioned to send more than mere ripples throughout the economy in the US and abroad. The foreclosure crisis was to become ground zero for the worst, most protracted recession since the Great Depression, which would have significant effects on human rights.

The global "Great Recession" of 2008, its global reach, and the human rights enterprise

By 2008, the Great Recession was clearly in full swing after more than three decades of extended economic growth and unprecedented heights of stock-market values. Stock markets in the US and abroad tumbled in a free fall to levels not seen in decades, and at alarming rates. Millions of people lost their homes; tens of millions of workers, including those with high levels of education and training, lost their jobs; manufacturers closed their doors, either in bankruptcy or in desperate attempts to relocate to cheaper locations; financial institutions, including some of the biggest household names in banking and investment like Lehman Brothers, faced bankruptcy themselves or became targets for mergers and takeovers.

This was not the first time that the structure of the financial industry had been at the epicenter of economic meltdown; nor was it the first time that meltdown was not restricted to the United States. Indeed, even before formal deregulation of the US banking industry began in the 1980s, the unregulated international banking market allowed financial institutions to engage in predatory lending practices with developing countries similar to those used on private homeowners here. Banks intently sought to place development loans in countries that were struggling for escape from the domination by the international aid regimes of the World Bank, the International Bank for Reconstruction and Development, and the International Monetary Fund. These aid-regime members all placed severe restrictions, specifying precise projects in which the loans could be invested, and therefore wrested control of domestic policymaking in these countries. Private banks placed no such restriction on their loans: borrowing nations were free to use the loans in any way they saw fit. Private bank loans thus offered an irresistible escape route from international aid regimes, and, in their zeal to place these loans, banks aggressively reassured the borrowing countries that they would have no problem servicing the debt. The price of developing countries' emancipation from the international debt regimes came at a horrible price: after 1973, developing countries' combined global debt grew by over 500 percent, to almost half a trillion dollars (McNally 2010: 127), just in time for the oil crisis of 1973 to plunge economies throughout the world into severe recessions. In response to the crisis, banks sharply increased the interest rates for these loans, sending developing countries tumbling over the brink.

The International Monetary Fund reappeared at their doors, imposing a standard austerity package that required, among other things, a severe devaluation of the troubled economy's currency, a discontinuation of imports with a simultaneous significant increase in exports to generate dollars in income, and a sharp reduction if not elimination of social welfare expenditures in favor of devoting the bulk of the gross national product to servicing the private bank loans. The combined crushing debt burdens of developing countries, and their subsequent if reluctant acceptance of the austerity package, threatened the economies of the wealthier, industrialized, and post-industrialized countries that could ill-afford the tsunami of cheaper goods coming from these struggling economies combined with the loss of exports to them. But the greater economic wallop was felt in developing countries. In effect, tremendous economic resources were being siphoned out of developing economies and sent to private banks in the industrialized and post-industrialized West.

Schaeffer (2003) illustrates how this played out in the example of Argentina, where debt grew from $40 billion to $132 billion between 1982, at the dawn of the debt crisis, and 2001:

> At IMF request, the government introduced repeated austerity programs. But its debts grew anyway, despite its two-decade effort to repay them. The most recent austerity program, announced in 2001, required the government to cut salaries and pensions for government workers. Teachers have not been paid for months, schools can no longer afford to boil water to make powdered milk for malnourished children, and pubic health officials no longer vaccinate dogs for rabies, leading to a widespread outbreak of the disease. (Schaeffer 2003: 110)

In short, the austerity program, intended to clean Argentina's economic house, resulted in severe social and economic consequences that ironically thwarted any economic recovery: unpaid teachers means children will not be educated and teachers will not be able to purchase consumer goods; malnourished children and a disease epidemic undermine the continued development of a strong and healthy workforce that in turn could be better positioned to contribute to the growth of a robust economy. And Argentina was hardly alone in its economic woes. UN reports suggest that what happened in Argentina was widespread, and a result of lop-sided or "selective" capitalist development. Where a neocolonial approach to global capital would point to state actors in managing imperialist systems as the key to the problem, Schaeffer's (2003) concept of "selective globalization" suggests a more structural explanation: capitalism works to centralize privately appropriated capital and wealth at the expense of impoverished populations who are systematically excluded from opportunities for financial independence.

But where the concept of "selective globalization" suggests that crushing debt and economic crises (and consequent inability to ensure human rights) beset impoverished states more so than wealthy and advantaged states, the restructured global "free market" means that powerful states are actually similarly constrained. A notable feature of the global economic system is that this neoliberal, "free-market" model has bound states, their economies, and their banks in problematic dependent relationships. What started as mortgage and credit crises in the US has now become a global recession in what seemed like an instant. As a result, global populations continue to suffer, including those in more powerful states such as the US, China, and several members of the European Union.

The process of resource drain to the Western private banks accelerated under the "debt for equity" swaps that ostensibly were designed to help ease developing countries' debt burden but that in essence gave creditors a claim on valuable resources as the price of "forgiveness" of debt (McNally 2010). And, because of enduring high interest rates, developing countries found themselves unable to pay off their debts, even when they maintained minimum regular repayments, much like individual credit card users find that minimum monthly payments to the banks mostly pay off interest owed, not principal.

In the zero-sum game of fiscal budgeting, when increasing funds are devoted to debt servicing, other parts of the budget will have to be decreased. Enrichment of private banks that preyed on developing countries' loss of power in international aid regimes came at the expense of global South countries, and at the expense of the human rights of their citizens as social welfare programs were slashed and poverty deepened. Consequently, hunger and homelessness accelerated, infant mortality increased, and health epidemics spread at alarming rates unseen in the West, often wiping out significant proportions of the population. Governments responded to the subsequent civil unrest of food riots, social protest, and political challenges by violently clamping down on protestors. Thousands were jailed, beaten, maced, "disappeared," or otherwise silenced by police forces intent on restoring political stability at all costs. Free speech, free press, and free assembly were commonly eliminated in the process.

The most recent severe economic contraction in the US that began in 2008 similarly was not contained within its borders. National economies around the world plunged into the depths of economic crisis, including erstwhile prosperous European economies like Greece, Spain, Britain, Italy, Portugal, and Ireland, and oil-rich economies like Dubai. All faced the daunting task of balancing beleaguered budgets plagued by a loss of tax revenues because of rising unemployment in the face of increased pressures to address rising expenditures and debt to support the huge costs of post-9/11 military and security programs, corporate welfare, and social welfare. Bond markets, panicked by the endless reports of deepening economic crisis, downgraded the bond ratings of national economies; investors fled their bonds in droves, further aggravating the problem and threatening to plunge some of the biggest economies in the world into default and bankruptcy (Taibbi 2011). The party was clearly over. But was it over for all? Whose party was over, and who would pay the bill for the party?

Faced with the horrendous prospect of a global economic meltdown, the world's wealthiest nations' central banks embarked on the biggest bank bailout in history, spearheaded by the US Federal Reserve, pumping a transfusion of trillions of dollars directly into banks and into stimulus packages to encourage consumer spending. "All told, governments in the world's largest economies anteed up something in the order of $20 trillion – an amount equivalent to one and half times the U.S. gross domestic product – via a massive intervention without historical precedent" (McNally 2010: 2–3).

Oddly enough, none of these governments demanded changes in how financial institutions did business as a quid pro quo for bailing them out. And worse, at least in the US, the same financial institutions that benefited from the federal bailout within months announced mind-boggling bonuses for the executives who had led these institutions, and the national economy, to disaster (Taibbi 2011; Ferguson 2012). The Great Bank Bailout did seem to avert an unthinkable national and global Great Depression, but did not erase the problem: "the bank debt that triggered the crisis in 2008 never went away – it was simply shifted on to governments . . . the bank crisis morphed into a sovereign debt crisis . . . it *mutated* [emphasis in original]" (McNally 2010: 4). And now, with all the risks and costs of the bailout firmly on the shoulders of the state, the burden and the costs of ensuring private largess shifted to those who had never benefited from that largess or, worse, were unimaginably harmed by the institutional arrangements that enriched the few at the vast expense of the many.

This global recession differs from previous recessions in significant ways affecting human rights: unlike earlier in the twentieth century, the most recent incarnation of globalization has increasingly exposed pensions, retirement savings, and other forms of working-class economic security to "the market" (Albo, Gindin, and Panitch 2010). Unlike before, public pensions (such as the California Public Employees' Retirement System, for example) and others (such as the Teachers' Insurance and Annuity Association-College Retirement Equities Fund (TIAA-CREF)) are basically packaged, invested, and traded on the market by financial institutions like everything else. Workers' own deferred wages are now being used by financial institutions in ways that ultimately serve to contradict their rights and their future security. The worker now can hardly avoid being reduced to a poker chip in the capitalist casino.

Moreover, the Great Recession, brought to us with the use of the workers' own combined deferred wages as part of the arsenal, served to compromise workers' rights. Witness the political and rights discourse fallout from the recession on public employee unions and pensions, which have been framed as an overindulgence created by overly powerful unions. Legislation to decertify public unions in Wisconsin, Michigan, Ohio, and Indiana became the first salvos to discredit unions in general, in the name of balancing beleaguered budgets. Once again, the interests of capital accumulation, finance, and the overall political economy trumped human rights. While the federal government bailed out the very institutions that had sent the national and international economies tumbling in a free fall, none of the key instigators was prosecuted. Banks had received billions of dollars that they then deployed into bonuses for their executives, rewarding behavior that reaped bank profits by misleading investors. And the compromise of workers' rights came at the hand of the very state that was supposed to enforce human rights as delineated by international human rights agreements and conventions.

Human rights implications

Averting a global economic meltdown with a bank bailout came at a hefty price, borne unequally. Philip Beresford (2010) of *The Times* of London noted that the wealthiest members of society did not feel the economic collapse as anything other than a hiccup, but that the rest of society will feel the severe pain of austerity budgets for some time as the state struggles to reduce the deficit amid sharply reduced tax revenues: "The rest of the country is going to have to face spending cuts, but it has little effect on the rich because they don't consume public services" (available at <http://www.wsws.org/en/articles/2010/04/rich-a29.html>). As commonly happens under austerity measures, the budget cuts were most harshly foisted on the backs of the poor and working class with significant reductions in spending for anti-poverty measures like Food Stamps and school meal programs, low-income housing subsidies, Medicaid, public education, public transportation, jobs programs, and the like (Taibbi 2011). Periodic debates in the US Congress and state legislatures over whether or not to raise the minimum wage were framed not in terms of the desperate need for a living wage for workers, but in terms of the cost to profit-making of businesses. "This is not the time to impose more costs on businesses" was the common refrain, indicating a failure to appreciate that the right to food and adequate shelter was being compromised in the name of private profit maintenance. Similar positions were echoed in places like Greece, where repeated convulsive resistance to austerity has been met with state violence and sharp rebuke of demands for human rights as the state sought to find economic stability.

Arguments about extending entitlements to unemployment insurance similarly revolved around the cost of the extensions rather than the right of workers to a decent living, having been laid off through no fault of their own. Severe cuts in school budgets and the consequent layoff of badly needed teachers occurred without a wider view of the right of children to an adequate and affordable education. Pitched political battles over universal healthcare became framed, particularly in the 2012 presidential election season, in terms of the cost of the program, especially for employers, rather than in terms of the right of everyone to adequate healthcare. And nowhere was this issue understood as one of *public* health affecting everyone; it was individualized, with the affluent able to access first-rate care no matter what, and everyone else subject to their own limited or non-existent ability to pay. The right to education, food, housing, health, and the like was once again framed as the sole responsibility of individuals to provide for themselves. In a cruel twist, the right to a living wage that would make that possible was also under attack as "too expensive right now" for employers.

But while it's true that the wealthy do not consume public services such as Temporary Assistance to Needy Families, Food Stamps, public transportation, public education, Unemployment Insurance, and Medicaid, McNally (2010: 5) rightfully points out that the rich actually *were* and continue to be affected by the deep spending cuts the state made in the name of budget deficit reduction, in that these cuts were key "to the massive transfer of wealth from the poor to the rich that funded the rescue of the world banking system, the bailout of corporations, and the salvage of the investment portfolios of the wealthy" (see also Taibbi 2011; Ferguson 2012).

By 2012, the stock market had bounced back nearly to the levels it enjoyed before 2008, and corporate profits and corporate executives were once again logging hefty numbers, even if employment lagged and struggled to inch upward. Although the stock market indicated a recovery was under way, the data on unemployment, and underemployment, indicated that the "human recession" stubbornly remained a harsh reality for millions of people, including for military veterans returning from multiple deployments to Iraq and Afghanistan in support of wars that reinforced the enrichment of the few.

Moreover, the austerity measures adopted to balance the beleaguered budget will actually aggravate the global recession because the initial indicators of a weak recovery were prompted by trillions of dollars in state stimulus expenditures to encourage spending, stimulus investments which have now expired. Whatever shot in the arm the stimulus expenditures initially provided is no longer available, and so consumer spending on new cars and home renovations will trickle away, as will public spending on infrastructural improvements (spending which would have stimulated job creation). The loss of stimulus infusion, therefore, means that both private and public economic spending will be sharply curtailed, prompting yet more austerity measures to balance the budget. We have already seen the global reverberation of this in Greece, Spain, Britain, Ireland, and elsewhere in 2010 and again in 2012.

The "recovery" was, in short, unsustainable without state spending. "Even the World Bank, which strongly advocates austerity, has openly conceded it will dampen growth" (McNally 2010: 6). Even Paul Krugman (2012), an earlier architect and staunch defender of trade strategies of the 1980s and 1990s that relied on market forces and the imposition of austerity, has now admitted these policies were a resounding failure in the US and abroad; the expected "rising tide" of extended economic prosperity did not "raise all boats" after all. Cutting taxes for wealthy individuals and corporations, on the assumption that they would invest these cuts in new job creation, did not result in new, full-time, gainful employment; instead, this approach resulted in enrichment of the most affluent at the expense of the human rights of most. More people became downwardly mobile, unemployed and under-employed, homeless, hungry, and increasingly unable to afford healthcare and education (see also Stiglitz 2012). Krugman now notes that history actually favors the Keynesian strategy of print-ing and spending more money: government investments in public works projects, education, and the like, which put more people to work, invested in critical infrastructure, and increased individuals' spendable incomes, which would ultimately stimulate the private sector of manufacturing and services. He has, in fact, criticized the Obama administration's stimulus response to the Great Recession as inadequate: whatever economic stimulus infusions there were did not in fact encourage consumers to spend or corporations to invest; instead, both were far more likely to use the stimulus money to reduce debts rather than invest or purchase goods, and therefore became the indirect intermediaries shoveling federal money into the hands of the banks, the very institutions initially responsible for the crisis in the first place (Taibbi 2011; Ferguson 2012). The gap between wealth and poverty not surprisingly has widened significantly, at the great expense of basic human rights.

This discussion of global restructuring and human rights sug-gests that the structure of the political economy, both nationally and globally, played a significant role in the Great Recession of the twenty-first century: the collective position of financial institutions as the controllers of the unique and critical resource of finance capital enabled them to constrain the discretion of the state, both domestically and internationally, at the expense of human rights. To ignore their interests was not an option for the state. That structural relationship, however, was not without influence by business dominance. Recall the key role of players like Paulson, Gaithner et al. in applying pressures to discipline and remind legislators of their limited power to ignore capital accumulation objectives and imperatives, and the peril of doing so. Note their success in securing state policies, in the guise of crisis management that remained consistent with those objectives, all at the expense of human rights.

But this is not the full story: the structural position of financial institutions and the importance of the political economy, as well as their dominating business handservants, were not all-powerful. Pressures from below to reassert human rights continued to percolate up from below to affect the process.

Human rights and resistance in the face of recession and owning class impunity

It is noteworthy that the human rights violations resulting from the Great Recession were not simply or even primarily violations by the state (as many international human rights accords would imply), but rather violations prompted by private economic actors (corporations) alone and in concert with or enabled by the state and its policymaking power. But also noteworthy is that none of these actions occurred without resistance from below. And some of the resistance has been so strong, and growing, that it has become impossible for the state or private actors to ignore. Employed as part of a theoretical lens, the human rights enterprise enables us to appreciate the push and pull of the process of human rights, resistance, and human rights from below, even and especially in the age of the Great Recession and consequent austerity.

Challenges to predatory lending, the key spark igniting the economic catastrophe of the Great Recession, have intensified in community activism and direct action, and in the rise in watchdog organizations in local communities and states. Local activist organizations, such as Connecticut Fair Housing, advocate for people in danger of foreclosure, helping them to navigate the legal process in their battle to retain the roof over their heads. Others take more direct action in challenging and resisting foreclosures. In 2008, the Nashville (Tennessee) Homeless Power Project adopted the strategy of exercising their modern squatters' rights to reclaim vacant Housing and Urban Development (HUD) homes on property that had been re-zoned for development of luxury housing. They underscored their intent in this direct action with their assertion that they were not going to leave the reclaimed homes voluntarily.

Organizers pointed out that the group had already quietly taken over many vacant houses in the city, and vowed to continue to do so until all the homeless had homes (Barbieux 2008).

That same year, a Chicago sheriff refused to evict tenants from rental properties whose absentee owners had defaulted on mortgages. Sheriff Tom Dart noted that many of these tenants had in fact paid their rents regularly and on time, and were unaware that the landlords collecting their rents had stopped using that money to pay the mortgages, pushing banks to foreclose the buildings in which they lived. "Where mortgage firms see pieces of paper, my deputies see people . . . [E]victions are part of our job. What isn't part of our job, however, is to carry out work on behalf of the multi-billion-dollar banks and mortgages industries," he told reporters (<Turning Left2008http://www.suntimes.com/news/oth erviews/1211633,cst-nws-evict09. article>). Here, law enforcement employees whose very job is to enforce laws designed to protect private property and private profit recognized violations of basic human rights of the many for the profit of the few, and they refused to comply.

Pressures from below have begun to percolate up to the ranks of legislatures and the judiciary. In addition to the direct actions of local resistance, lawyers have joined resistance from the bottom up, adopting effective and aggressive legal strategies to challenge foreclosures. Judges are becoming less inclined to automatically support predatory banks' interests if they discover the slightest anomaly in the procedures and paperwork of the mortgages in question. Courts increasingly view these anomalies as violations of statutes designed to protect the rights of borrowers, such as the Truth in Lending Act, Fair Debt Collection Practices Act, and Real Estate Settlement Procedures Act. Judges who find statute violations have allowed the borrower to cancel the loan, which effectively stymies the foreclosure. When that happens, a new mortgage must be negotiated, and any payments the borrower has made must be credited entirely toward the principal of the mortgage (the bank does not get any interest); the borrower can refinance the balance of the principal at better terms than the original, predatory loan. At least 36 states have passed legislation against predatory and subprime lending (Seidenberg 2008). Cities have also passed local ordinances limiting the rates that lenders can charge and creating watchdog lists of predatory lenders. Of course, the process is not without pushback from lenders or from their federal supporters. While some of the local ordinances have been enforced (Chicago), others (such as Cleveland) have been met with high resistance from lenders and overturned by the Feds. But that pushback is not at all surprising; nor does it crush resistance from below, whether that resistance comes in the form of direct action or more formal, legal challenges.

Direct actions and legal challenges are part of a growing resistance to predatory lending as a violation of economic rights. One of the challenges confronting their efforts is to reframe the social construction of subprime lending from the popular characterization of being an unfortunate and unanticipated symptom of a temporary but deep economic downturn, to a framework identifying the predatory nature of these practices as a human rights violation and pointing out their role in igniting the Great Recession.

In Cleveland, community organizers took on house "flippers" who worked hand in hand with predatory lenders. Flippers are speculators who buy rundown, often foreclosed, houses cheaply and then resell them at a huge profit to new prey of unsuspecting buyers with the aid of predatory lenders. Organizers brought the worst offender of the house "flippers" to the attention of the judge in the city's housing court. The organizers got the Building and Housing Department to cite the flipper for code violations on a house he was trying to resell without making important repairs. When the flipper failed to show up for his court appearance, the judge found him at a local donut shop and placed him under house arrest for 30 days in one of his own "dilapidated structures." Shortly after he completed his sentence, the flipper relocated his flipping business to Columbus, Ohio. It didn't take very long for word to travel between community organizations: the flipper was convicted of fraud in Columbus (Kotlowitz 2009). Clearly, struggle in the human rights enterprise to prevent the isolation and deprivation of extreme poverty and racial discrimination happens not just through the courts and the UN, but also more locally, through communities' refusal to wait for federal policy and UN agreements to catch up to their plight, when they resort to direct action instead.

Moreover, predatory lending is not only a violation of economic rights. Predatory lending has eroded the single most important source of most people's access to wealth in the US: homeownership. And the dispossession has been most pronounced among people of color. Whiteness itself becomes property that can be translated to economic rights and economic profit (Beeman, Glasberg, and Casey 2010). It is no surprise, then, that the racialized wealth gap is wider now than it has ever been. Predatory lending, coupled with centuries of dispossession, has all but eliminated the most significant source of wealth for people of color as a process of institutionalized racism became embedded in the structure of the economy. Organizations such as the National Community Reinvestment Coalition are beginning to socially reconstruct our understanding of predatory lending as an issue of racialized economic injustice, and therefore an issue of civil rights as much as economic rights.

The prism of the intersection of economic, social, political, and civil rights is significant: economic justice continually affects other human rights issues, such as educational opportunity, access to adequate housing, and improvement of one's standard of living. Economic justice is the key to making civil, social, and political rights real and meaningful. And the security of the roof over one's head, without predators cynically engineering the eventual loss of that roof in the service of private profits, is an important part of economic justice.

Beyond the issue of predatory lending, the struggle for human rights from below has been expanding in direct actions like Occupy Wall Street in the US and elsewhere. Although the popular press continually complained that the movement lacked focus and a clear message, the message was in fact quite clear: the growing and fundamental gap between extreme wealth of the few (the "1 percent") at the expense of the extreme poverty of everyone else (the "99 percent"). The movement had been galvanized by the Great Recession and the growing frustration that even those, like

Mark and Diane, who had done everything they were supposed to do to "get ahead" (earning a college education, working hard, sacrificing, obeying the law, serving the country in the military), suddenly found themselves intractably unemployed or underemployed and losing their homes to foreclosure. Others discovered the cost of college or buying a home simply out of reach financially. Still others found their life savings and investments toward retirement evaporate in the casino mentality and corruption of Wall Street and corporate greed, while the initiators of the economic debacle enjoyed tremendous profits and personal gains. The Great Recession may have ushered in the end of the party, but the party continued on for the 1 percent; the bill for the party was handed to the 99 percent.

So was born the Occupy Wall Street movement. Rather than simply demonstrate and picket to express their discontent, participants literally occupied the streets, setting up tents in Zuccati Park in the heart of Wall Street and refusing to leave. Their direct action quickly spread: occupiers were setting up tent cities in parks and other public spaces all over the country, in opposition to inequality and injustice. Many became full, organized communities, with libraries and public soup kitchens (feeding local homeless denizens whom they gladly fed along with the protestors), warming tents, clean-up crews to keep the areas litter-free, medical tents, security crews to protect the protestors, etc. Cities and municipalities responded to this disruption of business as usual by citing anti-vagrancy laws and health code ordinances against serving food without a license, as well as citing disturbance of the peace, and sent in police to clear the areas. After police cleared out occupiers in many cities, often using extreme violence to do so in places like Oakland, California, occupiers claimed that while it may be possible to physically remove them from the park, the ideas could not be eradicated. And others took even more direct action, addressing the right to housing by taking over foreclosed homes and apartments.

Meanwhile, other direct actions challenge the deprivation of the right to something as basic as food. Groups like Food Not Bombs provide meals to the hungry and homeless in public spaces like parks and commons. They collect food from dumpsters behind supermarkets, catering halls, dorms, and restaurants, and recycle it by cooking nutritious meals. Local governments try to stop them by criminalizing their response to hunger, citing public nuisance, anti-vagrancy, and public health laws. Middletown, Connecticut, cited their lack of a Health Department permit to handle and provide food, for example. Food Not Bombs fought back, arguing that churches and parent organizations who sell home-baked goods at bake sales or who hold pot-luck fundraising dinners are not required to obtain these permits, and the parks and commons are public spaces for public access and use. After a protracted court battle, Food Not Bombs won the right to fill the void the state left open and continue to feed the hungry and homeless (Shannon 2011).

The significance of the human rights enterprise and the notion of human rights well beyond formal legal instruments are largely missed by dominant paradigms in human rights scholarship. Sociological perspectives, particularly political sociology, offer theories of the state that allow us to critically contextualize the state and formal, legal approaches to "doing human rights." As a result, we are better able to explain the inconsistent role of the state in realizing human rights practice in agreement with international instruments, and as detailed again in chapter 3, the history of human rights struggles being waged against or in spite of the states charged with their protection.

The point of the human rights enterprise is that human rights are an expression of shifting power relationships in process. In action, they're not a thing that is given or taken away, that once won no longer requires vigilance to maintain. They emerge from struggle – a demand of and challenge to the status quo – exerting pressure from below, sometimes taking direct action, always troubling the institutions, resisting and challenging the denial of rights by private interests and the state. The Great Recession set human rights issues in a stark contrast; analyzed as a power struggle and expression of the human rights enterprise, opportunities for action and meaningful human rights praxis emerge. We will return to these specific questions of praxis in the following chapters.

What makes resistance and pressure from below particularly effective in the defining and realizing of human rights? In the next chapter we will examine social movement theory and the history of civil rights in the US, to analyze the role and forms of resistance that tend to drive the broader human rights enterprise.

3

The Human Rights Enterprise

A Genealogy of Continuing Struggles

June, 2013: Anti-racist activists watched with horror as the Supreme Court handed down three decisions that strike at two important pillars of the civil rights struggle in the US. The first decision – on the Voting Rights Act – reverted power to local officials to decide what is "fair" in terms of voting rights procedures. Many civil rights activists felt their sacrifices were set back, including United States Congressman John Lewis, who was a leader in the Civil Rights Movement (Jeltsen 2013). In the second decision, the Supreme Court sent the *Fisher* v. *University of Texas-Austin* case back to the federal court on the grounds that they had not adequately scrutinized previous rulings on the consideration of race in admissions decisions. In the original case, a student charged the University of Texas-Austin with discriminating against her as a white woman who was somehow disadvantaged by the university's affirmative action policies that encourage and facilitate the enrollment of students of color (but also, ironically, white women). The ruling is being seen as a fundamental challenge to current affirmative action policies – one of many legal legacies of the Civil Rights Movement. According to the majority opinion of the court, the onus is now on the universities to demonstrate that race-neutral alternatives to affirmative action will not meet similar goals (Hamilton 2013). In a further move, in 2014, the Supreme Court upheld the state of Michigan's and seven other states' attempts to ban affirmative action in admissions to public universities (Liptak 2014).

July 2013: George Zimmerman was found not guilty of murdering African-American teenager Trayvon Martin in a very high-profile jury trial. In February 2012, Zimmerman – a self-appointed neighborhood watchman – saw Martin with his hoodie up in a light rain walking through a residential complex. Zimmerman called the police, suggesting that Martin looked suspicious. After ignoring several attempts by police dispatchers to persuade him to not follow Martin, and stay in his vehicle, Zimmerman pursued the teen, got out of his car, and a brief conflict ensued that ended in the point-blank shooting dead of Martin, who was found to be carrying only a drink and bag of Skittles candies. The jury decided that under Florida's stand-your-ground laws, the killing was justified. Even as a groundswell of protest developed, connecting the case to systemic racism and the historical legacy of excusing the murder of unarmed, innocent African-American men like Emmett Till, Medgar Evers, and Oscar Grant, public discourse still questioned the role of "race" in the case or in other cases where stand-your-ground laws were employed (Alvarez and Buckley 2013).

As we reflect on the human rights enterprise as a terrain of struggles, these legal decisions in the summer of 2013 alone provide a starting point for understanding the linked nature of historical and contemporary human rights struggles for racial justice. Taken together, the verdicts of these cases seem to indicate that the US does not need strong laws and continuing political commitment to monitor and eliminate racial discrimination. However, for millions of people around the country who are interested in eliminating racism, these decisions represent an unraveling of three key pillars of the Civil Rights Movement – voting rights, rights to equal education, equal protection under the law – which are also fundamental human rights, according to the IBHR. The civil rights struggles in the mid-twentieth century led to the passage of federal laws (and federal commitment) to end discrimination in political participation, enable access to education and housing, and provide protection from violence. The US has invoked these laws repeatedly to indicate its success in meeting the standards laid down by the International Convention on the Elimination of Racial Discrimination (ICERD). In this chapter we focus on the struggles that led to the passage of mid-twentieth-century civil rights legislation, and the struggle to substantively claim these rights, as well as the implications of these verdicts in 2013 and 2014.

In the previous chapters we discussed the human rights enterprise, emphasizing that rights are obtained through ongoing struggles for power, resources, and political voice. We focus here on struggles to obtain racial justice – through the process of claiming legal and substantive rights – and we juxtapose these struggles against the contradictory role of states to enable *and* fiercely resist such claims for rights. We use the insights of political sociologists, specifically, social movement scholars who have argued that mere grievances against unjust systems do not lead people to mobilize for change. People organize to claim rights, but not all types of mobilization lead to successful outcomes. Nor are rights guaranteed over time – we return to this point in chapters 4 and 5. The people involved in the movements, their organized ability to persuade other people to support their cause, the material and non-material resources they invoke to support their struggle, and the context in which the struggle unfolds are germane to our understanding of the human rights enterprise.

We begin this chapter with a brief introduction to some key concepts in social movement literature that will help us to understand the anatomy of struggles to define and realize human rights. Following this, we present the struggle over human rights and racial justice in the US, focusing specifically on the struggles related to the Civil Rights Acts (1964, 1965, 1968) of the 1960s. We then discuss some of the continuing struggles for racial justice today.

Social movement scholarship and some key definitions

In order to understand the struggle for racial justice, we use some of the concepts developed by scholars who study social movements and collective action.[1] *Social movements* are collective efforts oriented toward change; they involve organizations and show some degree of continuity; they support extra-institutional and institutional protests, claims-making, lobbying, and related activity; social movement participants share the broad goals of the movements, even though they might differ about the specific tactics and emphases; their success depends on the degree of overt or covert resistance they encounter (McAdam and Snow 1997). Social movements often involve multiple organizations and networks, and are "focused on changing one or more elements of the social, political and economic system within which they are located" (Ballard, Habib, and Valodia 2006: 3). Social movements attempt to wrest power to make and re-make institutions, to produce and disseminate ideologies to alter how people think of their concerns and options, to set agendas and policies, and to alter patterns of interactions that translate policy and law into everyday realities. Social movement scholars have highlighted three broad aspects of mobilization that are particularly important for understanding the struggles regarding human rights: structures of opportunities, including the constraints on mobilization; resources and tactics that movement agents/actors command in order to mobilize others; and the ways in which they frame their understanding of injustice.

Political opportunity structures

One of the key puzzles about human rights struggles is that of understanding the conditions under which they emerge. Are there external factors that make it possible or difficult to organize protests and movements? Prior to the 1970s, scholars speculated that *relative deprivation* led to movements for social change. They argued that when groups saw they were deprived relative to others, they were likely to protest and mobilize for change (Gurr 1970), actions also encouraged if their expectations of their material conditions were far removed from their real material conditions (Davies 1974). These scholars understood that conditions of deprivation alone do not lead to mobilizations; often mobilization occurs when people develop a sense of being worse off than others, or when they think things ought to be better than they are and that it is possible to change conditions.

While the broad theme of relative deprivation remains important, it implies a "spontaneous combustion": somehow, people reach the same conclusion about the unacceptability of their material conditions at the same moment in time, articulate the situation in common terms, agree on the need for change, and agree on strategies to address accomplishing that change. The analysis lacks an understanding of what ignites a shift from malaise to action: what influences or enables dissatisfaction to coalesce and become action? To address this problem, scholars have focused more systematically over the past four decades on *political opportunity structures* that enable or prevent movements for change (Oberschall 1973; Smelser 1962; Ballard, Habib, and Valodia 2006). Political opportunity structures are "consistent – but not necessarily formal, permanent or national – dimensions of the political environment that provide incentives for people to undertake collective action by affecting their expectations for success or failure" (Tarrow 1994: 85). Political opportunity structures include "openness or closure of the institutionalized political system, stability or instability of elite alignments that typically undergird a polity, presence or absence of elite allies, and the state's propensity and capacity for repression" (McAdam 1997: xxvi). As we discussed in the last chapter, state actors can provide opportunities through their engagement or disengagement. In their account of the American farmworkers' movements, Jenkins and Perrow (1977) pointed out that public agencies and officials have their own interests to protect against insurgents, and these interests often bring them into alignment with powerful private-interest groups. Similarly, the ability of the powerful to use violence to repress struggles, control the media to shape public opinion, or repress the voices of protest, affects the direction and relative success of movements in profound ways. At the same time, activists organizing for change can play important roles in defining and opening up political opportunities. For instance, in South Africa, the sheer scale of state repression created significant barriers for the organization of movements to dismantle apartheid. However, the scale of injustices brought political parties, NGOs, churches, and other groups together on the shared objective of dismantling apartheid. Even though the emphases and choice of practices differed among these groups, the sum of their collective actions constituted a mass resistance. These struggles, in turn, created further political opportunities to challenge and dismantle apartheid (Ballard, Habib, and Valodia 2006). We will show that a similar process worked for the US-based struggle for racial justice.

Overall, attention to political opportunity structures helps us to understand the impact of external factors on collective action, especially the ways that social movements have to respond to changing political opportunity structures.

Resource mobilization (RM)

While it is important to consider the conditions that promote, constrain, or suppress resistance, social movements do not emerge because of these external factors. A crucial dimension of any movement consists of the material and non-material resources it can mobilize to build and sustain its agenda and actions (e.g., W. Gamson 1971 [1990]; J. Gamson 1996; McCarthy and Zald 1976; Piven and Cloward 1979; Tilly 1978). RM scholars examine the source of the resources that allow groups to mobilize, and how these resources are organized (Morris and Mueller 1992). For instance, scholars have studied the financial resources of movements to trace which groups and individuals support a specific movement (e.g., Haines 1984). They examine the ways that ideas are disseminated; for instance, a rapidly growing literature examines the role of the Internet in disseminating ideas and information (Pudrovska and Ferree 2004; Narayan, Purkayastha, and Banerji 2011). Scholars have also paid a great deal of attention to the networks that sustain or impede movements. Who is drawn into the movement? Social movement scholars have documented the importance of pre-existing informal networks held together by strong bonds as basic building blocks of movements (Mueller 1994). Snow and his colleagues (1980) have argued that individuals do not join a movement simply because they're motivated to do so; often the key issue is that they are available to participate because of their structural location. Do movements have the internal organization to sustain movements? In his analysis of lunch-counter sit-ins of the 1960s, in which people of color deliberately staged strategic civil-disobedience actions against segregation by sitting at 'whites-only' restaurants, Morris has pointed out these actions of civil disobedience were not successful prior to the 1960s because many Civil Rights Movement groups did not have the internal organization to mobilize sufficient people to sustain the tactics. Scholars have also examined the role played by different parts of the state in fostering or stifling movements (e.g., Opp and Roehl 1990).

Strategies, frames, and identities

Social movements often challenge entrenched social structural arrangements and they organize outside conventional channels to make their claims. Thus, social movements have to work out the *strategies* that will be useful for their cause. They also have to convince people to understand and support their perspective and actions. As Tarrow (1994) has argued, movement leaders select from a toolkit of "repertoires of contention," based on their understanding of what is likely to work in that context. Indeed, the "weapons" and tactics vary, from non-cooperation and non-violent confrontation, to strikes and violent confrontation (Chabot 2002; Gamson 1990; Scott 1985). Indeed, Gamson (1990) documented how often unruly groups – those who use violence and strikes – have better than average success. But Chabot (2002), Brown (1991), Parikh (2001), Hassim (2006), Katzenstein (1995), Scott (1985), and others have demonstrated the possibility of change through the use of non-violent tactics. Overall, these repertoires are often chosen, much like a chess game, as the social movement activists attempt to offset the power of their opponents (McAdam 1983). As we will discuss later in the chapter, some prominent civil rights organizations strategically chose non-violent marches and boycotts as the strongest "weapon" to publicly challenge violent repression by the state; other groups focused on challenging racial segregation through courts, while others chose to claim rights on the ground, by attempting to desegregate lunch counters, or register people to vote.

Social movements have to mobilize people who will be active in the movement and gather larger support for their cause. The research on *frames* and *identities* attempts to explain how people become involved political actors and supporters of movements. Snow and Benford have pointed out that social movement organizations and their supporters regularly "frame or assign meaning to and interpret relevant events and conditions in ways that are intended to mobilize potential adherents and constituents, to garner bystander support, and demobilize antagonists" (1988: 198). Further research on frames has identified processes of frame alignment or the mechanism through which social movement organizations attempt to link their interpretations to those of prospective adherents. For instance, Tarrow (1983, 1994) and Klandermans (1984, 1988) describe agents within social movements who draw on existing mentalities and political culture to manipulate symbols to create collective action frames that will mobilize others on behalf of the movement. This process of meaning-making via frames is crucial to the emergence, sequencing, and tactical repertoires of social movements (Morris and Mueller 1992; Tarrow 1983). These frames have to be sufficiently powerful to counter the power-elites' framing of the same issue. For instance, during a crucial point in US history, as the National Association for the Advancement of Colored People (NAACP) was advocating for economic, social, and political and civil human rights, they found that the government and powerful sections of American society had begun to successfully stigmatize their demand for economic rights as anti-American "communism." As we describe later in the chapter, this influenced the organizers to consciously orient their frame toward civil rights claims to highlight the lineage of their demands within the US constitutional framework (Anderson 2003).

At the same time, participation in collective actions and social movements often leads to the development of *collective identity* or "a shared definition of a group that derives from its members common interests, experiences, and solidarity" (Taylor and Whittier 1992: 105). Collective identities generate the development of a heightened consciousness of the problem, goals, meanings, and environment of action, an understanding of the boundaries or the social structures that create differences between challengers and the dominant group-opponents (e.g., Melluci

1989; Taylor and Whittier 1992; Touraine 1985). Such collective identities are often filtered and reproduced through movement organizations (Gamson 1996). Groups use their consciousness of the problem, the boundaries, and their knowledge of common symbols and repertoires of actions, to resist the existing structures of domination. The classic example of this concept would come from Marxist notions of the class consciousness necessary for the success of anti-capitalist movements. Through following the Civil Rights Movement, one could point to the development of racial consciousness. Scholars pointed out that the rising tide of "black pride" – a collective identity worked out through shared struggles, a sense of shared political and cultural aspirations, and a sense of group self-determination – was one of the critical binding factors of the struggles for racial justice. Despite differences of tactics, resources, and numbers of constituents who were mobilized, the development of this collective identity provided inspiration for the ongoing struggles (Lawson 1997).

As we examine the struggles for racial justice, we use social movement concepts – political opportunity structures, resources, repertoires, frames, and collective identities – to document the efforts by ordinary people to claim rights in spite of the state's attempt to oppose such claims.[2] At the same time, we show that states can play contradictory roles through their different units affirming some legal rights, while other state units organize massive violent resistance to movements that claim these rights substantively. Equally important, we show that getting laws passed is simply one step in the process to claim, let alone exercise, rights. Long after legislations affirmed the right of racial minorities to vote, attend integrated schools, and access housing and jobs on equal terms with whites, continued white resistance on the ground (white supremacist organizations and lynch mobs like the Ku Klux Klan, southern "dixiecrats," white "race riots," and so forth) made it difficult to access these rights. These substantive rights – rights that can be accessed every day without hindrance or opposition by states and/or dominant groups – had to be claimed through new phases of activism. Consistent with our human enterprise approach, we show different strands within the Civil Rights

Movement were able to create a consciousness about entrenched inequalities and suffering that had been normalized or relegated to private arenas, away from the public eye. "Ordinary" people mobilized material and non-material resources to sustain their actions, successfully deployed frames that won more supporters to their cause, and, at times, were able to use the dynamic interplay between local, national, and international forces to create political opportunity for their cause.

How were people mobilized for these movements? What kind of resources did the movement use? What were the contexts and opportunity structures within which they mobilized? How did they frame their claims?

Anatomy of a human rights struggle in the US: anti-racism and civil rights

In 1964, the US passed the Civil Rights Act to formally prohibit discrimination on the basis of race, color, religion, sex, or national origin. In 1965, it passed the Voting Rights Act that prohibited states from imposing any "voting qualification or prerequisite to voting, or standard, practice, or procedure . . . to deny or abridge the right of any citizen of the United States to vote on account of race or color."[3] The passage of these Acts – which we will refer to as the civil rights legislations – put some legal reforms in place to address formal racial discrimination in the US. But these landmark pieces of legislation are neither an endpoint of centuries of struggle for racial justice, nor a logical outcome of a democratic Constitution devoted to life, liberty, and freedom. As Tsesis argues:

> (t)he American Constitution's use of generalities, about equality, the general welfare, and due process, has helped . . . [however] both equality and liberty have often been mere abstractions used as catchwords for political gain; real progress has often come when these principles inspired action for the sake of fairness and general improvement. The most effective change arrived through the efforts of coalitions capable of winning popular and political support. (2008: 3)

While the passage of laws is a significant achievement, a human rights enterprise approach reminds us that it is important to also consider the processes through which rights are claimed substantively. Scholars such as Evelyn Nakano Glenn (2002) have documented that substantive rights can only be exercised through power struggles to break through powerful ideologies and practices that enforce racial/gendered/classed boundaries in everyday life. For instance, the segregated buses in the South did not have lines demarcating who would sit where – powerful cultural norms and ongoing practices constructed and enforced those lines of racial segregation. Or, when we examine the status of residential segregation at the end of the twentieth century, we find that housing segregation has been declared illegal, but actions by people, specifically white flight from neighborhoods as racial minorities move in, lead to the same outcome: persistent residential segregation that has been described as American apartheid by Massey and Denton (1993).

Anti-racist struggles:
relative deprivation, opportunity, and context

The period between the formal ending of slavery in 1865 and the passage of the civil rights legislations of the 1960s, often referred to as the era of Reconstruction and Jim Crow, was marked by the passage of a number of formal laws and policies which codified the oppression of racial minorities – black, brown, yellow, and other categories of non-white people – in the United States. Jim Crow laws enforced racial segregation in all aspects of life. Such racial segregation targeted blacks, "Orientals," and Latinos, forcing them into segregated schools, housing, and jobs, while constituting them as less than equal in matters of civil and political participation. Violence and intimidation, including lynching, for decades a widespread practice used to intimidate and kill African Americans, with murders, enforced removals – for example, of Native Americans off their lands, or Japanese Americans to internment camps – and mass incarceration are among the repertoire of practices used to uphold a racially segregated socio-economic-political system. Robin D. G. Kelley (1993) has pointed out that even though they lived in a democracy, African Americans, especially the working class, did not actually experience the beneficial outcomes of living in a liberal democratic nation-state. Thus, the movements for racial justice had to be organized within a harsh and repressive system that existed within a democratic nation-state.

During the period when the UDHR was being crafted, American veterans – black, Japanese American, Latinos – who had fought against Nazism, fascism, and imperialism during World War II – returned home and found little had changed in the apartheid conditions under which they were expected to live (Lawson 1997). Their sense of relative deprivation intersected with the discontent of people who continued to experience discrimination at home throughout the war years. The disruptions of the world wars coupled with the continuing infamy of lynching (by racist groups who were abetted by local police forces that either actively participated or looked the other way) and segregation (enforced through interactional violence and institutionalized legal might) had led to a significant migration of black Americans to the North. However, internal migration would not solve racism since the North enshrined its own set of racial barriers. By the early 1940s, a variety of organizations had begun to insistently demand fair housing, education, and rights to political participation.[4] Philip Randolph organized the first March on Washington in 1941. In 1942, Congress for Racial Equality (CORE) developed the direct-action tactics for fighting segregation (Meier and Rudick 1973). By 1947, organizations such as the Committee Against Jim Crow in Military Service and Training threatened to organize African Americans to boycott the army. Even prior to the landmark school desegregation case – *Brown* v. *Board of Education* – school segregation was being challenged by a variety of Latino and Asian-American groups through federal courts (Robinson and Robinson 2005; Strum 2010).

Given these early organizing efforts, it is not surprising that African-American leaders would be interested in seeking racial justice through the emerging international institution: the United

Nations. However, the political opportunity to claim rights through international mechanisms was complicated; it was a rapidly shifting terrain where national and regional politics intersected with political international trends. As the UDHR was being crafted, a strident opposition to the United Nations and the emerging human rights charter (including its attention to racial justice) began to gain ground in the US. Many prominent groups like the American Bar Association and the American Medical Association vigorously opposed the idea of a human rights charter (Lauren 1998; Peck 2011). They argued that a human rights charter would undermine American sovereignty and democratic institutions. Through the 1960s, a politically energized, deep opposition to racial equality was evident in different parts of the country, but especially in the South. Along with the entrenched racial regimes in many parts of the country – regimes which were enshrined through local laws and defended through violent action by states and white supremacist groups – these political discourses, which were critical of human rights, began to weaken the opportunity structure for claiming rights for racial minorities.

However, at the national level, there were glimmers of a political opportunity to advocate for racial justice during Truman's electoral campaign. During the political struggles between President Truman and Henry Wallace, the latter attracted a large number of black voters and the support of many prominent black leaders. They were better poised than ever before in US history to speak powerfully about injustices and demand freedom and rights. In the end, Truman won the elections, but not before he started emphasizing a civil rights platform at home. As D'Angelo (2001) has pointed out, three of the four presidential candidates, including the President, had announced they regarded civil rights and black equality favorably; this contributed to a slight shift in political discourse that later paved the way for Supreme Court decisions that struck at the heart of the architecture of racial segregation between 1948 and 1954.

These political opportunities created further space – albeit highly contested – for the Civil Rights Movements of the 1950s and 1960s. The effectiveness of block votes by African Americans was apparent during the Johnson presidential election success, and this opened up further political opportunities that led, ultimately, to the passage of the Civil Rights Act of 1964. Overall, the legal challenges, resistance mobilized through organizational activity among African Americans,[5] and the growing role of the federal government combined to focus the public's attention on the need to change institutionalized discrimination in American society.

International political opportunity structures, intersecting with the political opportunity structures at the national level, were also critical for the success of anti-racist and Civil Rights Movements. Throughout the early twentieth century, groups from different countries – leaders of colonies who were organizing independence movements against their European colonial masters, as well as leaders of racial minority groups in countries such as the US – had started coming together to challenge racism as a system and ideology. They organized conferences and were able to draft proclamations such as "Colonial and Subject Peoples of the World – Unite" (Lauren 1998: 206). In 1900, the Pan African Congress met to discuss ways to combat discrimination based on race; it was at this conference that W. E. B. Du Bois made his celebrated speech about the problem of the "color line." By 1907, Mohandas (later known globally by the honorific name "Mahatma") Gandhi had drawn international attention to the racial discrimination against Indian immigrants in South Africa by resisting the 1907 Asiatic Registration Act. A series of uprisings against colonial powers became evident in Asia and Africa through the early twentieth century; each of these struggles spoke the language of racial discrimination.[6]

Different nation-states, including Germany, South Africa, the United Kingdom, France, and the United States, had framed and justified their racist agendas – the extermination of Jews, the need to violently control colonial subjects in Africa, Asia, or Latin America, slavery, and apartheid within nation-states – through deployment of racist ideologies about superior groups who had to control, civilize, enslave, or exterminate inferior groups. Not surprisingly, representatives of colonized societies and the racial minority groups from Western nation-states criticized their governments in international platforms as they came together in shared discourse, strategies, and struggles. Gerald Horne (2008) points out that African Americans "virtually denuded of rights . . . were compelled to seek succour and allies globally" (2008: 3).

Eleanor Roosevelt's chairpersonship of the UDHR charter committee provided a unique opportunity for African Americans to claim human rights (and elimination of discrimination against racial minorities) within this international platform.[7] African-American leaders realized that as a prominent member of the human rights commission, the US was also vulnerable to criticism in this international arena. A series of pressures from NGOs served as an international "public" airing of unjust social conditions that the US was reluctant to acknowledge officially. W. E. B Du Bois and the NAACP were actively involved in the early forays over the writing of the human rights charter, linking the struggle of African Americans in the US to a global majority of "colored people" fighting racism (Lauren 1998; Horne 2008). The struggle continued through the phase of crafting UDHR.

Carol Anderson (2003) points out that even this international political opportunity was created through sustained struggles. Eleanor Roosevelt repeatedly sided with US policymakers at the expense of African-American rights. Even as demands for racial justice – achievable through a tapestry of political, civil, economic, social, and cultural human rights – gained favor at the international level, Eleanor Roosevelt was asked by the US government to focus her efforts on a declaration of principles, rather than enforceable commitments, and keep agreements to a tentative level (Lauren 1998). She complied. Like other powerful nation-states, the US was willing to speak about rights in principle, or protest rights violations in other nation-states, but was extremely reluctant to have its own record subject to similar scrutiny. Recognizing the efforts of the US government to control the public airing of its record on racism, W. E. B. Du Bois sent his complaint about the long history of racial discrimination in the US to the press and the UN in 1947, to maintain the political momentum to demand racial justice. However, other powerful nation-states began to resist the potential power of the UDHR by framing their concerns about the impact of this charter on their national sovereignty. Anderson (2003), among others, documents that the US delegation realized it could not afford to have its human rights record debated publicly. John Foster Dulles devised a human rights plan that would satisfy Southern Democrats, a powerful group opposing the claims of African Americans.

> [A]midst an unequivocal statement guaranteeing freedom from discrimination on account of race, language, religion, or sex, Dulles inserted an amendment that "nothing in the Charter shall authorize . . . intervention in matters which are essentially within the jurisdiction of the State concerned." The American and Soviet delegations immediately accepted Dulles' stroke of genius. (Anderson 2003: 48)

Of course, this clause, as NGOs protested, would not prevent future holocausts, address human rights abuses suffered by racial minorities in the US, or stop the discrimination or abuse that colonial subjects faced daily. Designating states as the primary arbitrator of human rights effectively restricted the political opportunity structure that seemed to emerge in the early phases of crafting this charter.

Understanding the need to keep seeking global rather than national allies, the NAACP wrote to the Human Rights Commission in 1948 to induce other nations to persuade the US to be just to its racial minority groups. India joined the NAACP and the Indian Rights Association to proclaim "Treatment of Negroes a Blot on U.S." (Lauren 1998: 207).[8] The effect of these networks is evident in the ways in which the UN general assembly could discuss racism during its earliest sessions. Vijaylakshmi Pandit (the first female leader of a nation-state's delegation to the UN, and later the first President of the UN General Assembly) raised the issue of apartheid against Indians in South Africa at the UN General Assembly. While General Smuts angrily declared apartheid in South Africa was an internal national matter, it opened up the political space within the United Nations to raise further charges of racism against a variety of nation-states.[9]

By the 1950s, the political opportunity to claim human rights was dealt a severe blow within the US. In the 1950s, as the US engaged in the Cold War, it was interested in wooing international partners, including the former colonies that were joining the bloc of Non-aligned Nations led by India and Indonesia (Prashad 2007). Since many of these nations had been vocal about racism, the US was forced to engage and manage some of the most contentious debates about racial justice and human rights. But this international political-opportunity structure intersected with the political context within the US. Within the country, the McCarthy era, the Cold War, and the Korean War unleashed a period of anti-communist nationalism. Groups that had advocated economic, social, political, and civil human rights for racial minorities found that the political opportunity to voice these holistic claims for human rights was eroding fast. The Soviet Bloc had championed economic, social, and cultural human rights, while political and civil rights had been the hallmark of the Western nations. If the civil rights groups pushed for economic and social human rights, they would be branded communist. If they pushed for civil rights, they would be downplaying their demand for economic rights.[10] Within this intersecting international and national context, groups like the NAACP chose, for pragmatic reasons, the frame of civil rights as the vehicle to demand racial justice.

Anti-racism struggles: resources, frames, and mobilization

A large number of books, treatises, and media document the Civil Rights movements in the US (see, e.g., D'Angelo 2001 for an overview; Wexler 1993 for first-hand accounts of the movement). These analyses have consistently emphasized the courage of individuals – women, men, and children – in the face of a violent, repressive state. Long before the struggle for racial justice and human rights became a mass movement, a variety of ongoing resistances became established in black communities. Frances Fox Piven (2008) has argued that because large numbers of African Americans worked in homes, fields, and factories, their white employers were dependent on their service; this interdependence generated a form of power for the African-American employees who could, *collectively*, interrupt this relationship. For instance, black domestic workers would threaten to quit their jobs just before important social affairs being hosted by their employers, or they would resist wearing uniforms (and assert their right to choose their attire). The success of these strategies depended on the collective "non-availability" of other workers, which itself depended on networks of information and collective support for these resistances. These seemingly small actions and victories helped to build these workers' collective identity, based on their consciousness of the problem, the boundaries, and their knowledge of common symbols and repertoires of actions to resist the existing structures of domination. Later, under the aegis of the Student Non-violent Coordinating Committee (SNCC), various pan-African organizations, and even later under more militant organizations like the Black Panther Party (BPP), the black power movement similarly mobilized a heightened sense of racial consciousness and sense of self-determination. Despite the class differences between these groups – the marginalized workers and the students – and the specificities of the process through which their political consciousness emerged, the development of these collective identities played an invaluable role in mobilizing African Americans to claim their legal and substantive rights, despite fierce opposition over the next few decades (Carmichael and Hamilton 1967).

Documenting different facets of the movement, historians like Robin D. G. Kelley (1993) have recorded black working-class resistance in the Jim Crow South. Due to the harsh system under which they worked, many of the oppositional tactics of workers were "submerged."[11] Kelley notes that even within the harshest working conditions, black workers used a range of daily actions such as delaying, immobilizing machinery, and absences to oppose the power structures. They constructed jokes, folklore, caricatures, and a range of submerged cultural transcripts of resistance. This culture and network of overt and submerged resistance within Jim Crow contexts contributed the people and material resources – however meager – for the larger political struggles.[12] African-American workers' unions organized many of these resistances; for instance, the Brotherhood of Sleeping Car Porters collectively articulated the grievances of black workers. Later, during the Montgomery bus boycotts, they sent money – however small the amount – for black workers who had to organize rides to get to their workplaces. Black workers used the segregated spaces – bars, street corners, barber shops, and salons – to create congregations of people who would exchange ideas and collectively reject the ideologies of the powerful. These segregated spaces became relatively safe contexts for constructing politicized collective identities that could be mobilized for different types of resistance, protests, and organizing.

Since African Americans lived in segregated housing, their journey to work often traversed the boundaries of segregated white and black worlds. Not surprisingly, public transportation emerged as one of the political spaces to showcase the resistance to segregation. Rosa Park's refusal to give up her seat, an action that challenged the color-line on Montgomery buses, was part of a long history of black women challenging this form of segregation in the South. To that point, between 1941 and 1942, many women were arrested for sitting in the "white section" of the bus (Kelley 1993). Some of their resistance was non-violent; at other times, physical altercations developed as drivers and passengers tried to push African Americans off the buses. The Women's Political Council (WPC) organized in 1949 to mobilize black women's vote; they also used the tactics of lodging several complaints with the City Commission about the ongoing humiliation of black female passengers.

The choice of Rosa Parks as the emblem of the resistance to segregated buses is an excellent example of strategic deployment of a *frame* to mobilize larger numbers of people for racial justice. The choice of Parks was a result of careful decision-making by E. D. Nixon (the Montgomery President of the NAACP) and Jo Ann Johnson, an active member of the WPC. The WPC had mobilized the local black community after the arrest of Claudette Clovin, a black teenager, who also refused to give up her seat on the bus. But other groups did not want to frame their protest with Clovin as the primary symbol of resistance; they anticipated that the press and white supremacists would reframe the issue by making Clovin's teen motherhood the subject of discussion. Unlike Clovin, Parks was an older woman, a civil rights volunteer whose private life would stand up to the harshest scrutiny by the opposition.

NAACP leader E. D. Nixon brought the planned bus boycott to the attention of church leaders and church members. The black churches were places where many African Americans gathered, so the message of a bus boycott was sent through these nodal points to garner more support. Nixon framed the resistance as an opportunity to support the women who had worked tirelessly for the community (and the church) and were now challenging one source of their daily humiliation. The movement then drew upon existing community networks as a key resource to organize the boycott as well as to mobilize volunteers who would provide rides – "car pools" – to the workers and court arrest for "running illegal taxis." Additional resources – leadership, press mobilization, money, organizing experience, and knowledge emerged through the networks of a variety of black organizations. John White (1990) describes how the $3,500 needed every week to keep the car pools running was sustained through donations; for instance, $100 came from the porters in Chicago, $25 from the porters of Jacksonville, and small sums were donated by community members. Small as these amounts appear today, for the marginalized black workers, these represented significant resources.

A growing number and variety of organizations, such as the Southern Negro Youth Conference (SNYC), the NAACP, the Southern Christian Leadership Conference (SCLC), the Student Non-Violent Co-ordinating Committee (SNCC), and the Congress of Racial Equality (CORE), had emerged by the 1960s. Each of these organizations pursued a slightly different set of objectives and strategies, mobilizing different networks – students, church members, workers – and material resources to challenge racial injustice.

The resources, strategies, and tactics of these groups were very different. For instance, over time, the NAACP became known for legally challenging racist laws or petitioning bodies (such as the United Nations Human Rights Commission as we mentioned earlier).[13] Founded by highly educated black and white intellectuals, the NAACP created a centralized operational structure that concentrated on "mainstream tactics": press releases, speeches, lobbying pamphlets, and challenging racism in courts (Morris 1984). *Brown* v. *Board of Education*, the landmark school desegregation case, was one of a long line of legal challenges that the NAACP mounted to tear down the entrenched racist edifice of the US.[14] Even though it rarely attracted more than a small percentage of African Americans as dues-paying members, its prominent legal challenges often coalesced with other efforts – including direct action by other groups – to challenge segregation.

The NAACP's centralized structure, operating procedures, and access to prominent leaders were also valuable resources for local organizers: it provided opportunities for local leaders to acquire organizing skills, and networks through which resources were pooled. The NAACP included leaders like Ella Baker, who led the attempts to involve ordinary people in the movement, to create a group-centered leadership, and maintain bridges with the Students Non-violent Coordinating Council (SNCC) and the Southern Christian Leadership Conference (SCLC).[15] Since its success with *Brown* v. *Board of Education*, the NAACP became the target of sustained attacks by organizations and Southern state governments. In an attempt to stop the NAACP from operating, these entities brought injunctions against the chapters on the spurious grounds of subversive activities. Nonetheless, these sustained attacks drained the NAACP units of resources, so that they were left with little money to support other organizations.

In contrast to the NAACP, the SCLC mobilized community- and church-based networks for non-violent mass protests, boycotts, and marches. A prominent resource of the Civil Rights Movement was the development of the techniques and philosophy of non-violent direct action. Just as African-American leaders had used multi-country networks to open up political opportunities in the international political context to discuss racism, the SCLC leaders used some of the innovative tactics of Gandhian movements that had been used successfully to confront violent, repressive states in South Africa and India. Since the NAACP, the United Negro Improvement Association (UNIA), and the Fellowship for Reconciliation (FOR) – three organizations with very different ideas about the specific ways of challenging racial injustice in the US – were generally positive about the Gandhian repertoire, they reinvented and implemented non-violent tactics in the US.[16] These tactics fit with the SCLC constituency and political frame. Faced with opponents – states, white supremacist groups – that did not hesitate to use extreme violence, the SCLC civil rights leaders framed their struggle to show that the powerful were using brutality against peaceful, non-violent activists, young and old. By the time of the Selma demonstrations, a larger section of Northern whites had been persuaded by this framing of non-violent activism against violent repressive regimes. A majority were ready to support the Voting Rights Act.

Black churches in the segregated South acted as significant nodes of organized networks in the movement (Morris 1984). Even as they reflected social divisions within African-American communities – church networks often reflected class and religious preferences – the churches were central to submerged networks as they catered to the spiritual and emotional needs of oppressed groups. Their repeated themes of cooperation and the need to give to worthy causes could be mobilized in the cause of justice. Since their members were often connected through a range of church activities, they disseminated information efficiently. They provided ideal places for the formation of collective identities that propelled members into movements. Like Martin Luther King, several leaders emerged from the ranks of church leadership; they commanded the stature to mobilize their constituents. "Their displays of courage, dignity, integrity, and burning desire for freedom earned the approval of the black masses because such values were deeply embedded in the social fabric of black society. The words they used were effective because they symbolized and simplified the complex yearnings of a dominated group" (Morris, in D'Angelo 2001: 154).

Unlike the church- and community-based groups mobilized by the SCLC, the students who joined the civil rights struggle focused on extending the political power at the grassroots level and getting federal government help to break the power of locally entrenched elites. The SNCC was mostly critical of the SLCC framing of the movement, their reliance on charismatic leadership, and their strategy of non-violent resistance without a long-term agenda for claiming substantive rights. The SNCC favored outspoken discourse and continuing direct action that would lead the movement to the next steps: to minimize the palpable fears of people who had experienced decades of violence and convince them to confront their oppressors. They wanted to create political, economic, and social conditions, and a groundswell of people who were ready to determine their own future as the path to actual equality and justice. Thus, SNCC members continued with their direct-action tactics, including desegregating lunch counters, voter registration drives, and empowering marginalized groups. The Selma marches organized by the SCLC actually drew upon the earlier work of the SNCC's voter registration drives and the creation of a politicized community of people who were ready to act to claim their rights. The SNCC activists were aware of the significant dangers that they and the groups they were mobilizing faced from brutal white supremacists. Lawson states, "In February and March 1963 [in Alabama] whites initiated a reign of terror against the SNCC. Arsonists attempted to burn its headquarters, and unidentified assailants fired shotgun blasts into a car carrying three voter registration workers ... vigilantes torched businesses ... and aimed gunfire into homes of ... youth active in suffrage drives" (1997: 85). For SNCC, voter registration often became direct action because of the violent opposition to their actions. Another group, CORE, which was also critical of many of the tactics of SLCC, mobilized black and white Freedom Riders who would challenge the South to comply with desegregation policies of interstate transportation, often facing the same types of opposition as the SNCC workers. The efforts of these student groups to empower people to claim substantive rights represent yet another set of tactics used within this terrain of struggle.

The increasing reach of the media, especially television, brought the confrontations of violent local governments with non-violent protesters, many of them children – the dogs, the beatings, the water cannons, dragging individuals along to wagons that would carry them to prison, the killings of activists, and all other violent means used to control these activists – to a national audience. To this end, the iconic images[17] of the Civil Rights movements – the Montgomery bus boycott following Rosa Parks's arrest (1955), the Little Rock Nine marching through hostile crowds to school (1957), the sit-ins organized by the SNCC to desegregate lunch counters beginning from the late 1950s, Ruby Bridges on her way to kindergarten surrounded by US marshals (1960), the children's marches in Birmingham (1963), and speeches by Martin Luther King and Malcolm X among others – inspired the black power movement. They also highlight the courage, commitment, and struggles of many ordinary people in the face of repressive state apparatus that were used to maintain racial hierarchy. These images were powerful frames to persuade many people to act for civil rights.

Since these groups framed their struggles differently, it is interesting to briefly examine why some frames were successful and others were not. August Meier and Elliot Ruddick (1973), among others, have speculated that the success of the Civil Rights Movement organized by Martin Luther King – measured arguably by more positive publicity by the media and acceptance by a larger swath of Americans – was due to the ways in which he was able to frame the movement. He was able to articulate the aspirations of African Americans in the manner of religious preaching that they were already familiar with; he also communicated these aspirations of African Americans by weaving together an eclectic set of messages from Christianity, Hinduism (via Gandhi), Hegel, and others, in a language that attracted many white supporters who felt less threatened by him. The SNCC's more radical challenge about the need to change fundamentally social and economic relationships, and SNCC's attempt to mobilize the grassroots so that they were empowered to determine their own future, made SLCC's approach appear as more tempered and consequently more acceptable to the white majority. Even though King was arguably quite radical in his approaches to race, capitalism, and imperialism toward the end of his life, his earlier speeches and actions appeared to reflect the views of a moderate who sought incremental change consistent with the promise of the US Constitution; his frame could be more easily aligned with existing frames about America's fundamental belief in justice and liberty. Consequently, white liberals, individuals, unions, and groups, who were generally supportive of racial equality through access to civil rights, directed their financial contributions to the Southern Christian Leadership Conference (see also Haines 1984). As the SLCC received more financial support, its stature within the movement began to grow until its message and strategies – highlighted through the media and political rhetoric as "the" Civil Rights Movement – began to eclipse the contributions of other groups.

In contrast to this successful frame for garnering support for civil rights (and emphasis on legal rights without a concomitant commitment to substantive rights), we earlier indicated the defeat of the substantive human rights frame advocated by the NAACP and other groups. Many of the NAACP members worked with Eleanor Roosevelt on the assumption that she would be a champion of their cause. Various African-American leaders like Du Bois had also issued direct appeals to the world. Some groups had drawn attention to racial injustice in the US by calling the treatment of African Americans *genocide*. However, the federal government used a successful counter-frame to defeat the Soviet Union's attempt to discredit the US[18] and to appease groups within the country that were leery of providing rights to racial minorities, especially economic rights. Government spokespersons like John Dulles began to emphasize the principles of the US Constitution, conflating civil rights with human rights; Eleanor Roosevelt continued to emphasize that the Human Rights Commission was not a tribunal and would not hear grievances – including those by African Americans; President Truman, attentive to local politics (and strident opposition to racial justice), expressed his commitment to desegregation only in terms of the Constitution. These three streams of discourses framed *human rights as much the same as civil rights* enshrined in the US Constitution, and, consequently, easily addressed within the structure of the American legal system. In addition, the political witch hunts of the McCarthy era silenced most voices that linked economic security – a claim for group rights within a just political-economic system – to communism and anti-Americanism.[19] Thus, powerful sections of American government and civil society successfully organized and sustained their opposition to the NAACP's human rights frames, and forced them to retreat from their claims for racial justice through holistic – political, civil, economic, social, and cultural – human rights. This resulted in frames that advocated deeper, longer-term structural changes to uphold human rights being successfully countered by more powerful frames deployed by entities who were interested in status quo or incremental changes.

These victories and defeats, the successes in wresting some power to change existing relations of domination and subordination, and being overpowered in other arenas make up the terrain of the civil rights struggle. The federal legislation in 1964, 1965, and 1968 reinforced the rights of all people to have equal access to voting rights and housing and over-rode a number of local legislations and practices that sustained racist structures. The movements leading to the civil rights legislation dismantled some of the inhumane racist edifices and policies that were part of the taken-for-granted life conditions within American democracy. For instance, the 1965 Voting Rights Act not only suspended literacy tests and poll taxes that impeded the right to vote, but also included a measure for states, with records of discrimination, to pre-clear any changes to the voting process with the federal government to ensure they did not discriminate against minorities.

It is instructive to briefly outline what was achieved in the 1960s. Undoubtedly, the dismantling of the most overt forms of racism within a repressive state structure was a significant victory for this human rights struggle. Yet, the framing of these victories as civil rights issues reinforced the ideology that other nation-states have human rights problems, while the democratic US only needs to adjust its civil rights and punish deviant individuals who commit crimes because of prejudices – this attitude, that the passage of laws addressed racial injustices, continues today. The repeated emphasis on the SCLC's civil rights frame, without a commitment to the dismantling of political-economic relations that would enable the marginalized to access substantive rights, paved the way for the emergence of *contemporary systemic racism* – marked by *color-blind ideology*, or "racism without racists" (Bonilla-Silva 2006). Civil rights legislation upheld equal opportunity, but did not address the deep structural adjustments necessary to ensure access and the dismantling of barriers for creating lives of human dignity.[20] The deeper, more abiding roots of racism – expressed through color-blind racism in everyday interactions, and institutionalized through the contemporary political economy – remain in place. As we discuss in the next section, these entrenched injustices continue in new forms today and require ongoing resistance.

This brief account of the struggle for racial justice illuminates several facets of the human rights enterprise. First, such struggles typically involve multiple organizations, using different resources, frames, and strategies, to challenge entrenched power structures and claim rights. Their relative success depends on the resources they are able to mobilize, the tactics and strategies they use, and the ways in which they are able to frame their demands. Second, as we mentioned in chapter 1, the roles of states are contradictory. As a guardian of human rights (as established through UDHR), the federal government was upholding its responsibilities during the Truman, Kennedy, and Johnson eras by granting some rights to racial minorities. At the same time, we confirmed the excessive force that state entities and powerful groups can use to repress struggles; these were clearly evident at the level of states. Third, examining human rights struggles through the lens of the human rights enterprise shows us that the rights emerged through significant struggle between those in power and those who mobilized on the ground, but these are dynamic power imbalances. Contexts and opportunities change, and resources and frames which are useful at one point in time may be overpowered in other contexts or time periods.

Racial justice in the twenty-first century

As part of its international commitment to human rights, the US signed on to the International Convention on the Elimination of all forms of Racial Discrimination (ICERD) in 1966, and ratified it in 1994.[21] While some of the most blatant racist structures of the early and mid-twentieth century were dismantled, new structures have been created and continue to lead to racial disparities in access to food, water, health, education, housing, jobs, voting rights, criminal justice (mass incarceration and the drug war specifically), and everyday experiences of racism.[22]

Indeed, as the US Human Rights Network recorded in its shadow report to the United Nations on US progress toward the elimination of racial discrimination, along with categorization and discrimination, new racial categories are currently being created such as equating Muslim-looking people with terrorists, and stratifying rights of non-white migrants by significantly curtailing their rights to due process (Purkayastha, Purkayastha and Waring 2011). The expansion of the reach of the government through the PATRIOT act and other "security" laws to detain people without trial, and the operation of secret FISA courts, continues to create unequal life chances for racial minorities. As the state expands the purview of its political powers to restrain and repress people under the rhetoric of security, it is able to control free speech, and people's ability to dissent or protest. We will return to these points, and their implications for fundamental civil and political human rights, in chapter 5. A new series of state laws has been instituted to allow the police to stop people on suspicion of illegal immigration.[23] These political restrictions are reminiscent of the type of laws that existed prior to the Civil Rights Act of 1964. Not surprisingly, new waves of hate crimes and systemic racism against Latinos, Sikhs, Muslims, "Muslim-looking people," and African Americans continue to deprive people of their substantive rights. Equally important, political protest and organizing has taken on new forms, often migrating to the web-sphere to organize protests and demand justice.

The contours of continuing structural racism are evident if we focus on the three decisions we outlined at the beginning of this chapter. The recent decision by the US Supreme Court to explicitly and implicitly strike down two landmark pieces of legislation that defined the Civil Rights movement – access to education and political participation – through Affirmative Action laws and Voting Rights Acts – represents the success of those who refuse to acknowledge contemporary racial inequality and injustices. These decisions are part of a continuing struggle over human rights.

Section 4 of the Voting Rights Act, which was struck down by the US Supreme Court in 2013, is a critical tool to address legal barriers that affect minority political participation. This section required nine states – Alabama, Alaska, Arizona, Georgia, Louisiana, Mississippi, South Carolina, Texas, and Virginia – and several localities to seek federal approval for proposed changes to voting laws or procedures. Pre-clearance was intended to ensure these states did not institute any process – including racial gerrymandering – to impede racial minority voters' political participation. By striking at the requirement for pre-clearance, the Supreme Court undermined federal oversight – the very commitment that ensured, in the 1960s, that racial-minority voters would get an actual chance to vote. The Supreme Court left the decision about the conditions under which voting takes place to states and local governments. In her minority opinion, Justice Ruth Bader Ginsberg said that the focus of the Voting Rights Act had properly changed from "first-generation barriers to ballot access" to "second-generation barriers" like racial gerrymandering and laws requiring at-large voting in places with a sizable black minority. She said the law had been effective in thwarting such efforts (Liptak 2013). Furthermore, this decision opens the doors for electoral redistricting (gerrymandering), to ensure that only the dominant and powerful groups are a numerical majority in most electoral districts and consequently retain electoral power. This possibility along with the significantly high proportions of incarceration of African Americans, which in turn disenfranchises them (Alexander 2010), leads to starkly negative effects on the ability of racial-minority voters to exercise their political rights.

Even as the Federal Justice Department prepares to sue Texas for some of its discriminatory redistricting, North Carolina passed House Bill 589 for Governor McCrory's signature in July 2013. According to the North Carolina NAACP, this bill contains some of the most draconian provisions erecting barriers to the right to vote, including vigilante poll watchers to challenge a citizen's right to vote in any jurisdiction in the state; preventing a county from having the flexibility to add more than one hour to the time for citizens to vote on election day; and imposing the most extreme voter identification requirements in the nation while refusing to recognize valid student and other types of reliable identifications (Sturgis 2013). We will return to this in chapter 4, as we discuss the shrinking rights of people in the face of greater power in the hands of banks and corporations.

It is important to pay attention to the implications of weakening the Voting Rights Act for the human rights enterprise. The American Civil Liberties Union (ACLU) correctly points out that literacy tests and poll taxes were among the pre-civil rights era laws designed to keep racial minorities from voting. Since 2008, a range of new policies, including requirements for certain types of voter IDs, restrictions on registration and early voting – which ensure that people without their own transportation or those who are unable to take time off from work or family commitments to get to the voting sites – continues to disenfranchise racial minorities (ACLU 2013). Supporters of the landmark civil rights legislation who wanted to ensure racial minorities could fully participate in the political process see this as a way of chipping away at these rights. Representative John Lewis, who was a leader in the SNCC – one of the organizations that were key to expanding the terrain of voter registration – described this decision, as we reported at the beginning of this chapter, as a strike at the heart of the Voting Rights Act.

Similarly in the *Fisher* v. *University of Texas at Austin* case, the Supreme Court sent a signal to the lower court that had sided with the university against Fisher's complaint. Texas has long been a legal battleground for Affirmative Action laws. In 1996, in *Hopgood* v. *Texas*, the court ruled that race-conscious policies could not be used and public universities in Texas went on to automatically admit the top 7 percent of each graduating class. This formula is built on the implicit notion of segregated schools so that the admission of top graduates leads to diverse classes. Fisher, who was among the top 12 percent of her class, did not meet the criteria for the University of Texas at Austin's automatic enrollment; nor were her credentials sufficient to admit her through the regular process. The federal court ruled in favor of the university. By sending the case back, the Supreme Court left open two questions: first, the question of who would decide whether the current standards were adequate – a task that would be decided by the local legislatures; second, the thornier question of how much diversity is sufficient and how this should be decided.[24]

In the voting rights case, the Supreme Court's majority explicitly framed racial injustice as being a thing of the past. But it promulgated the idea that state governments, irrespective of local cultures and politics, could be trusted to ensure fair voting procedures. Similarly, in the case of *Fisher* v. *University of Texas at Austin*, the Supreme Court left the decision to local authorities, while questioning whether race-neutral policies were available. These arguments – that resolutions at the local level are sufficient to address racism irrespective of the record of these locales – are reminiscent of the arguments that were used against the NAACP international petitions in the mid-twentieth century. There too, powerful forces insisted that national governments should be trusted to address racial justice, in spite of their record of failure on this issue.

This framing by the Supreme Court's majority, that structural racism is no longer an issue in the US, also seems to reflect the public opinion among the majority population (see also Pew 2013). Variants of a theme that narrowly links discrimination to the "behaviors of a few deviant individuals" seek to undermine the work of anti-racist groups that continue to point to structural discrimination. The powerful opponents of racial equality use their ability to disseminate their framing of the racial landscape in the US today through their control of well-financed think tanks and media. They decouple the patterns of unequal political representation or access to education (or health or housing) from the crucial role of laws and larger structures of domination and marginalization. Their success persuades many people that racial justice has "been done," even while the civil rights gains are being dismantled. By narrowly framing these issues as "African-American issues," these powerful frames and actions also succeed in drawing public attention away from the experiences of post-1965 immigrants and their children – especially Asian American and Latinos – who face many of the same barriers.[25] At the same time, the massive surveillance structures that we will discuss in chapter 5, along with the draconian effects of being imprisoned, even for political protests, mean that the political opportunity *and* right to protest visibly on the streets or even in the web-sphere is fragile at best.

These structural impediments are paralleled by violence in public places. Scholars continue to document many ways in which "race" remains relevant for organizing social relations in school yards (Aries 2008; Lewis 2003; Purkayastha et al. 2011). The killing of Trayvon Martin brings together the insidious effect of local laws and legalized availability of weapons. Trayvon Martin was shot dead by George Zimmerman, who successfully used Florida's stand-your-ground laws to escape murder indictment. Zimmerman, who is white,[26] assumed that the teenager – who was wearing a hoodie and was walking to his father's house with Skittles and water – was trespassing with criminal intent in this gated community. Despite advice from the police, Zimmerman got out of his car, had an altercation with Martin that left him with Martin's DNA under his nails, and shot him dead. Zimmerman argued that *he* feared for his life and Martin attacked him. Even though there was no DNA evidence on Martin to prove this alleged attack on Zimmerman, the jury acquitted Zimmerman. The activists, scholars, and commentators, who have worn hoodies and marched or written to protest this travesty of justice, point out that the verdict is only possible if people believe it is reasonable to fear black teenagers wearing hoodies, that they are essentially violent, and that these black teenagers cannot possibly be in white areas without nefarious intent (see also Feagin and Sikes 1994).

Those who think justice was done, point out that race was not relevant to this trial; the jurors simply interpreted the law. However, self-defense laws, which legally allow such killing, are based on cultural acceptance of these levels of violence to protect themselves in their everyday lives. These ideas intersect with gendered/ racist ideologies that shape people's decisions about who "looks suspicious," and whose very presence in a place makes people wonder why they are there. Much like Emmett Till's murder in 1955 for transgressing a color line, and the subsequent acquittal of the people who killed him (see Mettress 2002 for details on the Till case), Trayvon Martin's killing and Zimmerman's acquittal reflect cultural acceptance of killing of black children for transgressing the color lines in those locales. A Pew Charitable Trusts study shows a huge gap between black and white attitudes on the verdict, with only 30 percent of whites compared to 84 percent of blacks dissatisfied with the ruling (Pew 2013).

These killings have occurred against a larger pattern of violence against minorities, especially young males. The racist ideologies that construct young minority males as criminal, the disproportionate numbers of racial minorities who are imprisoned (see Alexander 2010), and physical and sexual violence in prisons consistently erode the human rights of racial minorities.[27] People who have been incarcerated are subsequently denied equal access to voting, jobs, housing, and other political, civil, social, economic, and cultural rights. At the same time, diversion of money from social welfare programs, significant expansion of new segregation through privatization of housing developments – gated communities, planned unit developments, Sun Cities – education, healthcare, and tax breaks for the rich create very different life chances for racial-minority groups.

A large number of organizations, including the Southern Poverty Law Center, Border Action Network, activist groups for immigrant and racial minority groups' rights (such as NAACP, MALDEF, AALDEF, DRUM), civil and human rights groups (such as ACLU, La Raza), have continued to struggle for racial justice. But the gains continue to be contested politically and through judicial activism.

Struggle for racial justice: concluding comments

Overall, this discussion of struggles over human rights provides substantive support for our historical argument, central to the human rights enterprise, that human rights have always been defined and realized through bottom-up power struggles, often against or in spite of the states charged with rights protection in the first place. Using social movement theories, we showed how these struggles tended to work within the United States, and what appeared to determine their success. We conclude this chapter with a brief description of the struggle for racial justice at the international level where the United States is required to submit reports of its progress on efforts to eliminate racial discrimination.

In order to review the framing of racial injustices today, it is interesting to contrast the US's 2007 country report to the UN (US CERD report), on the state of progress on eliminating racial discrimination, with the report submitted by NGOs.[28] The US's official review of the state of racial discrimination points to the passage of the Civil Rights Act(s) (of 1964, but also of 1965 and 1968) and subsequent legislation as proof of elimination of racial discrimination in the country; any remaining issues are attributed to acts of deviant individuals. But the US has been unwilling to face groups that are critical of this report. It refused to participate in two recent conferences on racism: the 2001 Durban conference on racism, and the 2009 Durban review conference. In close approximation of the tactics used by the leaders of the Civil Rights Movements, activists and NGOs have gathered at UN-sponsored conferences to publicly proclaim their views on the state of racial discrimination.

The 2008 Shadow Report's description of racism includes structural racism, immigrant rights, issues of the indigenous people, hate groups, police brutality, prisons, access to civil justice, voting rights, housing discrimination, homelessness, health, education, and a range of other issues (ICERD Shadow Report 2008). It focuses on structural *and* interpersonal forms of racism and identifies the shortcomings of the US official report. A key point of the

Shadow Report is that US laws do not meet the ICERD standards on combating racism. For example, the ICERD recognizes that discrimination results not just from deliberate acts on the part of the government, but also from actions and laws that have a differential impact on different racial groups. ICERD requires that both types of discrimination be eliminated. The Shadow Report points out that the US law, with a few exceptions, always considers the intent to discriminate (e.g., in hate crimes) as an important precursor for understanding discrimination, whereas ICERD's emphasis is on the effect. The ICERD also demands that governments take action to eliminate racial discrimination in the enjoyment of the right to work, the right to housing, the right to medical care, and the right to education – a range of economic and social human rights that are not recognized under US domestic law. Equally important, the Shadow Report emphasizes that the US has been, especially since September 2001, subjecting immigrants and refugees to systematic violations of their human rights. From immigration raids, racial profiling in a variety of spheres, and systematically denying immigrants their right to access jobs, housing, education, and healthcare, a new series of discriminatory measures has been institutionalized in the US in the twenty-first century, as the discrimination against African Americans continues.

The institutionalization of human rights at the international level helps to set up accounting systems that gauge the extent to which countries progress on human rights. The production of the Shadow Report – developed by a constellation of activist groups – is able to give voice and some political power at the international level to these groups' assessment of the US's progress (or lack thereof) on dismantling racism. This gap – the areas of disagreement between the two reports – becomes part of the data at the international level on the progress of a country toward eliminating racism and grounds for activism. Thus, the international platform remains important for reinforcing a country's record in a theoretically sound and empirically accurate way – where racism is not reduced to interpersonal bigotry and overt racial law/discourse, but instead persists through widespread institutionalization (structure) and mystification via color-blind ideology ("what racism?").

However, the structural conundrum remains; the same state that has enabled the erosion of many of the gains of the Civil Rights movement, and has enabled new forms of structural racism to be institutionalized, remains the arbiter and protector of human rights. It simply points to the need for grassroots resistance movements that are likely to be in conflict with states (and thus the legal regime).

Overall, this complexity defines and characterizes the human rights enterprise and the actual terrains of continuing struggles to realize human rights practice. As we indicated in chapter 2, what has changed between the mid-twentieth century and the early twenty-first is the resurging power of private corporations to move many aspects of social life to privatized arenas that are beyond the reach of much civil rights legislation, and the emerging sets of laws that legalize such actions. Thus, increasing pressure from below is an important feature of the human rights enterprise; so too is the subversion of advances by private corporations and retrenchment by the state, as seen by recent Supreme Court decisions and everyday practices such as racial profiling by police and stand-your-ground violence by individuals. In the following chapter, we examine the expanding rights, power, and influence of corporations and private wealth in the face of shrinking rights for everyday people. If the human rights enterprise is to succeed in any lasting or consistent way, such obvious imbalances of power and threats to democracy must be confronted.

4

Private Tyrannies

Rethinking the Rights of *"Corporate Citizens"*

Before we move forward, let's recap for a moment. In chapter 1, we began from the manifest observation that the world is far from achieving universal human rights practice, and that even in powerful states like the US, which played a primary role in the creation of the United Nations and international law, human rights carries little weight in law or public policy, and is relatively absent from public political discourse. We suggested that a critical sociology of human rights might help us to understand why human rights, when limited to the construction of international legal regimes that place states as the primary actors in charge of ensuring universal human rights practice, seems to fall far short of intended goals. In chapter 2, we employed political sociology – "critical theories of the state" – to illustrate *why* the state, particularly in the context of neoliberal global capitalism, is an unlikely champion of human rights, especially in the fairly common case where rights practice conflicts with the interests of capital. In chapter 3, we sought to illustrate our historical argument: that, in fact, human rights have been and continue to be defined and realized primarily through bottom-up power struggles and social movements, typically against or in spite of the very states (and other powerful interests) charged with rights protection in the first place. With no previous concept available to describe the complexity of human rights struggles in this regard, we offer "the human rights enterprise" in our work to conceptualize the broad global historical processes to define and realize human rights that include both formal legal terrains (the

115

UN, human rights instruments, international courts, and so forth) and the perhaps far more important terrains of bottom-up social movements (such as the civil rights and anti-apartheid movements) that often materialize as conflicts over power, resource, and political voice that tend to challenge the authority of law and the state. Chapters 2 and 3 also begin to explore the concept of "human rights praxis" – or our strategies for realizing human rights, given the lessons of history and previous attempts. Once we see human rights as the product of social struggle rather than simply the legal construction of rulers and states, we can examine and learn from the historical (civil rights) and contemporary (Occupy Wall Street) social movements most responsible for the rights we enjoy.

In chapters 4 and 5, we will continue to focus on contemporary human rights praxis. If the human rights enterprise can be understood as consisting largely of struggles over power where states play (at best) contradictory roles with regard to their international legal obligations, what are the most pressing power struggles of our day, particularly for those of us studying and working in the US? What should we do and how should we do it? In this chapter we suggest that one of these struggles must be in opposition to the massive consolidation of power and resources (threatening all aspects of equality and democratic decision-making at the local and global levels) achieved through the modern TNC and corporate banks. Ironically, challenging the power of big corporations and banks involves rethinking our legal notions of a legitimate "rights claimant." The question of "who counts?" when it comes to human rights was possibly the most important, controversial, and revolutionary notion offered by human rights instruments in the twentieth century, and we may once again find ourselves asking similar questions today regarding the rights and power of "corporate citizens."

Who counts?

If nothing else, the establishment of the UDHR in 1948 presented a rather profound statement about membership in the human species for its time. The original Articles 1 and 2 of the UDHR state that, "all human beings are born free and equal in dignity and rights," and that all are entitled to human rights "without distinction of any kind, such as race, colour, sex, language, religion, political or other opinion, national or social origin, property, birth or other status."[1] Though certainly flawed in substance and process – corrupted and complicated by the wounds of world war, the rise of nuclear weapons, an emergent Cold War, and anti-colonial struggles (Ishay 2008) – the UDHR as a discourse on human equality was potentially if not absolutely *counter-hegemonic.*[2]

In 1948, while African-American soldiers fought in US forces such as the Tuskegee Airmen during World War II, they returned to a state that embraced and brutally enforced white supremacy through racial segregation and Jim Crow laws that constructed African Americans as a subordinate "racial caste" (Wilson 1996; Alexander 2010). Former global powers such as the English, Dutch, and French violently sought to maintain colonial empires that were falling to resistance and expense on Asian and African continents, where French aggression in Algeria and Vietnam are notable examples. As illustrated in the previous chapter, the UDHR was drafted at a time of incredible racial oppression and anti-racist and anti-colonial struggle – not a time during which racial and ethnic equity was in any way a dominant worldview or common point of public policy.

At the close of World War II, the capacity for state-sponsored genocide and war crimes in the modern world was clear: Nazi Germany's use of death camps and an engineered, systematic genocide; Stalin's political purges, gulags, and forced migrations in the Soviet Union during the 1930s and 1940s; and the United States' bombing of German and Japanese cities, culminating with the first and only use of nuclear weapons, leveling the cities of Hiroshima and Nagasaki and murdering over 150,000 unarmed civilians. All of these efforts were made possible in part through nationalist, xenophobic, and racist ideologies, constructing "enemies" not worthy of human dignity, as is common in war.

Though the women's suffrage movements of the West in the nineteenth and early twentieth centuries afforded civil and political rights for privileged white women, 1948 certainly pre-dates the more contemporary feminist movements that speak to gender equity, or a critical deconstruction of patriarchy as a system and gender as a concept.[3] Women who previously had the freedom and opportunity to earn living wages in US factories, absent male workers during World War II, quickly found themselves constructed as subservient in the new "nuclear family" when war (and wartime production) subsided, and soldiers returned to the home, family, and workplace. Lesbian, gay, bisexual, transsexual, and queer (LGBTQ) populations – such a concept certainly did not exist at the time – were persecuted and systematically targeted in World War II, as were Jews, the Romany, and other marginalized racial/ethnic/religious populations. While the Kinseys' *Sexual Behavior in the Human Male* was published in 1948, and several gay rights organizations existed by the 1950s in the US and elsewhere, the actual decriminalization of various expressions of non-hetero sexuality (such as sodomy laws), and the wider public consciousness about sexual politics created in the wake of resistance such as the Stonewall Riots[4] did not occur until the 1960s and 1970s.

We do not mean here to ignore significant resistance at the time of the UDHR – notable critical sociologists such as W. E. B. Du Bois championed the centrality and importance of human rights during the drafting of the UN Charter as an anti-racist and anti-colonial effort (Ishay 2008). We only mean to point out the significance of the UDHR as an international, state-sponsored policy discourse, broadening the human concept to include as equals those who in daily practice experienced systematic, manifest inequality. The UDHR and the international human rights instruments to follow took a fundamental stance defining "humanity" in a way that was certainly against the dominant view – especially as an agreement between states in the formation of a new international legal structure.

When discourse appears as policy, it takes on a high level of perceived legitimacy because it has the backing of a state, or in this case a collective of states (Foucault 1977; Smith 2005). One clear contribution of human rights instruments and human rights as international law is their ability to provide a potentially counter-hegemonic discourse that carries with it a sense of legitimacy because they are the legal product of states. We agree with scholars like Arat (2008) in recognizing this unique feature of human rights instruments: on the one hand, they are a form of state discourse often representing powerful international agreement and the legal authority of states; on the other hand, they communicate a radical ideology emphasizing universal "equality in dignity" that may directly challenge the policies or legitimate authority of states, particularly when employed in social struggle and human rights praxis.

The expanded definition of humanity is central to human rights as a concept and to international human rights instruments, but *we should also note the stated boundaries of the concept as equally important.* In describing the Universal Declaration model,[5] Donnelly (2003: 25) argues that the rights listed in the UDHR should be understood as the rights of individual human beings:

> If human rights are the rights that one has simply as a human being, then only human beings have human rights; if one is not a human being, by definition one cannot have human rights . . . Collectives of all sorts have many and varied rights. But these are not – and cannot be – human rights, unless we substantially recast the concept.

What Donnelly refers to here are the limits to universal application of these rights concepts. They apply universally to all human beings (defined in revolutionary form for the time), and their legitimacy, or philosophical foundation, can only be found in the mutual needs of collective human survival and in forms of massive consensus (such as the drafting, debating, and signing of the UDHR and UN Charter) that construct what is required for one to live a dignified human life. In other words, human rights find their legitimacy in the shared human condition and in the sometimes shifting consensus on the definition of fundamental human dignity in real historical contexts. Though there is certainly an argument to be made here for expanding similar fundamental rights and dignities to other sentient beings (animal rights, particularly in regard to environmental protections), it is very difficult to argue the legitimacy of such rights if applied to legal constructs or non-living things. Human rights scholars have certainly spent considerable time debating the legitimacy of "group rights" vs. "individual rights" on the international level (Jones 1999; Donnelly 2003; Goodhart 2009), and we present here a similar conceptual boundary issue. Though it may seem moot to emphasize that human rights only apply to flesh-and-blood human beings, it may be one of the most crucial aspects of human rights as a legal and counter-hegemonic discourse in the pursuit of human rights practice.

In his description of the Universal Declaration model, Donnelly (2003: 23) makes a particular effort to mention that the listed rights apply to human beings and "not corporate entities." A great deal of scholarship, which also reflected and informed the anti-globalization movement,[6] demonstrates the historical processes through which corporations became the most powerful mechanisms in modern global capitalism, primarily through gaining the rights of people with few of the responsibilities – including rights to free speech and limited legal liability (Bakan 2004; Bond 2004; Bond and Manyanya 2003; Brecher, Costello, and Smith 2000; Klein 2000; McNally 2006; Parrenas 2001; Schaeffer 2003; Shiva 2000, 2001). This same literature documents the many cases where private corporate and financial interests (banks) with structural/legal obligations to profit often pose significant threats to human rights practice. In chapter 2, we discussed the extent to which these private interests can both constrain the actions of state governments and directly threaten the economic rights of global populations through processes of crisis, debt, and austerity (see also Graeber 2012; Albo, Gindin, and Panitch 2010; McNally 2011). As we will discuss below, corporations continue to enjoy expanded rights in the US through their legal and social construction as political subjects on a par with flesh-and-blood human beings. The boundaries of rights and to whom or what is a legitimate political subject, seen through a political sociological lens, include conversations about to whom/what such rights do *not* apply.

While the rights of corporations continue to expand, the constitutional and human rights of everyday folks in the US have arguably eroded. Such a pattern contradicts the letter and spirit of human rights instruments like the UDHR. Though there are certainly hopeful exceptions to be found in, for example, the progress of LGBTQ rights to marriage and military service in the US, the constitutional and human rights of women, the poor, and people of color are in many ways under threat as a result of US policies that, for reasons theoretically addressed in chapter 2, tend to reflect the narrow interests of the corporate owning class.

Corporate power and "personhood"

During the 2012 presidential campaign, GOP candidate Mitt Romney caught significant flack in the mass media for the following exchange with audience members at the Iowa State Fair:[7]

> *Romney:* Over the coming decades, are we going to be able to balance our budget and not spend more than we take in? We have to make sure that the promises we make in Social Security, Medicaid, and Medicare are promises we can keep. And there are various ways of doing that. One is we can raise taxes on people. And that's not the way that. . .
> *Audience members:* Tax Corporations!
> *Romney: [laughs]* Corporations are people, my friend.

Though political talking heads treated Romney's comment as a sign of his disrespect to working people, they failed to recognize over a century of questionable legal rulings on the matter of corporate rights. Legally speaking, Romney was correct. And since rulings like *Citizens United* v. *Federal Elections Commission* (2010), corporations would now have few limits on their ability to leverage unmatched economic might to sway elections or any political decision (such as state referendums or propositions) subject to a vote by the flesh-and-blood electorate.

What are corporations and what makes them so powerful? How is their "personhood" determined, and what does that mean for the rest of us real human beings? A considerable amount of research (Bakan 2004; Nace 2005; Hartmann 2010; Clements

121

2012) and documentary film (*The Corporation*, 2003) tells this story in far greater detail than space allows here. We will only present the overview and highlights of corporate power and personhood, as they have to do with effects on the practices and prospects of human rights and our broader arguments about best possible options for contemporary human rights praxis.

As defined by Clements (2012):

> A corporation is a government-defined legal structure for doing business. A corporation is created and defined by state legislatures to advance what the state deems to be in the public interest. Corporations as entities are government policy tools; only government makes incorporation possible. Unlike other associations or ways of doing business, a corporation cannot exist by private arrangement. (2012: 187–8)

In the US, businesses must apply to become "incorporated" under the specific laws of a particular state (such as Michigan, California, or Delaware). Structurally, corporations create a level of separation between those who share ownership of the business (shareholders, typically represented by a Board of Directors) and a class of managers (CEOs, CFOs, etc.) who actually run the business. First, as an economic institutional structure, this gives businesses the "capacity to combine the capital and thus the economic power, of unlimited numbers of people" through access to credit and the public trade of stocks and other related financial products (Bakan 2004: 8). Second, this structure sets the ultimate, and only, legal directive of any publicly traded corporation: to pursue profit on behalf of the *shareholders* (owners – those who own significant shares of a company, and affect the direction and actions of the corporation as a result). In the interest of our conversation here, we might see this in contrast with the needs of various *stakeholders* (anyone – typically including the tax-paying public – who is affected by the actions/decisions of a corporation, often without any ownership stake or decision-making power over that corporation) who are also affected by corporate pursuits of profit, though without democratic representation on corporate boards. In other words – pharmaceutical companies have no legal obligations to make us

122

healthier or create cures for disease; private news media have no actual legal obligation to inform the public; and private prison industries have no legal obligation to reduce crime rates. Publicly traded corporations in the US are required by law to work in the interests of the shareholders they represent – to make sure stock prices continue to rise in value, and their investments are protected by the decisions of those who manage the company (Bakan 2004).

When we speak of *privatization* in the context of global capitalism and global economic restructuring, it generally refers to turning certain social goals, such as education, public health, or incarceration/crime control, over to the "private sector" – private corporations. Central to neoliberal, "free-market" capitalism is the assumption that private-sector competition for market share and profit produce *both* profit for companies and the intended social goals for the consuming public. Unfortunately, as noted in a mountain of social scientific work,[8] corporate pursuit of profit often conflicts with the manifest social functions of their work: pharmaceutical companies earn a great deal of money creating customers and addicts rather than cures for harmful diseases; private prison industries – as demonstrated in contracts with states such as Arizona, Ohio, Louisiana, or Virginia demanding that newly constructed facilities remain filled to 90 percent + capacity (In the Public Interest 2013) – profit from increasing incarceration, not decreasing crime; and, perhaps most obviously, corporate members of the military industrial complex profit from war and fear, not "peace and security" (the central stated purpose of the UN and its Security Council). Further, consider the following about private vs. public approaches to public health in the US:

- The US has the most expensive healthcare system in the developed world.
- Of those with medical problems in the US, 42 percent skipped a doctor's visit or didn't buy needed medication due to cost in 2011.
- Common surgeries in the US cost three to ten times more than in comparable Western European countries.

- Though the US has one of the lowest average life expectancies in the industrialized world, the *public* Medicare program increased the life expectancy for its members by 3.5 years since it began in the 1960s (Buchheit 2013).

Here we see the central conflict discussed in chapter 2 emerge in greater detail: the contradictions between profit motives and rights protection play out in struggles to influence and/or capture the state and in the legal obligations of corporations to seek profit at all costs – even if that means violating rights practices, undermining democratic governance, or stripping environmental protections.

The benefits – "rights" – of incorporated businesses differ from state to state. For example, most TNCs, including 300 of the Fortune 500 list of the most powerful companies in the world and half of all publicly traded companies in the US, incorporate under Delaware state law because it is perceived as having the fewest limitations and liabilities for corporations while affording the most freedoms (Clements 2012; Nace 2005; Hartmann 2010). Some of the most significant rights and freedoms granted to corporations include:

(a) The ability to own and sell shares ("stock" – or partial ownership) of other firms. Like people, corporations are allowed to own and trade shares of other companies and financial institutions. This facilitates the increasing centralization of capital and conglomeration of corporations. The most telling example of this can be found in private media. In 1983 approximately 50 corporations shared the American media market; now approximately 7 corporations, including giants such as NewsCorp, Disney, Viacom, and Time Warner, control a startling 90 percent of mainstream media markets (Lutz 2012). A manifest challenge to the neoliberal myth of "free-market competition," this near-complete domination of what people hear, read, and watch in the US represents a challenge to the concept of a "free press," arguably necessary in democratic societies and for any meaningful constitutional

(1st Amendment) or human (UDHR, Article 19; ICCPR, Article 19) rights to the freedom of opinion and expression.

(b) The ability to sue and be sued in US courts. Discussed in pages to follow, this is how corporations expanded their rights as "people" in the first place. Their rights to bring suit expanded with international trade agreements like the North American Free Trade Agreement (NAFTA) that allow corporations to take direct legal action to sanction states for violating stated corporate trade interests. In sum, powerful TNCs have had little trouble expanding or exerting their influence via US courtrooms.

(c) Perpetual existence. Unlike flesh-and-blood human beings, as legal constructs corporations can live forever. While this might be seen as advantageous when it comes to developing products and technologies over several generations of workers, it can be extremely problematic when it comes to entrenched corporate interests. A perfect example here would be fossil fuel and petrochemical companies which dedicate significant resources to denying climate change and derailing alternative fuels and sustainable energy solutions (Adam 2009). The entrenchment of such powerful interests in preserving our pathological status quo threatens any effort to come up with energy solutions that will be necessary to ensure collective human survival (IPCC 2013), let alone universal human rights practice in the short term.

(d) The right to "free speech." Historically, corporations used "free-speech" arguments for everything from resisting the labeling of dangerous products to arguing for unlimited spending on political donations (Clements 2012; Nace 2005; Hartmann 2010). Similar arguments would be made in *Citizens United* v. *Federal Election Commission* (2010) to legitimate the right of corporations to spend much more, and more freely, to affect elections and political discourse in the US.

(e) Limited liability. One result of separating those who own a corporation from those who run it was to create an entity with the rights of a person, but none of the responsibilities or criminal accountability of one. The Delaware Corporations code states, for example, "The stockholders of a corporation shall not be personally liable for the payment of the corporation's debts except as they may be liable by reason of their own conduct or acts" (Clements 2012: 194).

There is no shortage of contemporary examples of startling corporate impunity to illustrate this point. In 2010 the Deepwater Horizon British Petroleum (BP) oil spill marked the largest and arguably most devastating accidental oil spill in the history of the petroleum industry. The catastrophe began with an explosion and sinking of the Deepwater Horizon oil rig, where 11 workers were killed. The crisis continued as oil flowed freely into the Gulf of Mexico for at least 87 days, discharging over 4.9 million barrels into the Gulf and on to the Gulf shorelines.[9] The environmental, economic, and human health effects of the spill continued to unfold – with "tar balls" and "tar mats" found on Gulf shorelines long after the spill began – closing beaches, destroying wildlife habitats, and crippling local fishing and tourism industries. BP settled with the federal government over criminal charges including 11 counts of manslaughter and a felony charge for lying to Congress.

Many may argue that BP made good on their deeds in paying a $4.5 billion settlement as a result, along with payments into another $42.2 billion trust fund for victim and civil suit payments (Fontevecchia 2013), but this misses the point entirely. To the most powerful corporations in the world, these kinds of economic settlements are easily weathered, come nowhere near the actual costs to stakeholders and the environment, and are treated simply as a cost of doing business. By the following year (2011), BP showed signs of recovery and earned record profits of over $25.7 billion (up from approximately $14 billion before the spill in 2009), in part due to increasing oil and gasoline prices (Macalister 2012).

Due to limited liability, corporations like BP – and, more importantly, their most powerful shareholders and decision-makers – are essentially able to buy their way out of meaningful public or criminal accountability. Consider for a moment what would happen to flesh-and-blood human beings like us, if we were found guilty of murdering 11 people, felony perjury before Congress, and causing irreparable damage to an entire international body of water, crushing the livelihood of millions of people and decimating wildlife in coastal communities. Certainly, in the country that incarcerates more people than any society in modern human history, individuals like us would expect considerable prison time if not calls for the death penalty if found personally, criminally responsible for such an act.

Private banks enjoy similar impunity in their pursuit of profit. In December 2012 state and federal prosecutors fined HSBC bank $1.92 billion in a court settlement for allegedly laundering money for Mexican drug cartels. Federal Justice Department officials refused to pursue criminal indictments because the British-based international bank was too large and powerful – wounding the "too big to fail" bank could destabilize the global economy (Protess and Silver-Greenberg 2012). To explain why this happens, one only needs to understand the state in the context of global capitalism as discussed in chapter 2 and the legal obligation of corporate businesses and banks to pursue profit discussed here. The structural focus on profit drives HSBC and other private financial institutions (also corporate in form) to bend and break the law if necessary to ensure short-term financial gains – which in this case meant direct investments in organized crime, terror, and systematic violence. Social costs, like the brutal public executions, organized violence, and state corruption that characterize the contemporary Mexican drug cartel, are externalized to the public, directly threatening human rights practice. Rather than prioritizing rights practice for drug-war torn communities in North America, the state acted (or failed to act) as would be predicted by state structuralist theory, in an attempt to stabilize capital markets, preserve the capitalist system, and not set precedents for criminalizing forms of capital accumulation.

As noted in Bakan (2004), this combination – the legal obligation to pursue profit above and beyond all other concerns, and the ability to do this work with virtual impunity (limited liability) – makes the modern TNC a kind of unaccountable tyranny (see also Chomsky 2007a). They hone massive amounts of resource (capital) and human energy (labor) for the sole purpose of pursuing profit, and seek to externalize all forms of cost ("externalities") – including the environmental or social effects of their products and activities. These externalized costs – whether the environmental effects of an oil spill, or the cost of a massive bank bailout – are often shouldered by the general public, deeply affecting the quality of life and human rights prospects of everyday people. Such externalized costs also deplete public monies to support the range of human rights, especially economic and social rights through publicly supported programs.

The modern concept of the corporate "person" that affords incorporated businesses their unique position of rights without reasonable responsibility or accountability can be found in US case law since the nineteenth century. Most scholars point to the (1886) case of *Santa Clara County* v. *Southern Pacific Railroad*, where the Southern Pacific Railroad claimed in an attempt to avoid certain taxes that it was a "person" under the newly minted 14th Amendment to the Constitution, originally meant to give meaningful protection under the law to newly freed slaves (Clements 2012; Bakan 2004; Nace 2005; Hartmann 2010). Though the court did not actually make any constitutional decision in this case (Clements 2012), that didn't stop corporate lawyers and corporate-friendly courts from using the *SCC* v. *SPR* decision as a precedent for corporate personhood over the next century. To wit, between 1890 and 1910, corporate interests invoked the 14th Amendment approximately 288 times in cases claiming the rights of a "person" under constitutional law. During this same period, estimates suggest that only 19 African Americans successfully invoked 14th Amendment rights in US courts (see Bakan 2004; *The Corporation* 2003; Grossman, Linzey, and Brannen 2003).

The most notable recent example of expanding the rights of corporate personhood is likely the 5–4 decision in *Citizens United* v. *Federal Election Commission* (2010), where in 2010 the Supreme Court overruled previous legal precedent (*Austin* v. *Michigan Chamber of Commerce* 1990; *McConnell* v. *Federal Election Commission* 2003), suggesting that the government could not restrict independent political expenditures by corporations or labor unions. Justice Kennedy's remarks in the majority opinion were widely reported: "If the First Amendment has any force, it prohibits Congress from fining or jailing citizens or associations of citizens, for simply engaging in political speech" (Liptak 2010). Though part of the dissenting opinion, Justice Stevens commented on the trajectory of case law on corporate personhood: "we have long since held that corporations are covered by the First Amendment" (Liptak 2010). Still, he and other dissenting Justices articulated the conceptual manipulation required to place corporations on par with human beings as rights claimants:

> ... corporations have no consciences, no beliefs, no feelings, no thoughts, no desires. Corporations help structure and facilitate the activities of human beings, to be sure, and their "personhood" often serves as a useful legal fiction. But they are not themselves members of "we the people" by whom and for whom our Constitution was established. (*Citizens United* v. *Federal Elections Commission* 2010)

Justice Stevens is not the first Supreme Court Justice to question the growing political economic power of corporations in modern society. Justice Rehnquist made clear decades earlier the concern that the unique economic privileges of corporations may serve to threaten democracy:

> A state grants to a business corporation the blessings of potentially perpetual life and limited liability to enhance its efficiency as an economic entity. It might reasonably be concluded that those properties, so beneficial in the economic sphere, pose special dangers in the political sphere. (Clements 2012; *First National Bank of Boston* v. *Bellotti* 1978)

Corporations' structural focus and legal obligations on the pursuit of profit above and beyond all other concerns directly threaten human rights through socially and environmentally devastating externalities that affect the state and state policy in all the ways discussed in chapter 2 and severely constrain the state in its ability to prioritize rights practice and fulfill its legal obligations – particularly when it seems to conflict with the interests of capital. Justice Rehnquist's comments demonstrate obvious concerns that the power of corporations can easily eclipse the needs of actual people, and threaten if not completely corrupt the democratic process. The stated positions of Justices Rehnquist and Stevens above also mirror the construction of legitimate rights claimants under human rights instruments: that "associations" of people or legal fictions cannot be constructed on a par with flesh-and-blood human beings as political subjects deserving of equal protection under the law.

The Justices' concerns seem to have been legitimate. Corporate size and economic might dwarf that of many states. In 2009, 44 of the world's 100 largest "economic entities" were corporations (the rest were states), with Walmart topping corporate charts as the 25th largest economic entity on the planet – sporting greater revenue than the GDP of at least 171 other countries (Keys and Malnight 2013). In 2011 the top 500 TNCs pulled in record profits of over $29.5 trillion – with Royal Dutch Shell, Exxon, Walmart, and British Petroleum weighing in as the largest, most powerful companies. Further, corporations and the similar corporate form that structures large banks/financial institutions have functioned to consolidate resources and power in the hands of a very few. This contradicts the dominant notion that publicly traded companies somehow spread out and democratize ownership through the sale and trade of stock.

First, consider research on corporate mergers and consolidation noted in our earlier illustration of private American media conglomerates. In their study of "Global Corporate Control," Vitali, Glattfelder, and Battiston (2011) point to a "super entity" of 147 TNCs that actually control about 40 percent of the total economic value of all the world's TNCs combined. They suggest further that this consolidation of corporate ownership – consider it a form of international ownership disparity – is even greater than measures of international wealth disparity. Such a comparison is telling when one considers the scope and growth of wealth disparity in recent years. The richest 1 percent of the global population own 40 percent of the world's wealth and increased their incomes by

60 percent over the past 20 years. The richest 10 percent of the global population hold 85 percent of the world's total assets, while the bottom 50 percent of the global population hold less than 1 percent of global wealth (Randerson 2006; Marshall 2013; Oxfam 2013). As the most gruesome display of international wealth disparity, Oxfam (Fuentes-Nieva and Galasso 2014) reported that the 85 wealthiest *individuals* on Earth now enjoy more wealth than the entire bottom half of the global population – over 3.5 billion people – combined.

Things look quite similar at the national level, where the share of national income earned by the top 1 percent in the US has doubled since 1980, the top 10 percent of earners in China earn a whopping 60 percent of total national income, and inequality in the UK "is rapidly returning to levels not seen since the time of Charles Dickens" (Oxfam 2013). This is why some researchers refer to current wealth disparity trends as a new "guilded age" where the world is essentially divided between impoverished working masses and a super-rich, relatively small owning class (Eichler and McAuliff 2011). International human rights and humanitarian organizations point to this staggering global wealth inequality as a manifest challenge to fundamental human dignity and social sustainability. In a report tellingly titled "The Cost of Inequality: How Wealth and Income Extremes Hurt Us All," Oxfam (2013) argued that the resources of the wealthiest 100 people on Earth (approximately $240 billion) would be enough to "end world poverty four times over" (p. 2). The World Economic Forum's Global Risk Report agreed, rating inequality as a top global risk for global peace, stability, and security in 2013 (Howell 2013).

Second, these most powerful corporations and financial institutions are owned and controlled by a relatively small number of people – referred to as the "Transnational Capitalist Class" (TCC) (Burris and Staples 2012). The TCC consists of a powerful network of actors who sit on the boards of multiple corporations and financial institutions, while also enjoying revolving-door[10] employment in many of the world's state governments, large universities, and most influential think tanks. Studies of the TCC tend to examine "interlocking directorates" (Mintz and Schwartz 1985)

– or the overlap in board membership between these powerful institutions that allow a small network of people to call the shots in the private sector. Since powerful TNCs are global in scope and overshadow the economic influence of many state governments, "the elites who own and control these corporations [the TCC] will also cease to be organized or divided along national lines . . . [their] social networks, affiliations, and identities will no longer be embedded primarily in the roles they occupy as citizens of specific nations" (Burris and Staples 2012: 324; see also Marshall 2013).

In short, the modern TNC and the small group of powerful players who run and own them are decreasingly bound by law or allegiance to any particular nation-state (Armaline and Glasberg 2009; Robinson 2001). This is extraordinarily problematic for the success of human rights as an international legal regime that expects states to protect and choose human rights practices over the interests of individual capitalists or broader interests of capital accumulation where they would conflict (Armaline and Glasberg 2009). How is the state to rein in the actions of banks and TNCs that may challenge them in economic size and influence?

Corporations and the further corruption of democratic governance

Powerful TNCs continually demonstrate their ability to affect state policy to ensure their own economic interests. Whether one examines the shared interests pursued by trade agreements like NAFTA or transnational state[11] structures (Robinson 2001, 2004) that emerged with global economic restructuring (such as the International Monetary Fund, World Bank, or World Trade Organization), the method of international corporate governance and decision-making is hardly democratic or representative of global populations. This lack of democratic decision-making that characterized economic globalization in the late twentieth century inspired the anti-globalization movement, contemporary anti-capitalism, and, as discussed in chapter 1, an emergent critical sociology of human rights. At the time controversial trade agreements like NAFTA purposefully shut out workers, unions, indigenous populations, and environmentalists to set policy that would favor capital interests; resistance that began with the Zapatista uprising in 1994 quickly spread to global cities like New York, Paris, Tokyo, Seattle, Toronto, and Genoa by the turn of the twenty-first century as an international movement against corporate power over national and international policies.

Undemocratic, non-transparent, unaccountable dominance of international trade by the most powerful corporations, financial institutions, and states most certainly persists in similar form today. The World Trade Organization, rather than becoming more transparent and democratically representative of global populations since its inception, still operates in relative secrecy. According to economist Joseph Stiglitz (2013), "The goal is a managed trade regime – managed, that is, to serve the special interests that have long dominated trade policy in the west . . . the more general point . . . is that trade agreements typically put commercial interests ahead of other values." These "other values" most certainly include the human rights and environmental prospects of the global masses, largely excluded from the conversation.

The dangerous and anti-democratic precedents set by NAFTA continue and are being reproduced today in efforts to expand "free-trade zones" and corporate influence over international trade. The Trans-Pacific Partnership (TPP), currently in its final stages of private negotiation since its start under the Bush administration in 2008, represents the contemporary international trade agreement now focused on expanding free-trade zones to the Asian Pacific. While the Obama administration claims that the TPP is primarily about expanding trade and stimulating broad economic growth, the US already holds individual free-trade agreements with most prospective TPP countries, and only five of the TPP agreement's 29 chapters covers issues of trade – the rest is essentially designed to expand the rights of corporations against the sanctions and controls of TPP states (Wallach 2012). In June 2012, a chapter of the TPP draft agreement was leaked[12] to the press. The chapter, still part of the negotiated TPP agreement, suggests that the TPP would continue the "investor-state dispute resolution" also employed under NAFTA. According to reporting by *The Nation* (Wallach 2012), these "extra legal" systems directly challenge the national sovereignty of TPP and UN member states:

> ... it empowers corporations to sue governments – outside their domestic court systems – over any action the corporations believe undermines their expected future profits or rights under the pact. Three-person international tribunals of attorneys from the private sector would hear these cases. The lawyers rotate between serving as "judges" – empowered to order governments to pay corporations unlimited amounts in fines – and representing the corporations that use this system to raid government treasuries. The NAFTA version of this scheme has forced governments to pay more than $350 million to corporations after suits against toxic bans, land-use policies, forestry rules and more.

Trade agreements like NAFTA and TPP demonstrate corporations' ability to exert power over the policies and actions of states in pursuit of profit and market share. This ability is bolstered through corporate rights as "people" or political subjects with "rights" to be leveraged against states, let alone against the human rights and interests of populations of stakeholders that these states may or may not meaningfully represent.

The ease with which powerful TNCs and financial institutions affect policy and practice at the national level is readily apparent in the US. Despite all the talk about corporate taxes harming economic growth and the availability of sustainable employment, powerful corporations pay very little into the US tax base, particularly when offset by forms of corporate welfare discussed in chapter 2. The nominal corporate tax rate is 35 percent in the US and the effective rate (minus deductions and credits) is about 27.1 percent (27.7 percent is the global average). Though the largest 1,000 US corporations can certainly afford it – they hold an estimated $1 trillion in cash reserves (Reich 2013) – it's clear that powerful corporations pay nowhere near their expected tax rates. In fact the top 10 most profitable companies, including some of the most profitable in world history, paid an average rate of 9 percent in federal taxes in 2011. The most profitable of these companies at the time, Exxon Mobil, paid only 2 percent (Chevron: 4 percent; Apple: 11 percent; JP Morgan Chase: 14 percent) (Eichler 2012; Nerdwallet 2012). Still, President Obama and challenger Mitt Romney both promised to lower this rate (Newman 2012) during the 2012 presidential election in their plans to improve the American economy, suggesting the continued ideological dominance of this free-trade, "hands-off" approach to regulating TNCs in American government.

The non-democratic, non-transparent collusion between corporations and policymakers demonstrated through bodies like the WTO at the international level also takes place at the national and state level in the US. The American Legislative Exchange Council (ALEC) was co-founded in 1973 by some of the same people who founded conservative think tanks like the Heritage Foundation. The group of business leaders (representing over 200 corporations and corporate interest groups) and policymakers (over 2,000 of them – a third of the nation's total legislators) work to develop, promote, and lobby for policies friendly to the agendas of its corporate membership, and have come to wield "undeniable influence" on state and federal policies covering a variety of economic and social policy issues (Hodai 2010; Olsen 2012). Technically a non-profit organization, ALEC is overwhelmingly funded by its corporate members: in 2008, $5.6 million of its total $6.9 million annual revenues were corporate donations (Hodai 2010). ALEC-approved "model legislation" tends to follow standard right-wing prescriptions for economic growth: fighting progressive forms of taxation, cutting public services (so they can be privatized), weakening private- and public-sector unions, and fighting "government regulation" – including environmental protections and regulations on potentially dangerous financial practices like those that led to the Great Recession in 2008 (Fisher 2012). While proponents of ALEC-sponsored legislation argue that these distinctly neoliberal approaches are good for the economy, research suggests that states in the US whose laws reflected the ALEC economic agenda between 2007 and 2010 reported lower per capita and median family incomes and rising poverty rates (Fisher 2012).

In 2010, journalists such as Beau Hodai (2010) exposed how ALEC facilitated Arizona's controversial anti-immigrant SB 1070 legislation that allows for and encourages "reasonable suspicion" interrogations by police (also called the "breathing while brown" provision), widely seen by human rights and civil liberties organizations as a "problematic" form of racial profiling where "lawfully-present aliens [*sic.*] would be impermissibly burdened by the law" (Human Rights Watch 2011: 4). Arizona's SB 1070 was submitted to ALEC's Public Safety and Elections Task Force by the bill's sponsor and task-force member, Arizona state senator Russell Pearce (R-Mesa). In order for the bill to be endorsed by ALEC (and thus labeled "model legislation"), it had to undergo a 30-day review by the task-force membership. Executive membership on the task force includes a who's who of the prison industrial complex and growing private (corporate) prison industry: Corrections Corporation of America (CCA), the American Bail Coalition, The National Pawn Brokers Association, and Prison Fellowship Ministries (Hodai 2010). Other private prison corporations, such as Geo Group, also populate ALEC corporate membership.

To be perfectly clear, this endorsement process allowed for the punitive immigration bill to be revised and endorsed by the very private corporate interests who would seek to profit from expanding policing and incarceration of undocumented immigrants in the United States. The private prison industry has increasingly shifted its focus to providing private contract services to the Department of Homeland Security (DHS) and to the Immigrations and Customs Enforcement agency (ICE):

> From January 2008 to April 2010, CCA spent $4.4 million lobbying the DHS, ICE, the Office of the Federal Detention Trustee, the Office of Budget Management, the Bureau of Prisons, and both houses of Congress. Of the 43 lobbying disclosure reports CCA filed during this period, only five do not expressly state intent to monitor or influence immigration reform policy or gain Homeland Security or ICE appropriations. (Hodai 2010)

Through organizations like ALEC or the US Chamber of Commerce (Gibson 2013b), corporations are able to pool their already massive resources to influence if not directly manufacture US domestic and foreign policy.

State policy is then greatly and directly influenced by corporations who, by law, have only their own economic imperatives in mind. One specific result is that immigration policies like Arizona SB 1070 are written purely for the purposes of increasing arrests and detention center populations, rather than policy that might represent some sustainable approach to immigration reform, let alone protect the civil and political human rights of migrant populations as articulated by the ICCPR or the International Convention on the Protection of the Rights of All Migrant Workers and Members of Their Families (MWC).

At what cost? Shrinking constitutional and human rights for real people

Corporate businesses and financial institutions are by far the most powerful private economic actors on Earth. Their size, power, and influence over the states charged with controlling and regulating their actions are determined a great deal by their construction as "people," "corporate citizens," or rights claimants under the 14th Amendment of the US Constitution. Their single legal and institutional imperative is to produce (often short-term) profit for shareholders, and this drives them to externalize the social, economic, and environmental costs of their activities to others – typically the public stakeholder. While mainstream economists and politicians continue to tout the myth of free-market solutions to solving social problems, the profit motive of corporate banks and businesses often drives them to contradict their manifest social functions.

Further, as discussed here and in chapter 2, corporations are driven to influence directly if not completely capture the state in their pursuit of profit and market share – this is made much easier with Supreme Court decisions like *Citizens United* v. *Federal Elections Commission* (2010) that expand the already problematic rights of corporations as "people" and strip the ability for the public or the state to limit corporate influence over government. Human and constitutional rights practices are doubly brutalized here: corporations' unyielding pursuit of profit often results in the direct violation of constitutional and human rights for entire populations and/or communities, as seen in the BP oil spill or the graft, fraud, and greed to blame for the mortgage meltdown and the Great Recession of 2008 (Ferguson 2012).

Simultaneously, the raw size and power of TNCs and corporate banks, bolstered by their legal construction as "people," allow them to capture or outmaneuver the state governments explicitly charged with prioritizing and protecting the human rights of their people according to international law. Here we see our critique of dominant approaches to "doing human rights" through the legal actions and responsibilities of states come back into focus. As the Canadian sociologist Dominique Clement (2011: 127) asserts in agreement, "Human rights advocacy is inherently directed toward state power; rights discourse is thus a potentially poor vehicle for limiting economic or private power." This is in large part because of the inability or unwillingness of states to choose human rights practice when in conflict with the interests of capital or the perceived stability of the capitalist system. TNCs and big finance are the legal fictions and structural mechanisms for owning class interests to escape the influence of democratic governance by flesh-and-blood human beings, thus also under-mining the influence of legal human rights regimes (such as the UN or EU) or human rights as a legal discourse that invokes the responsibility of states to ensure rights practices and the rule of law.

We've spent considerable time here establishing the dangers of giving corporations the powers and rights of human beings, noting that interpretations of US constitutional law by the Supreme Court and international human rights law by human rights scholars directly conflict when it comes to the consideration of corporations as "people." Further, as the rights of corporations continue to expand under US constitutional law, the constitutional and human rights of actual human beings in the US continue to shrink in contrast. Let us briefly consider the following as notable, recent examples:

Economic rights

Chapter 2 details the extent to which economic and social human rights to employment (UDHR, Article 23; ICESCR, Article 6), Social Security (UDHR, Article 22; ICESCR, Article 9), an adequate standard of living (UDHR, Article 25; ICESCR, Article 11), health/healthcare (UDHR, Article 25; ICESCR, Article 12), and food (ICESCR, Article 11) are all threatened by economic collapse due to the fraud and unchecked reckless greed of TNCs and global banks. Researchers in the years following the crash in 2008 (Hedges and Sacco 2012; Smiley and West 2012) have done a great deal to document the carnage left behind by the largest upward distribution of wealth in recent history in areas called "sacrifice zones": "Those areas in the country that have been offered up for exploitation in the name of profit, progress, and technological advancement" (Hedges and Sacco 2012: 11).

These sacrifice zones now include major cities that used to represent the strength of US industry and organized labor. In July of 2013 the city of Detroit filed the largest municipal bankruptcy in US history ($18 billion in "unpayable debts"), where an appointed emergency manager is now overseeing the cutting of public services and auctioning of public resources (privatization) to settle the city's financial woes. While it is difficult to blame Detroit's problems on a single cause, it is clear that the same big banks behind the recession were also behind the swindling of municipalities and public pension funds in cities like Detroit, as illustrated by Pyke (2013a; see also Pyke 2013b; Garofalo 2012):

> Detroit paid nearly half a billion dollars in fees to firms for engineering financial products that were bound to hurt the city, because the world's biggest banks were manipulating a key interest rate underlying those products. Similar bank manipulation in Alabama eventually forced JP Morgan Chase to cancel billions of dollars of debts the city of Birmingham never should have owed. (Pyke 2013a)

To be clear, cities and pension funds are not struggling across the US because workers are too greedy or because there is an insurmountable structural impediment to making good on the promises to pensioners. Pension funds and municipal investments were used as the gambling chips of the big banks and hedge funds – folded into increasingly complicated and unstable financial products such as the now infamous subprime mortgage-backed securities. When the financial house of cards collapsed in 2007 and 2008, the tax-paying public stakeholder, who never received a financial bailout, was left holding the bag (Albo, Gindin, and Panitch 2010). Cities and public employees have since been asked to shoulder both the losses to municipal and pension funds, and the tax burden of bailing out TNCs (e.g., auto bailouts) and the very banks responsible for the crisis (TARP, for example).

The rights of people of color

In chapter 3, we discussed the civil rights movement in the US leading up to the Civil Rights Acts of 1964, 1965, and 1968 as an illustration of the human rights enterprise in action, where human rights were defined and realized through grassroots organization and resistance from below, often waged against or in spite of the US government. Also mentioned in the chapter is the recent erosion of these hard-fought victories, namely, in the 5–4 Supreme Court decision in June of 2013 to invalidate section 4 of the Voting Rights Act (1965) that required many former confederate states and other historically problematic voting districts to receive federal clearance on any changes to voting laws or procedures (Liptak 2013).

The effects of this decision were immediately apparent as states such as Texas and North Carolina put forth voter ID laws and redistricting plans that would disenfranchise the most marginal populations of voters: students and young adults, the old, the disabled, the poor, and disproportionately people of color. Shortly following the Supreme Court decision, North Carolina passed some of the most strict and sweeping voting restrictions since the civil rights movement after only three days of public legislative debate. According to reporting by *The Nation* and local investigative journalists, the effects the law will have on democratic participation in North Carolina are quite clear:

The bill mandates strict voter ID to cast a ballot (no student IDs, no public employee IDs, etc.), even though 318,000 registered voters lack the narrow forms of acceptable ID according to the state's own numbers and there have been no recorded prosecutions of voter impersonation in the past decade. The bill cuts the number of early voting days by a week, even though 56 percent of North Carolinians voted early in 2012. The bill eliminates same-day voter registration during the early voting period, even though 96,000 people used it during the general election in 2012 and states that have adopted the convenient reform have the highest voter turnout in the country. African-Americans are 23 percent of registered voters in the state, but made up 28 percent of early voters in 2012, 33 percent of those who used same-day registration and 34 percent of those without state-issued ID (Berman 2013b; see also Berman 2013a)

In fact, efforts to disenfranchise populations of color in the polls were well under way for the 2012 election cycle, where states with Republican-controlled legislatures passed voter ID laws and other restrictive measures that the Brennan Center of New York predicted would strip the right to vote from over 5 million people on election day (Slater 2012; Weiser and Norden 2012). Though there is still no evidence that "voter fraud" is a significant social problem in the US, and since voter ID laws disproportionately disenfranchise the poor and people of color, Attorney General Eric Holder made a telling historical connection, calling them the equivalent of a modern "poll tax" more common during Jim Crow segregation (Slater 2012).

The rights of women

Similar to the erosion of the civil rights of people of color, we are also witnessing a parallel erosion of the rights of women in the United States. The trend is so apparent that politicians, activists, and NGOs openly refer to a "war on women" in the US. The ACLU (2013) defines this policy trend as:

a wide range of policy efforts designed to place restrictions on women's health care and erode protections for women and their families. Examples at the state and federal level have included restricting contraception; cutting off funding for Planned Parenthood; state-mandated, medically unnecessary ultrasounds; abortion taxes; abortion waiting periods; forcing women to tell their employers why they want birth control, and prohibiting insurance companies from including abortion coverage in their policies.

As we see on the terrain of voting rights, many of these restrictions to women's reproductive rights – undeniably part of their human rights to life (UDHR, Article 3; ICCPR, Article 6) and to health/healthcare (UDHR, Article 25; ICESCR, Article 12) – have been waged in states with Republican-controlled legislatures, with significant backing from wealthy individuals, corporations, and religious organizations (Stewart 2013). The curtailing of women's reproductive rights is an apparent public health issue. One in three women in the US will have an abortion in her life[13] and the US has the highest unintended pregnancy rate among developed nations (Guttmacher Institute 2013).

The struggle over women's reproductive rights was most recently highlighted in a legislative stand-off over Texas Senate Bill 5, a restrictive bill that would "ban abortions after 20 weeks of pregnancy, require abortion clinics to meet the same standards that hospital-style surgical centers do, and mandate that a doctor who performs abortions have admitting privileges at a nearby hospital" (Fernandez 2013). Such restrictions would effectively halt abortion services for many women in the large state of Texas, since only five of the existing 42 reproductive health clinics offering abortion services could remain in operation as a result of the bill (Fernandez 2013). The bill was met with massive public outcry and grassroots resistance that packed the halls of the Texas legislature in June of 2013. Backed by public support and a handful of Texas state legislators, democratic State Senator Wendy Davis successfully put the brakes on SB 5 through a 13-hour filibuster from the Texas Senate floor. This was a short-lived victory. Days later, Governor Rick Perry added SB 5 for reconsideration during a special session of the legislature. Despite massive public resistance, the Republican-dominated legislature and Perry administration successfully pushed the bill through and it was signed into law by mid-July – not even a month after Senator Davis's successful filibuster.

Silencing democratic dissent (civil and political rights)

It is perhaps most concerning that the re-authorization of the National Defense Authorization Act (NDAA) and the recently passed Federal Restriction Buildings and Grounds Improvement Act (HR 347, the so-called "Trespass Bill") curtail the constitutional (1st Amendment) and human (UDHR, Article 19; ICCPR, Article 19; UDHR, Article 20; ICCPR, Article 21) rights to expression and assembly. As discussed in chapter 1, the latest NDAA expansion gives executive and military powers to detain anyone, including US citizens on US soil, indefinitely without judicial review, based only on "suspicion" of activities that could threaten national security – powers that the ACLU and many legal scholars claim are demonstratively unconstitutional (Anders 2012). HR 347 took the coercion of public protest a step further, effectively outlawing assembly in the vicinity of public officials guarded by the Secret Service, expanding "restricted zones" and the ability for Secret Service personnel to arrest protesters in these zones, even if they were not aware of the legal restriction. Penalties for violating HR 347 include felony arrest, fines, and up to 10 years in federal prison (Molloff 2012). Beyond further restricting public protest at already highly restricted areas like the White House grounds, it is difficult to predict the broader effect that HR 347 will have on public protest in the US. That said, what many may not realize is that the trespass bill also potentially criminalizes protest of the corporate-driven transnational state (Robinson 2001) that determines the rules and boundaries of the global economy. It effectively outlaws protesting G-8/G-20 meetings, IMF or WTO meetings, and any significant event bringing together heads of state on US soil where Secret Service personnel would most certainly be present, and "restricted zones" would be employed.

The increasing criminalization of peaceful, previously legal public dissent is now a global trend. In response to a Toronto police order to "take back the streets" in confrontation with G-20 protests in 2010, where over 1,000 residents, journalists, protesters, and human rights monitors were physically coerced and placed in detention in a 36-hour sweep, the International Network of Civil Liberties Organizations (INCLO) released a report (Turner 2013): "Take Back the Streets: Repression and Criminalization of Protest around the World." The report analyzes and consolidates case studies from Argentina, Canada, Egypt, Israel, and "occupied territories" (Palestine), Kenya, Hungary, South Africa, the UK, and the US. The case studies represent very different social, cultural, and political contexts. However, the report (Turner 2013: 1) finds disturbing similarities when it comes to "direct state repression" of legal public protest: "mass arrests, unlawful detentions, illegal use of force and the deployment of toxic chemicals against protesters and bystanders alike. At other times the state action is less visible: the increased criminalization of protest movements, the denial of march permits, imposition of administrative hurdles and the persecution and prosecution of social leaders and protesters."

The implications of this trend amount to serious challenges to the human rights enterprise, since the grassroots movements that have been so central in the defining and realizing of human rights in our societies can now be legally crushed, even in our most "rights protective" Western democracies. Could the civil rights movement, including the march on Washington, happen today, under these conditions? Would the "battle of Seattle," the massive public resistance by one of the broadest coalitions in US history (the diverse anti-capitalist left, environmentalists, organized labor, indigenous populations, feminists, anti-racists, and so forth) that characterized the anti-globalization movement have a chance in the face of such expanded repression? Did we not witness the repeated coercion of Occupy movements from New York City to Oakland, California, in the very ways described in this report?

According to an earlier study (Knuckey, Glenn, and MacLean 2012: vi) by the Global Justice Clinic (New York University, School of Law) and The Walter Leitner International Human Rights Clinic (Fordham Law School), identical repression was used against Occupy Wall Street protesters. Included were:

144

(a)ggressive, unnecessary and excessive police force against peaceful protesters, bystanders, legal observers, and journalists; obstruction of press freedoms and independent legal monitoring; pervasive surveillance of peaceful political activity; violent late-night raids on peaceful encampments; unjustified closure of public space, dispersal of peaceful assemblies, and kettling (corralling and trapping) of protesters; arbitrary and selective rule enforcement and baseless arrests; failures to ensure transparency about applicable government policies; (and) failures to ensure accountability for those allegedly responsible for abuses.

What could be more telling about the contradictory role of the state in ensuring rights practice than effectively crushing some of the oldest civil and political rights in Western history, while also curtailing rights to confront policymakers with dissent and disagreement in response? The (INCLO) report states in agreement:

> History tells us that many of the fundamental rights we enjoy today were obtained after generations before us engaged in sustained protests in the streets: the prohibition against child labor, steps toward racial equality, women's suffrage – to name just a few – were each accomplished with the help of public expression of these demands. If freedom of expression is the grievance system of democracies, the right to protest and peaceful assembly is democracy's megaphone. (Turner 2013: 1)

Is this the end of civil and political rights?

The following chapter (5) details the many ways that some of the oldest civil and political rights in Western history, including the rights to due process[14] and protections from arbitrary arrest, detention, or exile,[15] are completely undercut by growth in the use and powers of the US police, military, and surveillance apparatus. It is now very difficult to discuss the salience of civil and political rights in the face of practices like the US drone war, where both US citizens and foreign nationals of any age can be targeted and assassinated in foreign sovereign territories, where there is no declared war theater, without notification, charge, or trial. All of this continues without meaningful consequences for those involved from any branch of US government or international legal regimes. Before addressing this powerful argument in some detail, we offer some tangible steps forward to address the problems of "corporate citizenship."

Opportunities for action

The contemporary human rights enterprise does and should include "radical" forms of resistance that directly confront domination by capital and the often repressive capitalist state. Since human rights are essentially claims on equality in human freedoms and dignity that demand democratic forms of social organization and some reasonable distribution of finite global resources, they currently stand in direct conflict with the trajectory of contemporary neoliberal capitalism and corporate friendly governance, state repression, and the staggering inequalities that result at national and international levels (Arat 2008; Armaline and Glasberg 2009). In this sense, the human rights enterprise and the critical sociological theory that informs it offer an appropriate lens for contemporary human rights scholarship and praxis. The human rights enterprise presents the ongoing process to define and realize human rights as a struggle over power and political voice where the state takes on problematic and contradictory roles relative to the needs of their public(s), the interests of private capital, and international legal obligations as articulated by, for example, human rights instruments or the UN Charter.

On the point of human rights praxis – human rights struggles informed by history and scholarship and human rights scholarship informed by social struggle – scholars have a role to play in fighting for the clarification of rights concepts, including who or what can be constructed as a legitimate political subject or "person" under the law. Our job as public intellectuals is arguably to create a counterbalance to (for example) political ideologies and Supreme Court decisions that grant rights to unaccountable corporations while constraining the rights, power, and political voice of actual human beings. Corporate power and personhood, often in partnership with the repressive states they ultimately seek to influence or capture, represent a direct challenge to human rights practice and the very concept of human rights itself, which began from the revolutionary conceptualization of a unique and shared *human* identity and experience discussed at the beginning of this chapter. Though we will get into further, specific implications of our work thus far for human rights praxis in the following chapter, we will end here with some possibilities for action when it comes to corporate power and personhood as a direct challenge to realizing human rights practice.

Others from the emergent sociology of human rights (Blau and Frezzo 2012) and from social-movement organizations (Gibson 2013c) have argued for constitutional solutions to bring US policy and practice in line with international human rights laws and standards. These arguments are sometimes treated as fantasy – not least because of the decreasingly democratic nature of modern governance articulated in this book. It is beyond the scope of our work here to debate the feasibility of significant constitutional revisions in the US, but we would like to identify strategies short of a new constitutional convention that could certainly address corporate domination.

Since the *Citizens United* decision of 2010, the "Democracy is for the People Amendment" proposed by Senator Bernie Sanders (I-VT) (Sanders 2013) and legislation from 16 individual states such as Oregon (McCarter 2013), demanding that Congress take on such a bill to overturn the decision, indicate significant resistance to expanded corporate power and personhood in the US. This legislation presents a starting point, where it would essentially overturn the effects of the *Citizens United* decision, but falls short in fully addressing the social and legal construction of corporate personhood that undergirds unchecked corporate power at the national and global level. The "Move to Amend" movement (MTA)[16] is an organized coalition of activists and organizations across the US, formed in 2009, "calling for an amendment to the US Constitution to unequivocally state that inalienable rights belong to human beings only, and that money is not a form of protected free speech under the First Amendment and can be regulated in political campaigns." MTA currently combines community organizing, political organizing, public education, and public protest/resistance to garner public support and focus resources toward stripping corporate personhood at state and federal levels.

Clearly, the contemporary campaigns to curb corporate power and personhood represent grassroots resistance with the aim of fundamentally changing the power relationship between corporations and human beings under the law. The MTA movement and similar campaigns of organization and resistance provide opportunities for meaningful human rights praxis: critical scholarship identifies corporate power and personhood as a massive impediment to human (and constitutional) rights practice in the US and beyond (recall, powerful US corporate banks and businesses are effectively global in reach and effect), and, as we would expect from an application of the human rights enterprise, avenues for curbing corporate domination emerge as grassroots social movements that struggle against or in spite of the dominant forces of capital and the state. Engaging in these resistance movements to clarify human rights claimants from unaccountable corporations then presents itself as a reasonable, productive opportunity for meaningful human rights praxis. In the following, final chapter, we will articulate more specific implications of our work and a critical sociology of human rights on contemporary human rights praxis – how we choose to study and "do" human rights. Further, we argue that contemporary US foreign and domestic policy now stand in direct contradiction to the oldest, most fundamental civil and political rights in the Western world. Human rights work in the US should revolve around these most troubling challenges, but should also be prioritized to address what are now threats to the survival of our species, let alone to any legal rights construct.

5

Current Contexts and Implications for Human Rights Praxis in the US

US policy confronts civil and political rights in the world

A critical sociological analysis of human rights would be incomplete were it not to interrogate a misconception common in the media as well as the extant scholarly literature, that the United States is somehow the "gold standard" of rights practice and that human rights tragedies occur elsewhere. We noted earlier that human rights scholars often use the concept of *American exceptionalism* to describe the complex and contradictory role of the US in efforts to define and realize human rights practices via international law. On the one hand, the US played a central role in the design and implementation of the United Nations and fundamental human rights instruments like the UDHR following World War II (Ishay 2008). The US has also on numerous occasions employed a human rights discourse to affect or intervene in the foreign affairs of other states, such as contemporary China or the former Soviet states at the close of the Cold War (Peck 2011). All of this would suggest that the US has viewed, and in some cases continues to view, human rights as meaningful if not legally legitimate. At the same time, in the US, "politicians, civil servants, members of the judiciary, academics, and pundits have long insisted that international human rights norms do not apply (or apply in only a limited manner) to the crafting, implementation, or evaluation of US domestic laws and public policy" (Hertel and Libal 2011: 1). In short, the role of the US government has been to champion international human rights law when it comes to the actions of literal and cultural (Said 1978) *others*, but to take exception when international law poses threats to US sovereignty, policy, practice, or dominant interests.

Nowhere is this US policy stance, and perhaps the fundamental problems of realizing human rights through legal regimes of modern nation-states, more clear than in recent history. As we pen this chapter, revelations about US targeted assassination programs (including but not limited to drone strikes), domestic and foreign surveillance programs, and expanded state policing and military powers through reinstatements of the PATRIOT and National Defense Authorization (NDAA) Acts[1] paint an Orwellian nightmare that would have been the content of comic books and conspiracy theorists a generation ago. We find ourselves on a surreal terrain of political conflict where some of the oldest-established civil and political rights in Western history, reaching back to the Magna Carta of 1215, are under great threat if not bled out completely on the altar of narrowly defined "national security" or "national interests" (Chomsky 2012). It is very difficult to argue, as do some in dominant human rights scholarship (Moyn 2010), that the contemporary history of human rights could be explained as a linear progression where global respect for "first-generation" civil and political rights continues to grow and spread since the inception of international human rights law, to the point that Western liberal rights practices border on "hegemonic" (Donnelly 2003). Further, as human-made climate change, grotesque resource and wealth inequalities, and nuclear proliferation threaten life on Earth as we know it, let alone international human rights standards (see, for example, Schellnhuber 2012; Chomsky, 2007a,b; Parenti 2011; Shiva 2000, 2001, 2008), it is difficult to see how the dominant approaches to defining and realizing human rights through legal regimes of participating states is somehow succeeding in the bigger picture.

A brief summary of recent revelations demonstrates the weakness of US constitutional and international human rights practice in the shadow of state and corporate power. It also suggests the need for a critical sociology of human rights, and a scholarly approach that defines struggles over human rights ultimately as struggles over power, resource, and political voice.

Targeted assassination, drone strikes, and "kill lists"

Rather than ending the second[2] "war on terror" waged by the Bush administration following the terrorist attacks in New York City on September 11, 2001, the Obama administration opted to shift war strategies in favor of what is now called the "drone war" or "drone program," while continuing the practices of rendition, incarceration, and torture without charge or trial (at Guantánamo Bay and other "black sites"), and the sacrifice of civil and political rights established through renewals of the PATRIOT and National Defense Authorization (NDAA) Acts (Hajjar 2012; Groeger and Currier 2010). Though major official combat operations have been largely scaled back in Iraq and Afghanistan, it is fundamentally inaccurate to say that the US no longer exercises a military footprint in these war theaters (Skahill 2013), still plagued by widespread violence thanks to exacerbated internal conflicts and the continued deployment of CIA and JSOC (Joint Special Operations Command) forces in these and bordering nations. More importantly, the removal of traditional ground forces from these regions of Southwest Asia and the Middle East has simply given way to a new technological strategy, employing "unmanned drone aircraft" and special forces (JSOC) to collect information (surveillance) and conduct targeted strikes without the commitment or logistical problems associated with full ground-troop deployment. But, unlike traditional warfare, drones open a new chapter in the psychological aspects of war and state terror, where civilian populations – even in countries where there is no stated conflict – live under the constant threat of death from above without warning, meaningful legal recourse, or remorse (International Human Rights and Conflict Resolution Clinic/Global Justice Clinic 2012).

Nearly all US military drones operated by both the defense department and the CIA are capable of surveillance, and armed drones are capable of striking targets from many miles away, using any number of lethal projectiles. Drone strikes are typically categorized as "personality strikes" or "signature strikes." Personality strikes refer to the targeted assassination of individuals, vetted through weekly meetings between the President and military advisors, called "terror Tuesdays." Almost as if looking through baseball cards representing a "who's who" of suspected terrorists in a particular region, the President is in the position to directly authorize the assassination or capture of anyone on the established "kill list" without legislative or judicial oversight (Becker and Shane 2012).

Clearly, the most well-known personality drone strike thus far was against American Muslim cleric Anwar al-Awlaki and Samir Khan on September 30, 2011 – both American citizens. The Obama administration began targeting al-Awlaki as he became more outspokenly radical (critical of US foreign policy to the extent of advocating violent resistance), particularly following the first Fort Hood shootings, and his relocation from Michigan to Yemen (Scahill 2013). These assassinations are one of many recent affronts to constitutional (5th Amendment, "due process") and international law (UDHR, Article 10; ICCPR, Article 14), where American citizens were targeted and killed by remote control without notification, charge, or trial in a foreign sovereign country with which there was no war or established combat zone. Even more disturbing, two weeks later a drone strike in Yemen *knowingly murdered al-Awlaki's 16-year-old son* (Abdulrahman al-Awlaki, also a US citizen) along with his 17-year-old Yemeni cousin, Ahmed, and other Yemeni civilians while at a barbecue. When confronted about the illegal slaughter of a US child with absolutely no tangible connection to terrorist organizations, former White House press secretary and senior presidential advisor Robert Gibbs coldly replied that the 16-year-old Abdulrahman should have picked "a more responsible father" (Rohrict 2013a).

So-called "signature strikes" give further reason for alarm and concern. "Signature strikes" are not targeted at a particular individual or individuals, but are meant to target suspicious-looking people doing suspicious things, as determined from surveillance and military intelligence agencies. The Obama administration has yet to release any meaningful account of how signature strikes are established as accurate or legitimate. How do you know the difference between a meeting of young would-be al-Qaeda militants and a family barbecue from 10,000 feet? Instead, the administration continues to insist that the drone and targeted assassination programs are extremely accurate and efficient with little "collateral damage" or civilian casualties. Similarly outlandish and inaccurate statements were made about "high-tech" targeting used in the first and second Iraq wars, justifying new wars and war tools by claiming their application was more efficient and humane.

In several public statements, the Obama administration claimed that civilian casualties from drone strikes number in the single digits (International Human Rights and Conflict Resolution Clinic/ Global Justice Clinic 2012). To the contrary, a 2012 collaborative study between the Stanford Law School and New York University School of Law – the only study of its kind to date – reports that "from June 2004 through mid-September 2012, available data indicate that drone strikes killed 2,562–3,325 people in Pakistan, of whom 474–881 were civilians, including 176 children" (International Human Rights and Conflict Resolution Clinic/ Global Justice Clinic 2012; Bureau of Investigative Journalism 2012). A qualitative study by Amnesty International (2013: 8) on civilian casualties of US drone strikes in Pakistan claims "these and other strikes have resulted in unlawful killings that may constitute extrajudicial executions or war crimes." Another report details civilian casualties due to zone strikes in Yemen (Alkarama Foundation 2013). These reports make two other important related points for us here. First, drone strikes are not accurate or efficient. Only 2 percent of all those killed by drone strikes have been "high-level" targets. As a result, the drone program may have the effect of exacerbating the rise of violent terrorism rather than selectively killing those who seek to carry out violent terrorist attacks. As noted in the drone study and reporting by the *New York Times*, "Drones have replaced Guantanamo as the recruiting tool of choice for militants; in his 2010 guilty plea, Faisal Shahzad, who had tried to set off a car bomb in Times Square, justified targeting civilians by telling the judge, 'When the drones hit, they don't see children'" (International Human Rights and Conflict Resolution Clinic/Global Justice Clinic 2012; Becker and Shane 2012). Second, the US government uses a manifestly problematic and disingenuous standard for determining whether or not casualties are innocent civilians or "militants." In the accounting of casualties in the drone and targeted assassination programs, the US government counts any adult male killed in a strike as a "militant" unless undeniable proof of their innocence is presented after the fact to exonerate the victim as a number (in the stats), but not as a human being (they're already dead!). Even more outrageous, investigative reporting on the drone program under the CIA revealed that US officials often "had no idea" who was being killed in signature drone strikes, making only superficial efforts to investigate and legitimate the strikes after their occurrence (Engel and Windrem 2013).

Finally, there doesn't seem to be any limit as to who can be targeted by the US government for assassination, "extraordinary rendition" (kidnapping), torture, and detention without charge or trial, following the re-authorization of the National Defense Authorization Act. According to analysts, at least one federal judge who attempted and failed to block the Act (Neumeister 2012), and many scholars and journalists who filed suit against the Obama administration over its re-authorization (Hedges 2012), NDAA in its new form "authorizes the U.S. government to carry out 'counter-terrorism' domestically and detain INDEFINITELY and WITHOUT TRIAL any U.S. citizen who is suspected of any sort of suspicious activity that could be deemed terrorism or supporting terrorism . . . these U.S. citizens could be shipped to one of our extraordinary rendition sites across the globe – like Guantanamo Bay" (emphasis in original document, Rohricht 2013a). Noted, so far unsuccessful, challenges to NDAA in its present form explicitly point out the high likelihood of such executive privilege being used against journalists and political dissidents who pose threats to US military interests. Recent revelations about unbridled, illegal, and unprecedented surveillance of domestic and foreign populations, and the fevered legal prosecution and media persecution of government whistleblowers seem to suggest their concerns are well placed.

Modern surveillance and the end of privacy

In a 5–4 decision in 2013, the Supreme Court found that police officers in the US can swab any and all arrested individuals to collect and permanently store their DNA records at point of arrest without a warrant to do so. Somewhat surprisingly, the strongest dissent in this decision came from conservative Justice Scalia: "Make no mistake about it: As an entirely predictable consequence of today's decision, your DNA can be taken and entered into a national DNA database if you are ever arrested, rightly or wrongly, and for whatever reason" (Goodwin 2013). This would normally have attracted great attention from the civil liberties crowd – and it did – but the story was quickly overshadowed a week later by a cascade of reports, largely published by investigative journalists for the *Guardian* newspaper, that reveal the extent to which the US government now secretly employs what might be the largest, most intrusive, most capable, and most privately outsourced surveillance apparatus in human history.

Revelations about US surveillance practices are far too complicated and numerous to outline in detail here, and they continue to unfold. Instead, we will simply highlight some important points for consideration based on what can be fully substantiated:

(1) The US government can and does collect the call records of US citizens and foreign nationals through accessing the networks of private phone companies. The collection of so-called "metadata" can be used to determine a great deal, including patterns of behavior, position, and movement without any need for a legal warrant – a necessary step for accessing, but not collecting, the "content" of calls (Mayer 2013). Rules to determine government access to the content of phone calls are articulated by the Foreign Intelligence Surveillance Act of 1978 (FISA) and several sections of the PATRIOT Act (section 215 in particular) that set the precedent

for "warrantless wiretapping" under the G. W. Bush administration. Officially, FISA outlines the legal procedures for physical and electronic surveillance of communications with foreign powers or actors, or by those suspected of terrorism or espionage against the US. The Foreign Intelligence Surveillance Court (FISC) makes decisions on whether or not certain levels of surveillance are allowed and to what extent.

The Obama administration and the US Justice Department claim that such surveillance is constitutional in that it continues to be subject to "checks and balances": the FISC must provide a warrant to *access* the content of calls (even though content may be *collected* without warrant), and members of Congress had the chance to challenge re-authorizations of the FISA and PATRIOT Acts, and chose not to. It is worth noting that though all members of Congress had the opportunity to be briefed on these surveillance programs, very few requested this at any point, not unlike their failure to read, let alone challenge, the original PATRIOT Act in 2001. Further, investigative reporting shows that the FISC denies a whopping .03 percent of all surveillance requests made by the federal government (Eichelberger 2013). The FISC is also classified – they have no obligation to share their decisions or the bases of their decisions with the public or any branch of government, with the marginal exception of the Senate foreign intelligence committee. This is in part due to the fact that vetting of cases and requests actually happens through the Justice Department, explaining the high "passing" rate and illustrating that the FISC fails to supply any reasonable judicial check on executive powers (Eichelberger 2013). Finally, even with the nearly non-existent oversight of NSA surveillance activity, and despite President Obama's claim on live television that no domestic spying programs existed and that all NSA activities have been well within the law (Easley 2013), the *Washington Post* (Gellman 2013) reports, "The National Security Agency has broken privacy rules or overstepped its legal authority thousands of times each year since Congress granted the agency broad new powers in 2008 ... Most of the infractions involve unauthorized surveillance of Americans or foreign intelligence targets in the United States."

Worries that warrantless access to cell-phone "metadata" would expand to local law-enforcement practice and domestic surveillance seem to have been well founded. In July 2013, the 5th US Circuit Court of Appeals found that a warrant was not needed to collect "cell-site" information from private cellular providers because such data are a "business record" (Kravets 2013). Further, leaked documents prove that the US Drug Enforcement Agency (DEA) repeatedly used NSA surveillance data in order to initiate and prosecute federal drug cases before covering up their trail (Shiffman and Cooke 2013), and purchased the private call records from cellular provider AT&T, dating all the way back to 1987, in order to pursue any number of drug cases in the US (Ball 2013).

(2) Reporting on leaked information from Edward Snowden – government whistleblower, former NSA analyst, and former employee of private military contractor Booz Allen Hamilton – revealed that the US government, in partnership with major tech companies such as Apple, Google, and Facebook, have and do monitor, in real time, the content and metadata of all Internet communication inside (and in some cases outside) the US: email, chat, social media, and use histories. Initial reporting was limited to the PRISM program (Greenwald and MacAskill 2013); however, we now know that US surveillance of all Internet communication has and does go well beyond the monitoring of communications with foreign entities or governments conducted for the purposes of terrorism or espionage.

Similar to the collection and monitoring of phone-call data, no meaningful forms of warrant or judicial oversight prevent US intelligence agencies from the real-time surveillance of *all* online communication. In fact, following revelations about the PRISM surveillance program, top officials from the EU, South Africa, Canada, and Pakistan voiced aggressive criticism of the Obama administration, vowing to investigate the extent to which their citizens' information was collected and permanently stored in violation of their own domestic privacy and surveillance policies, let alone international law. Further, they showed particular concern for private contractors' access to citizens' personal information, and the questionable legal right of US Internet companies to categorically store and share personal information with the US government in violation of EU or other foreign domestic policies (Travis, Osborne, and Davies 2013). To add insult to injury, a leaked NSA document "outlines how the NSA bugged offices and spied on EU internal computer networks in Washington and the United Nations, not only listening to conversations and phone calls, but also gaining access to documents and emails" (Breidthardt, Deighton, and Zakaria 2013).

According to any number of legal scholars, the actions of the NSA are plainly unconstitutional (4th Amendment) and violate international law[3] (UDHR, Article 12; ICCPR, Article 17). The remarks of Glenn Greenwald, who covered the leaks of NSA whistleblower Edward Snowden for the *Guardian* (Greenwald 2013c), stand in direct contrast to any notion of rights to privacy or protections from arbitrary search or surveillance: "The actual story that matters is not hard to see: the NSA is attempting to collect, monitor and store all forms of human communication." To be clear, this is not just about US citizens and foreign nationals – it applies to global communication networks. Millions of Brazilians found the NSA had in fact been collecting their email and phone records through operation "FAIRVIEW" (Greenwald 2013b). These secret surveillance programs – along with the pursuit of whistleblowers like Snowden – reflect what is now a *global* crisis in the right to expression, privacy, and protection against arbitrary search, seizure, or surveillance.

(3) The US surveillance apparatus is absolutely part of the massive and increasingly privatized military industrial complex. It demonstrates the solidarity of corporate and state power in the coercion and social control of those who seek to challenge state and owning class interests. Leaked PRISM slides explicitly state that corporations allowed the NSA to collect data directly from servers, despite previous claims otherwise by the state and corporate representatives (Robertson 2013). Leaks by Edward Snowden provided much more than evidence of illegal surveillance practices; they illustrated the extent to which NSA surveillance activities are outsourced to private, for-profit corporations like

Booz Allen Hamilton. Indeed, over a million civilian workers currently enjoy top federal security clearance as employees of private security corporations (Urie 2013). The leaks further demonstrate the incestuous relationship between the state and powerful corporations in order to coerce and monitor anyone they wish. Further evidence of collusion can be found with little effort:

> In the new American cyber-power, only the revolving doors have changed. The director of Google Ideas, Jared Cohen, was adviser to Condoleezza Rice, the former secretary of state in the Bush administration who lied [*sic*.] that Saddam Hussein could attack the US with nuclear weapons. Cohen and Google's executive chairman, Eric Schmidt – they met in the ruins of Iraq – have co-authored a book, *The New Digital Age*, endorsed as visionary by the former CIA director Michael Hayden and the war criminals Henry Kissinger and Tony Blair. The authors make no mention of the Prism spying program, revealed by Edward Snowden, that provides the NSA access to all of us who use Google. (Pilger 2013)

Once again we see the signs of a close relationship between states and capital (corporations, banks, and the broader owning class), as discussed in chapters 2 and 4. These close relationships constrain democracy, and set policy in pursuit of the narrowly defined interests of capital, often at the cost of human rights protections.

(4) There is no reason to believe that, as the US government claims, heightened security measures and the violation of civil and political constitutional and human rights are somehow a "trade-off" for safety from terrorist attacks. Statistically speaking, over 50 times more Americans die in a single year from preventable medical errors than have died from terrorist attacks of any kind since 1970 (Urie 2013). A much more plausible hypothesis, also detailed in reporting by the *Guardian* (Ahmed 2013; see also Hedges 2013), based largely on materials from the Department of Defense (DOD), is that such extensive security and surveillance measures are to prepare for "civil unrest" in opposition to dominant interests (neo-liberal capitalism) and in response to increasing environmental and refugee crises resulting from global climate change.

In 2013, US military law was changed explicitly to grant the Pentagon powers to directly intervene in the case of such civil unrest. According to these changes, "Federal military commanders have the authority, in extraordinary emergency circumstances where prior authorization by the President is impossible and duly constituted local authorities are unable to control the situation, to engage temporarily in activities that are necessary to quell large-scale, unexpected civil disturbances" (Ahmed 2013). Scholars (Potter 2011) and journalists (Federman 2013) have already documented the explicit use of expanded executive policing and surveillance powers to watch and prosecute environmental and other anti-establishment activists to date. Evidence and testimony from Edward Snowden to the Council of Europe demonstrated that the NSA has repeatedly "targeted either leaders or staff members in a number of civil and non-governmental organizations . . . including domestically within the borders of the United States" (Harding 2014). This should come as no surprise, given the long history of coercing dissent in the US by federal agencies, including the FBI's CONTELPRO and other attempts to suppress the civil rights and anti-war movements of the 1950s, 1960s, and 1970s. Time after time, we see the US and other powerful states seeking to squash social movements that are in fact responsible for realizing human rights in any meaningful way. These social movements are the heart of the human rights enterprise, and confront the contradictory historical position of the US and the state more broadly relative to formal human rights. Repeated attempts by the US to coerce and quell these kinds of social movements demonstrate the importance of the human rights enterprise and the fundamental critique of how human rights are formally "done" that is presented in this book.

(5) Of course, we only know about top-secret surveillance programs or other recent crimes of US empire because of those willing to leak classified information as whistleblowers, working in collaboration with formal media outlets such as the *Guardian, The Intercept,* or less traditional outlets for information-sharing such as the Wikileaks or Reddit websites. Despite Obama's claims as a presidential candidate that "acts of courage and patriotism, which

can sometimes save lives and often save taxpayer dollars, should be encouraged rather than stifled as they have been during the Bush administration" (Greenwald 2013a; Obama for America 2008), the Obama administration has so far prosecuted more government whistleblowers (six) under the Espionage Act than all previous US presidents combined. Notably, UN Security General Ban Ki Moon *also* demonized whistleblowers, describing Snowden's actions as "misuse" of his access to government surveillance records, in a foreign affairs committee meeting (Pilkington 2013). We find such statements troubling yet unsurprising when it comes to whether or not formal legal regimes can push powerful states toward universal human rights practice.

When he first leaked information on the PRISM program, Edward Snowden was well aware of the risk: "I understand that I will be made to suffer for my actions" (Greenwald, MacAskill, and Poitras 2013). Such a fate has already befallen Chelsea Manning, who endured solitary confinement in a military prison for three years before seeing trial (Rohricht 2013b) and being sentenced to another 35 years of imprisonment. Though Manning seems to have escaped execution, she could not escape torture and a lengthy prison sentence for revealing US war crimes,[4] and any number of nefarious practices by US military forces, the CIA, and private military contractors in Iraq and Afghanistan (Rohricht 2013a).

Journalists have also felt the heat of state coercion for their participation in reporting on documents leaked by internal whistleblowers. David Miranda, partner of journalist Glenn Greenwald who was the lead reporter on the *Guardian* coverage of Edward Snowden and NSA revelations, was forced to hand over all electronic devices, then held and questioned for nine hours by English officials, before re-entering the country. English spokespeople claimed that anti-terror legislation allowed them to temporarily suspend the rights of anyone entering the country suspected of terrorism or supporting terrorism – needless to say, no such evidence on Mr Miranda surfaced. Weeks earlier, the British Government Communications Headquarters (GCHQ – similar to the NSA) had forced and supervised the destruction of several hard drives of the *Guardian* newspaper in order to destroy leaked documents from

Snowden on the domestic and international spying programs (such as XKeyscore) in the US and the UK (Poitras 2013; Scheuermann 2013).

(6) The trampling of civil and political rights according to the US Constitution or international law is nothing new for populations of color – African Americans in particular – in the US and in much of the global South. Surveillance and the erosion of 4th Amendment protections, let alone civil and political human rights as a matter of international law, have defined the experience of people of color in the US under the wars on drugs and crime since the 1970s. In her now well-known work, *The New Jim Crow*, Michelle Alexander (2010) illustrates the case history of the US drug war, where 4th Amendment protections against illegal search/seizure/surveillance were steadily and incrementally eroded in order to expand the policing powers of the state to pursue those criminalized in the drug war – namely, the poor and people of color. In short, it would be inaccurate to say that the erosion of "first-generation" civil and political rights (whether enumerated by the Constitution or the ICCPR) is purely a feature of the "post-9/11 world." Arguably, this erosion began with the racist criminalization of African Americans through the US drug war and abhorrent practice of mass incarceration – where only 13 percent of the US population is African American, they represent nearly half of just under 2 million people currently incarcerated, and a vast majority of those criminally prosecuted under the drug war (Alexander 2010).

Parallel experiences are clearly documented in other areas of the racialized global South – including the South African apartheid regime (also supported by the US and US corporations for much of its history). Taking the stand at trial, Nelson Mandela – a former revolutionary who spent 27 years in prison for organizing sustained, aggressive resistance to the South African apartheid regime – had the following to say about the experience of black South Africans in 1964:

> Pass laws, which to the Africans are among the most hated bits of legislation in South Africa, render any African liable to police surveillance at any time. I doubt whether there is a single African male in

South Africa who has not at some stage had a brush with the police over his pass. Hundreds and thousands of Africans are thrown into jail each year under pass laws. Even worse than this is the fact that pass laws keep husband and wife apart and lead to the breakdown of family life. (Mandela 1964)

OK, all this is bad from a human rights perspective – but what's the point?

Constitutional and international legal rights to life, liberty, and security of person, protection against arbitrary arrest/detention/ exile/execution, privacy, trial, or tribunal (due process), and the presumption of innocence are far from assured in current contexts, almost anywhere in the world. In response, this book and our broader collection of work should be seen as an effort to investigate why dominant approaches to defining, realizing, and studying (scholarship) human rights have, frankly, achieved so much while falling so short. It helps us to answer the uncomfortable questions from our students in the United States and elsewhere who ask: "Why don't human rights seem to matter here?" A critical sociology of human rights places the nation-state, laws, and legal discourse, international decision-making structures like the United Nations or World Trade Organization, and other macro systems of privilege and oppression, such as contemporary systemic racism or patriarchy, in their proper contexts relative to the global capitalist economy. It also illuminates social struggles over power, resources, and political voice that develop against these institutions and structures. Critically conceptualized, we find states often unwilling or unable to fulfill the human rights obligations articulated by human rights instruments, even of their own design. This is in large part because of the constraints of capitalism and capitalists that tie states to capital accumulation interests. These interests often overshadow and outweigh, if not directly contradict or challenge, human rights practice and democratic governance in the broader sense. In the case of powerful nations like the US, the state is also a tool of empire and for aggressive expressions of realpolitik like the current military drone program or surveillance apparatus – complete mockeries of international law – all part of a "national security" strategy that also serves to facilitate dominant political economic interests abroad.

A critical sociology of human rights also examines the conditions under which human rights have been successfully realized to various degrees. Demonstrated by the civil rights movement in the US, the anti-colonial movements of the continents of Africa, Asia, or Latin America, and more contemporary, anti-capitalist "Occupy" and "anti-Austerity" movements across the world, struggles to define and realize human rights and fundamental standards of human dignity manifest as social movements from below. They are battles over power, resources, and political voice that play out on terrains of social struggle in specific historical and social contexts.

The role of the state in these contexts is historically contradictory at best. According to international law, itself a legal construction based on the agreement between sovereign nation-states, states are in charge of protecting, respecting, and fulfilling the obligations – rights practices – articulated by human rights instruments. However, when we look at the actual history of social struggles to achieve human or civil rights in the world, we find that these struggles are often waged against or in spite of the state. The civil rights movement in the US or the anti-apartheid movement in South Africa, for example – both of which took place after these countries helped draft the UN Charter and UDHR – were characterized by brutal, violent state repression of rights activists, not by the compassion of governments seeking to fulfill their international legal obligations to the global community or serve the rights and needs of their people. We also find states employing human rights discourse in hypocritical and disingenuous ways to achieve narrow national interests abroad, often involving obvious abuses of human rights and international law in the process. Such was the case when the US tried to legitimate the illegal invasion of Iraq in 2003, or during any number of other military aggressions ("police actions") associated with the global "war on terror" (Peck 2011).

It is through critical sociology – political sociology in particular – that we can explain these historical phenomena: the contradictory role of states relative to international law and human rights instruments, the variable meaning and effect of human rights as a legal regime and discourse, and the tendency of human rights to be defined and realized as struggles over power, resources, and political voice from below. Such a "sociology of human rights" has continued to emerge since at least the anti-globalization movement of the 1990s (Stammers 1999; Sjoberg, Gill, and Williams 2001; Blau and Frezzo 2012; Freeman 2011; Blau and Moncada 2005; Brunsma, Smith, and Gran 2012; Clement 2011; Armaline and Glasberg 2009; Armaline, Glasberg, and Purkayastha 2011), and has at least five unique characteristics worth reviewing again here: (a) law and legal discourse is seen as socially constructed and understood as an expression and source of institutionalized power; (b) the state and other formal bodies of institutionalized authority, such as the United Nations or International Monetary Fund, are approached critically and are fully conceptualized in appropriate structural context(s); (c) civil, political, economic, social, and cultural rights are seen as inextricably linked, particularly at the level of human rights practice or implementation; (d) sociologists, if public intellectuals, are presumably concerned with formal human rights regimes and international law to the extent that they tend to inhibit or facilitate human rights practice; and (e) sociologists share the historical perspective that human rights as a concept and practice are ultimately the product of social movements and social struggle.

When we apply a critical sociological lens to the history of human rights struggles, a rather complicated process emerges – what we call the human rights enterprise. The human rights enterprise includes but is not limited to the creation and implementation of human rights as a form of international law and legal discourse. It identifies the *totality* of movements to achieve universal fundamental human dignity as taking place inside and outside the legal arena, where the role of the state is often contradictory, and where social movements from below are most common and effective in actually realizing the rights more or less articulated in legal instruments. This collective force is presented as a living, organic process of counter-hegemonic resistance that seeks to tip balances of power toward equality, shared resources, democracy, sustainability, peace, social stability with purpose, and personal liberty.

In line with a long tradition of critical sociology, the *point* of a critical sociology of human rights would be to inform struggles to realize them in the lives of real people. Similarly, human rights scholarship should seek to learn from the actual experiences of those enduring human rights abuses and working to achieve rights practice – a canon of literature that arguably exists in multiple disciplines. This reflexive relationship between theory and action is what we call human rights praxis. We've spent a great deal of time arguing the relevance of a critical sociology of human rights. Below, we'd like to briefly and humbly summarize two of the possible implications of our work for human rights praxis, beyond those already presented in previous chapters.

Let's get our priorities straight

It seems obvious to us that any serious approach to human rights would hold threats to collective human survival, and the survival of thousands of other species that make up the ecological balance we depend on to live, as the highest priority. In this sense we are in agreement with those attempting to articulate environmental rights and intergenerational justice as human rights (see Hiskes 2008). What good are rights if we aren't around to enjoy them? Many scholars suggest the most significant threats to the survival of the human (and thousands of other) species include climate change (and related social problems of resource wars, refugee crises, and fundamental resource shortages), nuclear warfare, and unsustainable human population growth (see, for example, Shiva 2000, 2001, 2008; Chomsky 2007a; Parenti 2011). Stanford biologists Paul and Anne Ehrlich published a paper in the *Royal Society of Biological Sciences* (2013: 1) – not a particularly radical platform – where they discuss and hypothesize the inevitability of human species extinction if such threats are not immediately addressed:

> Today, for the first time, humanity's global civilization – the world-wide, increasingly interconnected, highly technological society in which we all are to one degree or another, embedded – is threatened with collapse by an array of environmental problems. Humankind finds itself engaged in what Prince Charles described as "an act of suicide on a grand scale," facing what the UK's Chief Scientific Advisor John Beddington called a "perfect storm" of environmental problems. The most serious of these problems show signs of rapidly escalating severity, especially climate disruption. But other elements could potentially also contribute to a collapse: an accelerating extinction of animal and plant populations and species, which could lead to a loss of ecosystem services essential for human survival; land degradation and land-use change; a pole-to-pole spread of toxic compounds; ocean acidification and eutrophication (dead zones); worsening of some aspects of the epidemiological environment (factors that make human populations susceptible to infectious diseases); depletion of increasingly scarce resources, including especially groundwater, which is being overexploited in many key agricultural areas; and resource wars. These are not separate problems; rather they interact in two gigantic complex adaptive systems: the biosphere system and the human socio-economic system. The negative manifestations of these interactions are often referred to as "the human predicament," and determining how to prevent it from generating a global collapse is perhaps the foremost challenge confronting humanity.

Anne and Paul Ehrlich and the community of natural scientists their work represents are joined by many critical economists who link the threats of climate change, environmental destruction, and all of the associated social problems to fundamental flaws in the global neoliberal capitalist system of production and consumption. These economists point out that neoclassical economic theories guiding neoliberal capitalism, such as the goal of endless growth while ignoring the reality of limited resources (there's only one Earth) lead us to max out our own biosphere by extracting, polluting, and consuming virtually without limit, all to support a model of permanent, constant capital accumulation (see, for example, Smith and Max-Neef 2011; Daly and Farley 2010).

It should be no surprise after reading this book that the contemporary movements to address species-threatening climate change and environmental destruction are clearly grassroots movements that employ forms of direct action and civil disobedience to affect public discourse and social change (Moe 2013). These social-movement organizations vary in size and strategy, from the Idle No More global indigenous movement against "CO2lonialism," to the often vilified "radical" environmental movement that would include "Earth Liberation" and "Animal Liberation" groups as well as the more moderate organizations like People for the Ethical Treatment of Animals (PETA), Greenpeace, or the emergent "anti-fracking" movement – many labeled and treated as terrorist organizations by the US and other powerful states (Potter 2011). In conjunction, biologists Anne and Paul Ehrlich assert that technological and scientific solutions must be accompanied by social movements reflexively informed by social science:

> Besides focusing their research on ways to avoid collapse, there is a need for natural scientists to collaborate with social scientists, especially those who study the dynamics of social movements. Such collaborations could develop ways to stimulate a significant increase in popular support for decisive and immediate action on the predicament. Unfortunately, awareness among scientists that humanity is in deep trouble has not been accompanied by popular awareness and pressure to counter the political and economic influences implicated in the current crisis. Without significant pressure from the public demanding action, we fear there is little chance of changing course fast enough to forestall disaster. (Ehrlich and Ehrlich 2013: 5)

Battles for the survival of the human species as a struggle for environmental rights and intergenerational justice are a part of and perhaps presuppose the human rights enterprise. These informed social movements represent forms of human rights praxis, as do associated movements against the neoliberal capitalist system that leans us toward ecological crisis.

Engage on all fronts

To emphasize the role of social movements from below in driving the human rights enterprise is not to discount the relative usefulness and at least temporary utility of formal, legal human rights regimes and the notion of international law. We are surrounded by notable examples of their relevance, even for the United States: (a) in fall 2013 the US and others backed down from direct military intervention in the Syrian civil war, moving to a more diplomatic stance, after UN diplomacy joined public disapproval in swaying the US Congress and Obama administration; (b) on October 28, 2013, the Inter American Commission on Human Rights (IACHR)[5] held a hearing on the conviction of Kevin Cooper, a death-row inmate in California, on what his attorneys claim was the denial of Cooper's rights to due process, racial equality under the law, and his right to life; (c) the UN special rapporteur on torture, Juan Mendez, is seeking to review the conditions of California prisons following the prison hunger-strike resistance that called attention to conditions in Secure Housing Units (SHUs) and Isolation Units (approximately 10,000 inmates) (St John 2013). Even in cases where the legal authority of international law is not recognized or immediately effective, human rights as a legal discourse provides a certain legitimacy for struggles from below – their claims are less easily tossed aside as groundless if an international community of states backs their position.

Further, as suggested by Christian Parenti (2011) and others, the challenges we face as a species – such as the threats of climate change or nuclear disasters – may require highly organized efforts and responses. The UN and other regional bodies provide a framework for a democratic sustainable future – a basis of organizing information and efforts to solve global social problems. Considerable progress can be made in current conditions within and through the existing legal regimes. In chapter 4, we clearly advocate revisiting and challenging the construction of corporations as people under US constitutional law as a crucially important point of human rights praxis. But to say dominant systems offer opportunities for change does not relieve us from the responsibility to name and address the structural impediments to human rights practice and ecological sustainability that may threaten life on Earth.

We've spent a great deal of this book illustrating the devastating effects of capitalism on human rights practice and the likelihood that states can or will fulfill international legal obligations to facilitate human rights practice. In chapter 2, we discussed the structural constraints of the capitalist state, or state within the global capitalist economy. In chapter 4, we discussed how rights discourse is twisted to socially construct corporations – now massive economic entities that join global finance as the primary mechanisms for owning class rule and capital accumulation – as humans. In chapters 1 and 3, we discussed the repeated contradiction of the US and other powerful states when it comes to choosing human rights practice over dominant domestic or foreign interests. Now, and in previous work (Armaline and Glasberg 2009; Armaline, Glasberg, and Purkayastha 2011), we join others in recognizing that the front lines of many significant social movements – the Arab Spring/Winter, the Occupy and anti-Austerity movements, Quebec's Red Square student movement, Idle No More and much of the climate movement, successful, massive teacher and student strikes in Mexico and Brazil, the anti-contemporary anti-war (Afghanistan, Iraq, Syria, Iran, drone war, covert wars, etc.) movement – *are organized and populated by anti-capitalists.* Even tertiary accounts of any and all of these most recent, relevant, social justice movements – all formally or informally (substantively) associated with the struggle to define and realize human rights, or the human rights enterprise – show the indicative black and red flags, red stars, and black hoodies associated with the global anti-capitalist left.

If praxis is to be taken seriously, we can't treat this as coincidence. We suggest that contemporary human rights praxis should be formulated in opposition to the exploitative and completely unsustainable system of global neoliberal capitalism. It is and should be a Gramscian (1971) form of counter-hegemony. In Michelle Alexander's groundbreaking work, *The New Jim Crow*

(2010), she presents an evidenced critique of the contemporary US criminal justice system as an institutionalized mechanism of racial social control – a new Jim Crow where African Americans are marginalized through the drug war, mass incarceration, and the "collateral consequences" of felony convictions and imprisonment, and, in many states, permanent political disenfranchisement of convicts and ex-convicts alike (Manza and Uggen 2008; Uggen and Manza 2002). In her discussion of solutions she asserts, "tinkering is for mechanics, not for racial justice activists" (2010: 217). She argues convincingly that fundamental changes would be required for meaningful results – and that the structural roots of oppression, in this case contemporary systemic racism, would have to be *explicitly named and confronted* to be addressed. In current contexts, human rights praxis requires explicitly naming and confronting capitalism and institutionalized forms of hierarchical rule that take a variety of state forms: fundamentalist states like Iran; liberal "democracies" like the UK, France, or the US; military dictatorships like those that previously ruled over Burma or Chile or may now rule over post-revolutionary Egypt; modern monarchies like Saudi Arabia; bureaucratic dictatorships (formerly "communists" in name) like China or North Korea; and so forth.

If we are to take seriously the challenges that face human rights practice and collective human survival, we must confront the social and ecological limitations of the current political economic system. We have to directly confront all forms of hierarchical rule that manifestly fail to provide the means of survival, let alone dignified rights practice, to the people they supposedly serve and protect.[6] Those of us engaged in human rights praxis can no longer be satisfied with "tinkering" with notions of endless economic growth or endless war. In other words, to be meaningful in current contexts, *human rights praxis is a revolutionary praxis* – where ensuring universal, dignified human survival is confronted by the hegemonic forces of capital and increasingly coercive states like the US.

And the clock is ticking . . . Climate change introduces a situation where the classic liberal/moderate strategies of slow incremental change are no longer an option – particularly for those living at or near sea level, or in areas expecting increased "extreme weather events" or social instability due to resource crises and massive dislocation (refugees). In a recent article titled "How Science is Telling Us All to Revolt," scholar activist Naomi Klein (2013) summarizes the positions of leading natural scientists on climate change and its connection to capitalism: "research shows that our entire economic paradigm is a threat to ecological stability . . . challenging this economic paradigm – through mass-movement counter-pressure – is humanity's best shot at avoiding catastrophe." To the chagrin of many human rights scholars and activists who cling to fantasies of market-based solutions, their privileged positions in well-heeled universities and NGOs, or to solutions that can somehow avoid sweeping social change that may be accompanied by risk and the unknown, it is now impossible to have it both ways – saying you are "for human rights" while denying the manifest challenges to human survival posed by the global political economic status quo. While the potential alternatives are without bounds, subject only to our collective creative capacities, anti-capitalism can no longer be denied as centrally important to the human species, let alone the human rights enterprise. This is a position articulated well outside the bounds of the current two-party system in the United States and the American mainstream media: voting Democrat will not save us. According to leading climate scientists, anti-capitalism is "no longer a matter of mere ideological preference but rather one of species-wide existential necessity" (Klein 2013). To address the global social problems at hand, we must act boldly and swiftly to find a sustainable course. Scholars, students, and stakeholders engaged in human rights work should be prepared to engage on all fronts, with the courage to consider the "radical" or "revolutionary" changes that might be necessary for a better world. Are you prepared to do your part?

Notes

Chapter 1 The Human Rights Enterprise and a Critical Sociology of Human Rights

1 US Constitution, 5th Amendment; UDHR, Article 10; ICCPR, Article 14.

2 US Constitution, 4th Amendment; UDHR, Article 9; ICCPR, Article 9.

3 It should be noted that sociological work on human rights subject matter – genocide, war and war crimes, and so forth – has existed for some time. This is quite different from sociological analyses and approaches to human rights as a concept or terrain of social struggle. We refer here to the development of work explicitly dedicated to a "sociology of human rights."

4 The "state" should be understood as the lasting structural mechanisms and institutions designed for the governance of a particular modern "nation-state" within its delineated borders. This could be considered in contrast to the "government" which refers generally to the people who occupy positions in the state structure, and carry out the day-to-day functions of state governance. In short, "the state" refers to the structures and institutions – such as the military or federal judicial system – while "the government" refers to the population of folks who populate state structures and institutions as employees and "public servants."

5 We use the phrase "define and realize" to indicate that the social construction of rights and realizing their practice in people's lives and the organization of human societies are two overlapping processes.

6 See, for example, Armaline and Glasberg 2009; Armaline, Glasberg, and Purkayastha 2011; Chomsky 2007a, 2007b, 2010; Bakan 2004; Dangl 2007; Shiva 2000, 2001, 2008; Monshipouri, Welch, and Kennedy 2003; Ishay 2008; Stammers 1999; Plummer 2006.

7 See, for examples, Lauren 2011; Donnelly 2003; Freeman 2011; Forsythe 2012; Landman 2002; Risse, Ropp, and Sikkink 1999.

173

8 This has been a particularly sticky issue when it comes to decisions about various forms of *humanitarian intervention* and the controversial principles behind the *responsibility to protect* (R2P) (Peck 2011; Forsythe 2012; Goodhart 2009).

9 For more on efforts to ratify human rights instruments at the local level in the US, including but not limited to "human rights cities," see Kaufman 2011 and Blau 2012.

10 Efforts to achieve "human rights practice" or to "realize human rights" do not refer to the effort to create a law or legal instrument. Where a legal aim might be to create a widely ratified instrument, such as the ICESCR, that claims everyone has the right to food, the aim of *human rights practice* is to make sure that everyone actually eats, as the right would suggest.

11 "Human rights legislation should not be judged solely on its potential for legitimation, but the law's capacity to fulfill a concrete mandate" (Clement 2011: 128).

12 The military industrial complex (MIC) is a term originally coined by US President – formerly General – Dwight D. Eisenhower, who explicitly warned that such a partnership could become powerful enough to threaten functional democracy and any prospects for world peace. Sociologically, the MIC can be understood as a confluence of interests between uniformed branches of the military, the aerospace-defense industry, so-called "private security" agencies, clandestine (CIA) and security agencies (NSA), members of the executive branch including the President ("commander-in-chief"), and the US Congress (which controls funding, resource appropriation, and declarations of war), created and reinforced by the state through its highly lucrative defense-contracting relations and through campaign financing laws that enable private industry (corporations) to strongly influence if not control related state policy. Put simply, the MIC is the consistent relationship between all of these folks for the purposes of furthering their individual and collective interests. Meeting their interests typically translates to the increase of war and weapons production in order to produce profit and demand for their products and services.

13 We are referring to 4th Amendment rights under the US Constitution and the right to privacy according to international (human rights) law, as articulated in UDHR, Article 12, and Article 17 of the ICCPR.

14 Also known as "economic globalization" or "globalization from above," a uniquely neoliberal ("free-market") approach to global economic development still dominant, though under challenge by contemporary social movements, since the oil and monetary crises of the early 1970s. (See Albo, Gindin, and Panitch 2010; McNally 2006, 2011, for excellent analyses of global neoliberal capitalism in its previous and currently persistent forms.)

Chapter 2 Power and the State: Global Economic Restructuring and the Global Recession

1 One might also refer to "left libertarian theory," "left socialist theory," or particular strands of anarchist theory like "libertarian socialism" or "libertarian communism."

Chapter 3 The Human Rights Enterprise: A Genealogy of Continuing Struggles

1 Social movement scholars offer many useful distinctions between terms such as "collective action," "collective behavior," and "social movements." Collective action mostly "occurs within institutions on the part of constituted groups who act in the name of goals" (Tarrow 1994: 2). Collective behavior refers to "extra-institutional, group problem-solving behavior that encompasses an array of collective actions, ranging from protest demonstrations, to behavior in disasters, to mass or diffuse phenomena, such as fads and crazes to social movements and even revolution" (Snow and Oliver 1995: 571). Social movements differ from collective behavior such as crowds, panic, fads, and crazes because of their change-oriented goals, semblance of organization, and temporal continuity (McAdam and Snow 1997: xxiv). We use the term "social movements" broadly to include collective action.

2 For complete reviews of different social movements approaches, see, for example, Morris and Mueller 1992, and McAdam and Snow 1997. For a discussion on substantive rights, see Glenn 2002.

3 The Civil Rights Act of 1968 was passed to address discrimination in housing, and to protect the rights of African Americans to vote. In 1988, 2001, and 2008, parts of the Civil Rights Acts were reaffirmed and extended (available at: <http://www.infoplease.com>). The Supreme Court struck down a significant plank of the 1965 Voting Rights Act in July 2013.

4 It is important to remember that even though Southern slaves were "freed" in the nineteenth century, a barrage of laws – including *Plessey* v. *Ferguson* which established the legality of "separate but equal" facilities, and other Jim Crow laws – ensured African Americans, Latinos, Asian Americans, and Native Americans remained unequal citizens of the United States. (For a gendered/racialized/classed social historical analysis of unequal citizenships, see Glenn 2002, or see <http://www.nea.org/assets/docs/HE/mf.pdf>.)

5 While we focus mainly on African Americans, both Latinos and Asian Americans were involved in civil rights struggles. For an introduction to the struggles of Asian Americans or Latinos, see, for instance, Ancheta 1997; Foo 2007; Gutierrez 2005; Rosales 1996.

6 For instance, Gerald Horne suggests, Indians (who were subjects of British

colonial rule till 1947) and African Americans "shared a common experience of opposition to racism and imperialism . . . that tended to bind them . . . This was part and parcel of a larger anti-racist and anti-imperialist struggle that encompassed millions globally, and that the defeat of Japan . . . along with the Cold War . . . set the stage for retreat of Jim Crow and the erosion of colonization" (2008: 3).

7 Even though Roosevelt's role is repeatedly lauded and conflated with the US official role in crafting UDHR, the actual record is mixed at best. For more details, see Anderson 2003.

8 As Gerald Horne suggests, until 1947 Indians (who were subjects of British colonial rule) and African Americans "shared a common experience of opposition to racism and imperialism . . . that tended to bind them" (2008: 3; see also n.6 of this chapter).

9 In his memoirs, Ahmed Kathrada – who was imprisoned for 27 years with Nelson Mandela, for his anti-apartheid activism – has written about the sense of elation among South African anti-apartheid activists when they heard that Vijaylakshmi Pandit had confronted Jan Smuts of South Africa about apartheid at this public international platform. Pandit's leadership on racism is tied to a longer history of Gandhi's experience with overt racism in South Africa and his initial experiments with using non-violent resistance as a repertoire for challenging repressive states. After he moved to India in 1913, Gandhi brought his non-violent resistance tactics to the independence movement that was in progress in India. As the British colonial machinery used increasingly harsh techniques to repress Indians, the theme of racism and human rights remained an ongoing issue among Indian leaders. This multi-country organizing against racism yielded other collaborations on tactics and strategies to confront repressive state powers.

10 In the interest of space we have provided a simplified version of this struggle to claim rights during the 1940s and 1950s. For a longer, detailed historical analysis, see Carol Anderson's *Eyes Off the Prize* to understand the struggles *within* the movement and *within organizations* as some civil rights leaders chose to purge real or suspected communists from their group's membership rolls.

11 For a longer discussion of weapons of the weak, see Scott 1985.

12 For a detailed history of working-class African Americans, see Kelley 1994.

13 Groups like the NAACP, with many local chapters and inspirational leaders, were involved in a variety of actions, including registering voters and direct action.

14 It is important to note that while the legal victory established the right to equal education, the substantive claim to this right was asserted on the ground by very young people who marched to school, surrounded by national guards, through violence-prone crowds. The iconic picture of Ruby Bridges (see <http://www.palmbeach.k12.fl.us/rooseveltms/portfolio/

cav_blk5/hillary_w/ photo. htm>), six years old, marching to school through jeering crowds, captures both the tactics of resistance and the violence that accompanied the desegregation of schools.

15 Baker worked with a variety of groups – the NAACP in the 1940s; the SCLC in the 1950s; later the CORE and the SNCC.

16 For detailed discussions on the Indian and African exchanges, read Gerald Horne's (2008) *The End of Empires: African Americans and Indians*, or Sean Chabot's (2002) treatise on the transnational diffusion of Gandhian repertoire. Based on his experience in both countries, Gandhi had changed both the substance and meaning of non-violent resistance, insisting that non-violent resistors engaged in direct action *despite* their capacity to use violent means of protest and resistance (Chabot 2002). Both authors point out that despite a general admiration of Gandhi's non-violent resistance, in the 1920s and 1930s, each of these groups also thought it would not be possible to use these tactics in the US because of cultural differences between India and the US. But, in the 1930s, Howard Thurman, Benjamin Mays, and Sue Bailey Thurman went to India and Sri Lanka where they met a large number of Indian nationalist leaders, including Gandhi. Horne emphasizes "the primary importance of the Black American mission to India in the 1930s . . . [was that] (t)he 'missionaries' came home imbued with the fire of non-violence" (2008: 113). Then these missionaries inspired another generation of movement leaders like Martin Luther King.

17 Many images are available for viewing at: <http://images.search.yahoo. com/ search/images?_adv_prop=image&fr=yfp-t-900-s&sz=all&va=civil+rig hts+images>.

18 Since many of the European colonies were just beginning to emerge as independent countries there were no countries from the global South that were in a direct power struggle with the US. Even though countries kept up the pressure on racism, they were not individually powerful opponents in the struggle for global domination (see also Peck 2011).

19 As we mentioned in chapter 1, many of the specific concerns that were raised repeatedly during the crafting of the UDHR were not formalized until much later. For instance, the International Convention on the Elimination of Racism (ICERD) was open for signatures in 1965, while the Convention on the Elimination of All Forms of Discrimination against Women (CEDAW) was not formalized till 1979. The mechanisms for enforcement of these Conventions remain weak at best.

20 It is important to remember that, in the 1960s, many groups had begun to question whether civil rights without economic rights would achieve freedom and equality; they began to talk about de facto segregation along with de jure segregation. The rise of Malcolm X and the black power movement raised significant questions about the entrenched capitalist political economic system that was built on the basis of racial hierarchies. Martin Luther King

also spoke about economic empowerment, but that message was never a powerful frame of the SCLC. More importantly, the black power movement and its critical role in creating a heightened sense of racial consciousness and pride played an invaluable role in mobilizing African Americans to claim their rights despite opposition over the next few decades (Carmichael and Hamilton 1967).

21 Arguably, other instruments – such as the International Covenant on Political and Civil Rights (ICCPR), which the US signed in 1977 and ratified in 1992, and the Convention Against Torture and other Cruel, Inhuman, Degrading Treatment or Punishment (CAT), signed in 1988 and ratified in 1994 – also attempt to ensure equal and humane treatment of those who are treated as "others" by states and dominant groups within states.

22 The literature on racism is too vast to enumerate here. Among some key sociological studies over the last few decades are: Bonilla-Silva 1996; Espiritu 2007; Glenn 2002; Feagin and Sikes 1994; Segura and Zavella 2007; Zinn and Dill 1984. A range of scholarly research continues to document disparities; they include, among other works, American apartheid in housing (e.g., Massey and Denton 1993; Oakley and Burchfield 2009), education (e.g., Aries 2008; Lewis 2003), rates of incarceration (e.g., Alexander 2010), and health (e.g., Hynes 2012).

23 The most notorious of these laws were the stop-and-search laws in Arizona. In May 2013 a federal judge ordered Sheriff Arpaio to stop targeting Latinos in his stop-and-search dragnet, ostensibly to find undocumented migrants. The issue before the judge was whether racial profiling was used to stop Latinos. This verdict indicated that Arpaio's department used racial profiling to stop and search Latinos *upon suspicion* that they might be undocumented migrants.

24 "How much diversity is enough" is an important and thorny question because the continuing quotas against high-achieving affluent Asian Americans, along with the failure to consider the rising numbers of Latinos, further complicate this question. Nonetheless, the focus on Affirmative Action laws and framing these as issues of blacks against whites draws our attention away from the deeper issue of structural advantages for white students.

25 Scholars have been very critical of the use of "model minority" Asian Americans as "proof" that individual-level striving is the best antidote to structural discrimination (see, for instance, Espiritu 2007; Purkayastha 2005; or Kibria 2011, for critiques of the model minority lens).

26 The mainstream media made a concerted effort to emphasize Zimmerman is Hispanic, ignoring the fact that people who are ethnically Hispanics or Latinos are of different races; being Hispanic does not automatically mean a person has lived the life of a racial minority. Two other pertinent issues are that Martin had been killed because he "looked suspicious" to Zimmerman,

a racist/gendered construction that people internalize in a racist society. Zimmerman was let go because his actions fit with the "race-neutral" laws that do not investigate who is targeted as suspicious and why, with the claim of the gun-wielding person's sense of vulnerability deemed to be sufficient (see also Bugado 2013).

27 Minority females are the fastest-growing sector of the prison population. Both males and females are susceptible to sexual violence.

28 Some of this material has appeared as a chapter – "From International Platforms to Local Yards: Standing Up For the Elimination of Racial Discrimination in the US" by Aheli Purkayastha, Bandana Purkayastha, and Chandra Waring – in *Human Rights in Our Own Backyard: Injustice and Resistance in the United States,* edited by William Armaline, Davita Silfen Glasberg, and Bandana Purkayastha.

Chapter 4 Private Tyrannies: Rethinking the Rights of "Corporate Citizens"

1 See the United Nations General Assembly Resolution 217 A (III), 1948, p. 76.

2 Broadly speaking, a counter-hegemonic ideology, worldview, or movement seeks to challenge, confront, and replace dominant "common-sense" ideologies that tend to reflect owning and or ruling-class interests in a society. The concepts of hegemony and counter-hegemony stem from the work of Antonio Gramsci (1971) and other neo-Marxist theorists, who imagined the revolutionary potential of civil society in the face of political economic domination.

3 Many countries in the global South had movements claiming women's rights by the nineteenth and early twentieth centuries also. As a result, many of the female representatives from Latin America and Asia (particularly India) demanded women's political, civil, economic, and social rights during the crafting of UDHR, along with demands for racial justice (Falcone et al. 2010; Kumar 1997). The trajectories of human rights in other countries often assumed diverse public forums.

4 On the morning of June 28, 1969, NYPD raided the mafia-owned "gay bar" of the Stonewall Inn. The Stonewall Inn was located in the Greenwich Village neighborhood – a center of the LGTBQ community in New York City at the time. Though raids of "gay bars" and the criminalization and persecution of LGTQ peoples were common at the time, this particular raid sparked massive, confrontational street protests that many consider the beginning of the modern "gay rights" movement.

5 See Donnelly's (2003: 22) "Universal Declaration model," a theoretical position arguing for the centrality and primacy of the UDHR in substantively defining international human rights. According to the model, the primacy,

legitimacy, and significance of the UDHR stem from it representing a considerably wide international consensus.

6 This refers to the period between (roughly) 1994, marked by the rise of the Zapatista movement in response to the North American Free Trade Agreement and neoliberal global economic restructuring, and the failed resistance to the Afghanistan and Iraqi Wars by approximately 2003.

7 See YouTube (retrieved on August 15, 2013, from <http://www.youtube.com/watch?v=E2h8ujX6T0A>) or C-Span for this video footage.

8 See, for example, Bakan 2004; Bond 2004; Bond and Manyanya 2003; Brecher, Costello, and Smith 2000; Klein 2000; McNally 2006; Parrenas 2001; Schaeffer 2003; Shiva 2000, 2001; Armaline and Glasberg 2009; Armaline, Glasberg, and Purkayastha 2011.

9 For data, see the National Commission on the BP Deepwater Horizon Oil Spill and Offshore Drilling Report, "The Use of Surface and Subsea Dispersants during the BP Deepwater Horizon Spill" (2010, retrieved on August 15, 2013, from: <http://media.mcclatchydc.com/smedia/2010/10/06/18/_Staff_Report_No._4.source.prod_affiliate.91.pdf>).

10 The "revolving door" refers to the tendency for legislators and regulators to be former and/or future executives of the private industries they are meant to regulate, oversee, and control. Examples would include former forestry and fossil-fuel company executives employed as regulators by the Environmental Protection Agency (EPA), former pharmaceutical executives employed by the Food and Drug Administration (FDA), or, in the opposite direction, former military brass employed as lobbyists and executives for private military contractors and weapons companies.

11 The transnational state refers to the international decision-making (governing) bodies and policy-setting financial institutions that have arisen during global economic restructuring since the 1970s, such as the World Trade Organization, International Monetary Fund, and World Bank. These international bodies typically consist of powerful state actors (rulers) and representatives from powerful private interests (owners), tend to be non-transparent to the global public, tend not to reflect democratic representation from global stakeholders or national publics, and in many ways are believed to supersede the power and reach of many nation-states, since they set many of the rules and standards for global trade and finance (Robinson 2001, 2004).

12 Full text of the leaked chapter can be found (retrieved August 15, 2013) here: <http://www.citizenstrade.org/ctc/wp-content/uploads/2012/06/tppinvestment.pdf>.

13 See the "1 in 3 Campaign" for this research and the resultant grassroots political campaign it currently inspires at: <http://www.1in3campaign.org/> (retrieved August 15, 2013).

14 US Constitution, 5th Amendment; UDHR, Article 10; ICCPR, Article 14.

15 US Constitution, 4th Amendment; UDHR, Article 9; ICCPR, Article 9.
16 See the Move to Amend website (2013) at: <https://movetoamend.org/>.

Chapter 5 Current Contexts and Implications for Human Rights Praxis in the US

1 See: <http://www.fincen.gov/statutes_regs/patriot/index.html> for these documents in full text.
2 The first "war on terror" was waged by the Reagan administration against democratically elected socialist governments in Central and South America. Notably, US officials such as Oliver North were accurately labeled as international war criminals in the overlapping controversies that defined what we now call the "Iran-Contra scandal" (Chomsky 2007a).
3 See Granick and Sprigman (2013) for several sample legal arguments.
4 The "collateral murder" video leaked by Manning, showing the indiscriminate killing of civilians and at least one journalist by American forces, is accessible via Wikileaks, and can be found at: < http://www.collateralmur der.com>.
5 The IACHR (Washington, DC) is a body created to oversee human rights practice in the western hemisphere by the Organization of American States – a regional legal human rights regime. The United States enjoys membership on these bodies, but does not recognize their legal authority or the authority of the Inter-American Court of Human Rights (San José, Costa Rica).
6 Remember, even some of the most fascist regimes claim that their authority is in part legitimated through some sort of trade-off or social contract – serving the material or spiritual needs of the people, and/or protecting them from any number of real or existential threats.

References

ACLU. (2013) "The Voting Rights Act: protecting minority voting rights." Available from: <http://www.aclu.org/voting-rights/voting-rights-act-0.>; July 13, 2013.

ACLU. (2014) "Guantanamo by the numbers." Available from: <https://www. aclu.org/national-security/guantanamo-numbers>; April 1, 2014.

ACORN, Pennsylvania. (2000) "Equity strippers: the impact of subprime lending in Philadelphia." Available until 2010 (when ACORN went bankrupt) from: <www.acorn.org/pressrelease/equity.htm#_ftn1>.

Adam, D. (2009) "ExxonMobil continuing to fund climate sceptic groups, records show." *Guardian*. Available from: <http://www.theguardian.com/enviro nment/2009/jul/01/exxon-mobil-climate-change-sceptics-funding>; August 13, 2013.

Ahmed, N. (2013) "Pentagon bracing for public dissent over climate and energy shocks." *Guardian*. Available from: <http://www.theguardian.com/ environment/earth-insight/2013/jun/14/climate-change-energy-shocks-nsa-prism>; August 1, 2013.

Akard, P. J. (1992). "Corporate mobilization and political power: the transfor- mation of US economic policy in the 1970s." *American Sociological Review* 57: 597–615.

Akard, P. J. (2005) "Now room for compromise: business interests and the politics of health care reform." *Research in Political Sociology* 14: 51–105.

Albo, G., Gindin, S., and Panitch, L. (2010) *In and Out of Crisis: The Global Financial Meltdown and Left Alternatives*. Oakland, CA: Spectre/ PM Press.

Alexander, M. (2010) *The New Jim Crow: Mass Incarceration in the Age of Colorblindness*. New York: The New Press.

Alkarama Foundation. (2013) "The United States' war on Yemen: drone attacks. Report submitted to the Special Rapporteur on the Promotion and Protection of Human Rights and Fundamental Freedoms while Countering

References

Terror." Available from: <http://en.alkarama.org/documents/ALK_USA
-Yemen_Drones_SRCTwHR_4June2013_Final_EN.pdf>; July 1, 2013.

Alvarez, L. and Buckley, C. (2013) "Zimmerman is acquitted in Trayvon
Martin trial." *New York Times*, July 2013. Available from: <http://www.ny
times.com/2013/07/14/us/george-zimmerman-verdict-trayvon-martin.html?
pagewanted=all>; July 14, 2013.

Amenta, E. and Halfmann, D. (2000) "Wage wars: institutional politics, WPA
wages, and the struggle for U.S. social policy." *American Sociological
Review* 65: 506–28.

Amenta, E. and Parikh, S. (1991) "Comment: capitalists did not want the Social
Security Act: a critique of the 'capitalist dominance' thesis." *American
Sociological Review* 56: 124–9.

Amenta, E. and Skocpol, T. (1988) "Redefining the New Deal: World War II and
the development of social provision in the US." In M. Weir, A. S. Orloff, and
T. Skocpol (eds), *The Politics of Social Policy in the United States*. Princeton,
NJ: Princeton University Press, pp. 81–122.

American Civil Liberties Union (ACLU) website. (2013) "Blog of rights: War
on Women." Available from: <https://www.aclu.org/blog/tag/war-women>;
September 15, 2013.

Amin, Sameer. (1997) *Capitalism in the Age of Globalization*. London: Zed Books.

Amnesty International. (2013) " 'Will I be next?': US drone strikes in Pakistan."
London: Amnesty International Publications. Available from: <http://www.
amnestyusa.org/sites/default/files/asa330132013en.pdf>; October 21, 2013.

Amster, R., DeLeon, A., Fernandez, L., Nocella, A. J., and Shannon, D. (eds).
(2009) *Contemporary Anarchist Studies: An Introductory Anthology of
Anarchy in the Academy*. New York: Routledge.

Ancheta, A. (1997) *Race, Rights and the Asian American Experience*. New
Brunswick, NJ: Rutgers University Press.

Anders, C. (2012) "Will Congress finally start to clean up the mess it made with
NDAA?" *ACLU: Washington Markup*. Available from: <https://www.
aclu.org/blog/national-security/will-congress-finally-start-clean-mess-it-made
-ndaa>; August 1, 2013.

Anderson, C. (2003) *Eyes Off the Prize: The United Nations and the African
American Struggle for Human Rights, 1944–1955*. New York: Cambridge
University Press.

Arat, Z. (2008) "Human rights ideology and dimensions of power: a radical
approach to the state, property, and discrimination." *Human Rights
Quarterly* 30(4): 906–32.

Aries, E. (2008) *Race and Class Matters in an Elite College*. Philadelphia, PA:
Temple University Press.

Armaline, W. and Glasberg, D. S. (2009) "What will states really do for us?
The human rights enterprise and pressure from below." *Societies Without
Borders* 4: 430–51.

References

Armaline, W., Glasberg, D. S., and Purkayastha, B. (2011) *Human Rights in Our Own Backyard: Injustice and Resistance in the United States.* Philadelphia, PA: University of Pennsylvania Press.

Associated Press. (2011) "Sharp rise in foreclosures as banks move in – business – real estate – Msnbc.com." *Msnbc.com – Breaking News, Science and Tech News, World News, US News, Local News.* Msnbc.com. NBC News, 13 October 2011. Available from: <http://www.msnbc.msn.com/id/44885991/ns/business-real_estate/>; December 4, 2011.

Austin v. Michigan Chamber of Commerce, 494 U.S. 652 (1990).

Baca Zinn, M. and Thornton Dill, B. (1994) *Women of Color in U.S. Society.* Philadelphia, PA: Temple University Press.

Bakan, J. (2004) *The Corporation: The Pathological Pursuit of Profit and Power.* New York: Free Press.

Bakunin, M. (1964) *The Political Philosophy of Bakunin.* G. P. Maximoff, ed. New York: Free Press.

Ball, J. (2013) "U.S. drug agency partners with AT&T for access to 'vast database' of call records." *Guardian.* Available from: <http://www.theguardian.com/world/2013/sep/02/nsa-dea-at-t-call-records-access>; September 2, 2013.

Ballard, R., Habib, A., and Valodia, I. (2006) *Voices of Protest: Social Movements in Post Apartheid South Africa.* Durban, South Africa: University of Kwa-Zulu Natal Press.

Barbieux, K. (2008) "That wacky Homeless Power Project of Nashville." Available from: <http://thehomelessguy.blogspot.com/2008/05/that-wacky-homeless-power-project-of.html>; September 5, 2013.

Becker, J. and Shane, S. (2012) "Secret 'kill list' proves a test of Obama's principles and will." *The New York Times.* Available from: <http://www.nytimes.com/2012/05/29/world/obamas-leadership-in-war-on-al-qaeda.html?pagewanted=1&_r=5&hp&>; April 1, 2013.

Beeman, A., Glasberg, D. S., and Casey, C. (2010) "Whiteness as property: predatory lending and the reproduction of racialized inequality." *Critical Sociology* 37: 27–45.

Benoit, D. (2007) *The Best-Kept Secret: Women Corporate Lobbyists, Policy, and Power in the United States.* Piscataway, NJ: Rutgers University Press.

Beresford, P. (2010). "The Sunday Times rich list 2010: rising from the rubble." *The Sunday Times*, April 25.

Berkman, A. (2003) *What is Anarchism?* Oakland, CA: AK Press.

Berlin, L. (2012) "Foreclosure crisis is far from over, report finds." *Huffington Post* (April 4). Available from: <http://www.huffingtonpost.com/2011/11/17/foreclosure-crisis-center-for-responsible-lending_n_1099120.html>; September 5, 2013.

Berman, A. (2013a) "North Carolina Republicans push extreme voter suppression measures." *The Nation.* Available from: <http://www.thenation.com/

References

blog/175395/north-carolina-republicans-push-extreme-voter-suppression-measures>; August 1, 2013.

Berman, A. (2013b) "North Carolina passes the country's worst voter suppression law." *The Nation.* Available from: <http://www.thenation.com/blog/175441 /north-carolina-passes-countrys-worst-voter-suppression-law#>; August 15, 2013.

Bhatt, E. (2008) *We are Poor but So Many.* New Delhi, India: Oxford University Press.

Blackmon, D. (1999) "Silent partner: how the South's fight to uphold segregation was funded up North." *Wall Street Journal.* Available from: <http://www.sla verybyanothername.com/other-writings/silent-partner-how-the-souths-fight-to-uphold-segregation-was-funded-up-north/>; July 26, 2013.

Blau, J. (2012) "Growing and learning human rights." In J. Blau and M. Frezzo (eds), *Sociology and Human Rights: A Bill of Rights for the Twenty-first Century,* Los Angeles, CA: Sage/Pine Forge Press, pp. 245–69.

Blau, J. and Frezzo, M. (eds). (2012) *Sociology and Human Rights: A Bill of Rights for the Twenty-first Century.* Los Angeles, CA: Sage/Pine Forge Press.

Blau, J. and Moncada, A. (eds). (2005) *Human Rights: Beyond the Liberal Vision.* Lanham, MD: Rowman & Littlefield.

Block, F. (1987) *Revising State Theory: Essays in Politics and Postindustrialism.* Philadelphia, PA: Temple University Press.

Block, F. L., Cloward, R. A., Ehrenreich, B., and Piven, F. F. (1987) *The Mean Season: The Attack on the Welfare State.* New York: Pantheon Books.

Bond, P. (2004) "Should the World Bank be 'fixed' or 'nixed'? Reformist posturing and popular resistance." *Capitalism, Nature, Socialism* 15(2): 85–105.

Bond, P. and M. Manyanya. (2003) *Zimbabwe's Plunge: Exhausted Nationalism, Neoliberalism and the Search for Social Justice.* London: Merlin Press.

Bonilla-Silva, E. (1996) *White Supremacy and Racism in the Post Civil Rights Era.* Boulder, CO: Lynne Reinner Press.

Bonilla-Silva, E. (2006) *Racism Without Racists: Color-Blind Racism & Racial Inequality in Contemporary America.* Lanham, MD: Rowman & Littlefield.

Bostic, R. and Robinson, B. 2005. "What makes Community Reinvestment Act agreements work?" *Housing Policy Debate* 16: 513–45.

Bradley, J. (2000) *The Community Guide to Predatory Lending Research.* North Carolina: Community Reinvestment Association of North Carolina.

Brecher, J., Costello, T., and Smith, B. (2000) *Globalization from Below: The Power of Solidarity.* Cambridge, MA: South End Press.

Breidthardt, A., Deighton, B., and Zakaria, T. (2013) "U.S. bugged EU offices, computer networks: German magazine." *Reuters.* Available from: <http://www.reuters.com/article/2013/06/29/us-usa-eu-spying-idUSB RE95S0AQ20130629>; June 29, 2013.

References

Brown, J. (1991) *Gandhi: Prisoner of Hope*. New Haven, CT: Yale University Press.

Brunsma, D. L., Smith, K. E. I., and Gran, B. (eds) (2012) *Handbook of Sociology and Human Rights*. New York: Paradigm Publishers.

Buchheit, P. (2013) "Eight ways privatization has failed America." *Truthout*. Available from: <http://truth-out.org/buzzflash/commentary/item/18126 -eight-ways-privatization-has-failed-america>; August 15, 2013.

Bugado, A. (2013) "White supremacy acquits George Zimmerman." *The Nation* Available from: <http://www.thenation.com/blog/175260/white-supremacy -acquits-george-zimmerman#ixzz2aXFijwv8>; July 15, 2013.

The Bureau of Investigative Journalism [TBIJ]. (2012) Covert War on Terror. Available from: <http://www.thebureauinvestigates.com/category/projects/ drones/>; June 1, 2013.

Burris, V. (1992) "Elite policy-planning networks in the United States." *Research in Politics and Society* 4: 111–34.

Burris, V. and Staples, C. (2012) "In search of a transnational capitalist class: Alternative methods for comparing director interlocks within and between nations and regions." *International Journal of Comparative Sociology* 53(4): 323–42.

Carmichael, S. and Hamilton, C. (1967) *Black Power: The Politics of Liberation in America*. New York: Vantage Books.

CERD Shadow Report. (2008) Available from: <www.ushrnetwork.org/cerd _shadow_2008.>; May 9, 2009.

Chabot, S. (2002) "Transnational diffusion and the African American reinvention of the Gandhian repertoire." In J. Smith and H. Johnston (eds), *Globalization and Resistance: Transnational Dimensions of Social Movements*. Lanham, MD: Rowman and Littlefield, pp. 97–114.

Chomsky, N. (2004) *Hegemony or Survival*. New York: Henry Holt and Company.

Chomsky, N. (2007a) *Hegemony or Survival: America's Quest for Global Dominance*. New York: Metropolitan Books.

Chomsky, N. (2007b) *Failed States*. New York: Owl Books.

Chomsky, N. (2010) *Hopes and Prospects*. Chicago, IL: Haymarket Books.

Chomsky, N. (2012) "Destroying the commons: how the Magna Carta became a Minor Carta. *TomDispatch.com*." Available from: <http://www.tomdis patch.com/blog/175571/>; June 1, 2013.

Chorev, N. (2007) *Remaking U.S. Trade Policy: From Protectionism to Globalization*. Ithaca, NY: Cornell University Press.

Citizens United v. *Federal Elections Commission*, 508 U.S. 310 (2010) Full text available from: <http://www.supremecourt.gov/opinions/09pdf/08-205. pdf>; August 15, 2013.

Clawson, D., Neustadtl, A., and Weller, M. (1998) *Dollars and Votes: How Business Campaign Contributions Subvert Democracy*. Philadelphia, PA: Temple University Press.

References

Clement, D. (2008) *Canada's Rights Revolution: Social Movements and Social Change, 1937–1982.* Vancouver, BC: UBC Press.

Clement, D. (2011) "A sociology of human rights: rights through a social movement lens." *Canadian Review of Sociology/Revue Canadienne de sociologie* 48: 121–35.

Clements, J. (2012) *Corporations are Not People.* San Francisco, CA: Berrett-Koehler Publishers.

Collins, J. M. (2000) "Analyzing trends in subprime originations: a case study of Connecticut." Washington, DC: Neighborhood Reinvestment Corporation.

Conlin, M. and Rudegeair, P. (2013) "Former Bank of America workers allege it lied to home owners." Reuters, June 14, Available from: <http://www.reuters.com/assets/print?aid=USL2N0EQ1KT20130614)>; September 5, 2013.

Cooke, Sarah and Kabeer, Naila (eds). (2010) *Social Protection as Development Policy: Asian Perspectives.* London: Routledge.

The Corporation. (2003) [DVD] Canada: [Directors] Mark Achbar, Jennifer Abbott, [Writer] Joel Bakan.

Courchane, M., Surette, B., and Zorn, P. (2004) "Subprime borrowers: transition and outcomes." *Journal of Real Estate Finance and Economics* 29 (4): 365–92.

Cowan, J. K., Dembour, M. B., and Wilson, R. A. (eds). (2001) *Culture and Rights: Anthropological Perspectives.* Cambridge: Cambridge University Press.

Daly, H. and Farley, J. (2010) *Ecological Economics: Principles and Applications,* 2nd edn. Chicago, IL: Island Press.

D'Angelo, R. (2001) *The American Civil Rights Movement.* New York: McGraw Hill/Dushkin.

Dangl, B. (2007) *The Price of Fire: Resource Wars and Social Movements in Bolivia.* Oakland, CA: AK Press.

Davey, M. and Greenhouse, S. (2011) "Angry demonstrations in Wisconsin as cuts loom." *New York Times,* February 16. Available from: <www.nytimes.com/2011/02/17/us/17wisconsin.html.>; September 5, 2013.

Desai, Ashwin. (2002) *We are the Poors: Community Struggles in Post Apartheid South Africa.* Durban: University of Kwazulu Natal Press.

Domhoff, G. W. (1970) *The Higher Circles.* New York: Vintage Books.

Domhoff, G. W. (1990) *The Power Elite and the State: How Policy is Made in America.* New York: Aldine de Gruyter.

Domhoff, G. W. (2005) *Who Rules America? Power, Politics, and Social Change.* New York: McGraw-Hill.

Donnelly, J. (1982) "Human rights and human dignity: an analytical critique of non Western conceptions of human rights." *The American Political Science Review* 76: 303–16.

References

Donnelly, J. (2003) *Universal Human Rights in Theory and Practice*. Ithaca, NY: Cornell University Press.

Donnelly, J. (2010) *International Human Rights*. Boulder, CO: Westview Press.

Dow Jones Report. (2008) Available from: <http://dowjonesclose.com/2008. html>; September 5, 2013.

Easley, J. (2013) "Obama tells Leno: 'We don't have a domestic spying program.'" *The Hill*. Available from: <http://thehill.com/blogs/blog-brief ing-room/news/315871-obama-we-dont-have-a-domestic-spying-program>; August 30, 2013.

Eckstein, R. (1997) *Nuclear Power and Social Power*. Philadelphia, PA: Temple University Press.

Ehrlich, P. R. and Ehrlich, A. H. (2013) "Can a collapse of global civilization be avoided?" *Proceedings of the Royal Society B: Biological Sciences*, *280* (1754): 1–9.

Eichler, A. (2012) "10 most Profitable U.S. corporations paid average tax rate of just 9 percent last year." *Huffington Post*. Available from: <http:// www.huffingtonpost.com/2012/08/06/most-profitable-corporations-tax-rate _n_1746817.html?ref=topbar>; August 8, 2012.

Eichler, A. and McAuliff, M. (2011) "Income inequality reaches guilded age levels, congressional report finds." *Huffington Post*. Available from: <http:// www.huffingtonpost.com/2011/10/26/income-inequality_n_1032632.html>; August 15, 2013.

Eichelberger, Erika. (2013) "FISA court has rejected .03% of all government surveillance requests." *Mother Jones*. Available from: <http://www. motherjones.com/mojo/2013/06/fisa-court-nsa-spying-opinion-reject-requ est>; June 10, 2013.

Engel, R. and Windrem, R. (2013) "CIA didn't always know who it was killing in drone strikes, classified documents show." *NBC News*. Available from: <http://openchannel.nbcnews.com/_news/2013/06/05/18781930-exclusive -cia-didnt-always-know-who-it-was-killing-in-drone-strikes-classified-docu ments-show?lite.>; June 6, 2013.

Erturk, Y. and Purkayastha, B. (2012) "Linking research, policy and action: a look at the work of the special rapporteur on violence against women." In M. Abraham and B. Purkayastha (eds), *Current Sociology*, pp. 20–39.

Esping-Anderson, G., Friedland, R., and Wright, E. O. (1986) "Modes of class struggle and the capitalist state." *Kapitalistate* 4–5: 184–220.

Espiritu, Y. (2007) *Asian American Women and Men: Love, Labor, Laws*. Lanham, MD: Rowman & Littlefield.

Falcone, S., Collins, D., Lodhia, S., and Talcott, M. (2010) "New directions in feminism and human rights: an introduction." *International Feminist Journal of Politics* 12(3–4): 298–318.

Feagin, J. and Sikes, M. (1994) *Living with Racism: The Black Middle-class Experience*. Boston, MA: Beacon Press.

References

Feagin, J. R. and Vera, H. (2001) *Liberation Sociology*. New York: Westview.

Federal Reserve Bank of New York. (1933) Banking Act of 1933. June 22, 1933. Available from: <http://fraser.stlouisfed.org/historicaldocs/1253/>; September 5, 2013.

Federman, A. (2013) "We're being watched: how corporations and law enforcement are spying on environmentalists." *EcoWatch*. Available from: <http://ecowatch.com/2013/were-being-watched/>; June 7, 2013.

Felice, W. (1999) "The viability of the United Nations approach to economic and social human rights in a globalized economy." *International Affairs* 75: 563–98.

Ferguson, C. H. (2012) *Predator Nation: Corporate Criminals, Political Corruption, and the Hijacking of America*. New York: Crown Publishers.

Fernandez, M. (2013) "Filibuster in Texas Senate tries to halt abortion bill." *The New York Times*. Available from: <http://www.nytimes.com/2013/06/26/us/politics/senate-democrats-in-texas-try-blocking-abortion-bill-with-filibuster.html?_r=0>; August 15, 2013.

First National Bank of Boston v. *Bellotti*, 435 U.S. 765 (1978) (Rehnquist, dissenting).

Fisher, P. (2012) "The doctor is out to lunch: ALEC's recommendations wrong prescription for state prosperity." *The Iowa Policy Project*. Available from: <http://www.iowapolicyproject.org/2012Research/120724-rsps.html>; August 15, 2013.

Flank, L. (2007) *Philosophy of Revolution: Towards a Non-Leninist Marxism*. St Petersburg, Florida: Red and Black Publishers.

Fontevecchia, A. (2013) "BP fighting a two front war as Macondo continues to bite and production drops." *Forbes*. Available from: <http://www.forbes.com/sites/afontevecchia/2013/02/05/bp-fighting-a-two-front-war-as-macondo-continues-to-bite-and-production-drops/>; August 15, 2013.

Foo, L. (2007) *Asian American Women: Issues, Concerns, and Responsive Human and Civil Rights Advocacy*, e-pub. Ford Foundation. Available from: <http://aapip.org/files/publication/files/aawp_full_reports.pdf>; August 15, 2013.

Forsythe, D. P. (2012) *Human Rights in International Relations*. Cambridge: Cambridge University Press.

Foucault, M. (1977 [1995]) *Discipline & Punish*. New York: Vintage Books.

Freeman, M. A. (2009) "Rethinking human rights, development, and democracy: the paradox of the UN." *Perspectives on Global Development and Technology* 9: 28–38.

Freeman, M. A. (2011) *Human Rights: An Interdisciplinary Approach*. Cambridge: Polity.

Fuentes-Nieva, R. and Galasso, N. (2014) "Working for the few: political capture and economic inequality." *OXFAM International*. Available from:

References

<http://www.oxfam.org / en / policy / working - for - the - few - economic-inequality>; February 2, 2014.

Galbraith, J. K. (1985) *The New Industrial State*, 4th edn. Boston, MA: Houghton-Mifflin Co.

Gamson, J. (1996) "Organizational shaping of collective identity." *Sociological Forum* 11: 231–61.

Gamson, W. [1975] (1990) *The Strategy of Social Protest*. Belmont, CA: Wadsworth, pp. 72–88.

Garofalo, P. (2012) "Interest rate rigging by big banks may have cost U.S. tax-payers billions of dollars." *Think Progress*. Available from: <http://think progress.org/economy/2012/12/19/1364661/libor-rigging-costs-taxpayers/>; August 15, 2013.

Gellman, B. (2013) "NSA broke privacy rules thousands of times per year, audit finds." *Washington Post*. Available from: <http://articles.washington post.com/2013-08-15/world/41431831_1_washington-post-national-secu rity-agency-documents>; August 30, 2013.

Gibson, Carl (2013a) "How to win the war on terror: repeal the patriot act." *Reader Supported News*. Available from: <http://readersupportednews. org/opinion2/277-75/17813-focus-how-to-win-the-war-on-terror-repeal-the-patriot-act>; August 1, 2013.

Gibson, Carl. (2013b) "'Bagful of cash' report exposing the U.S. Chamber of Commerce." *Reader Supported News*. Available from: <http:// readersupportednews.org/opinion2/279-82/18510-qbagful-of-cashq-report -exposing-the-us-chamber-of-commerce>; August 15, 2013.

Gibson, Carl. (2013c) "The 21st century declaration of independence." *Reader Supported News*. Available from: <http://readersupportednews.org/ opinion2/287-124/18246-the-21st-century-declaration-of-independence>; August 15. 2013.

Glasberg, D. S. (1989) *The Power of Collective Purse Strings: The Effect of Bank Hegemony on Corporations and the State*. Berkeley, CA: University of California Press.

Glasberg, D. S. and Skidmore, D. (1997) *Corporate Welfare Policy and the Welfare State: Bank Deregulation and the Savings and Loan Bailout*. New York: Aldine de Gruyter.

Glasberg, D. S. and Shannon, D. (2011) *Political Sociology: Oppression, Resistance, and the State*. Thousand Oaks, CA: Sage/Pine Forge Press.

Glasberg, D. S., Beeman, A., and Casey, C. (2011) "Preying on the American dream: predatory lending, the social construction of foreclosure and resistance to economic injustice." In W. T. Armaline, D. S. Glasberg, and B. Purkayastha (eds), *Human Rights In Our Own Back Yard: Injustice and Resistance in the United States*. Philadelphia, PA: University of Pennsylvania Press, pp. 34–45.

References

Glenn, E. N. (2002) *Unequal Freedom: How Race and Gender Shape American Citizenship*. Cambridge, MA: Harvard University Press.

Goldstein, D. (1999) *Understanding Predatory Lending: Moving Toward a Common Definition and Workable Solutions*. Cambridge, MA: Joint Center for Housing Studies of Harvard University.

Goodale, M. (2006) "Introduction, in focus: anthropology and human rights in a new key." *American Anthropologist* 108: 1–8.

Goodhart, M. (2009) *Human Rights: Politics and Practice*. Oxford: Oxford University Press.

Goodwin, L. (2013) "In dissent, Scalia joins with court's liberals to blast police DNA testing without warrant." *Yahoo News: The Lookout*. Available from: <http://news.yahoo.com/blogs/lookout/dissent-scalia-joins-court-liberals-blast-police-dna-184252969.html.>; June 6, 2013.

Gordon, U. (2008) *Anarchy Alive: Anti-Authoritarian Politics from Practice to Theory*. London: Pluto Press.

Graeber, D. (2009) *Direct Action: An Ethnography*. Oakland, CA: AK Press.

Graeber, D. (2012) *Debt: The First 5000 Years*. London: Penguin.

Gramsci, A. (1971) *Selections from the Prison Notebooks of Antonio Gramsci*, ed. G. Nowell-Smith and Q. Hoare. New York: International Publishers.

Granick, J. and Sprigman, C. (2013) "The criminal NSA." *The New York Times*. Available from: <http://www.nytimes.com/2013/06/28/opinion/the-criminal-nsa.html?pagewanted=all&_r=0>; July 1, 2013.

Greenwald, G. (2013a) "On whistleblowers and government threats of investigation." *Guardian*. Available from: <http://www.guardian.co.uk/commentisfree/2013/jun/07/whistleblowers-and-leak-investigations>; June 7, 2013.

Greenwald, G. (2013b) "The NSA's mass and indiscriminate spying on Brazilians." *Guardian*. Available from: <http://www.guardian.co.uk/commentisfree/2013/jul/07/nsa-brazilians-globo-spying>; July 8, 2013.

Greenwald, G. (2013c) "The crux of the NSA story in one phrase: 'collect it all.'" *Guardian*. Available from: <http://www.guardian.co.uk/commentisfree/2013/jul/15/crux-nsa-collect-it-all>; July 16, 2013.

Greenwald, G. and MacAskill, E. (2013) "NSA PRISM program taps in to user data of Apple, Google and others." *Guardian*. Available from: <http://www.guardian.co.uk/world/2013/jun/06/us-tech-giants-nsa-data>; June 7, 2013.

Greenwald, G., MacAskill, E., and Poitras, L. (2013) "Edward Snowden: the whistleblower behind the NSA surveillance revelations." *Guardian*. Available from: <http://m.guardiannews.com/world/2013/jun/09/edward-snowden-nsa-whistleblower-surveillance?CMP=twt_gu>; June 9, 2013.

Groeger, L. and Currier, C. (2010) "Timeline: how Obama compares to Bush on torture, surveillance and detention." *ProPublica*. Available from: <http://billmoyers.com/content/comparing-obama-and-bushs-records-on-wartime-civil-liberties/>; June 1, 2013.

References

Grossman, R., Linzey, T., and Brannen, D. (2003) "Model Amici Curiae brief to eliminate corporate rights." Available from: <http://www.ratical.org/corpo rations/demoBrief.html>; August 15, 2013.

Gruenstein, D. and Herbert, C. E. (2000) "Analyzing trends in subprime origina-tions and foreclosures: a case study of the Atlanta Metro area." Washington, DC: Neighborhood Reinvestment Corporation Available from: <www. nw.org/network/strategies/campaign/predatory/abt.pdf>; September 5, 2013.

Guerin, D. (1970) *Anarchism: From Theory to Practice*. New York: Monthly Review Press, pp. 128–30.

Gurr. T. R. (1970) *Why Men Rebel*. Princeton, NJ: Princeton University Press.

Gutierrez, J. (2005) *Making of a Civil Rights Leader: Jose Angel Gutierrez*. Houston, Texas: Arte Publico Press.

Guttmacher Institute. (2013) "Fact sheet: facts on unintended pregnancy in the U.S." *Guttmacher Institute*. Available from: <http://www.guttmacher.org /pubs/FB-Unintended-Pregnancy-US.html>; September 20, 2013.

Haines, H. (1984) "Black radicalization and funding of civil rights 1957–1970." *Social Problems* 32: 31–43.

Hajjar, L. (2012) "Wikileaking the truth about American unaccountability for torture." *Societies Without Borders* 7: 192–225.

Hamilton, R. (2013) "Supreme Court remands Fisher to Lower Court." Available from: <http://www.texastribune.org/2013/06/24/us-supreme-court-issues-de cision-fisher-v-ut/>; June 27, 2013.

Harding, L. (2014) "Edward Snowden: US government spied on human rights workers." *Guardian*. Available from: <http://www.theguardian.com/ world/2014/apr/08/edwards-snowden-us-government-spied-human-rights-workers?CMP=twt_gu>; April 9, 2014.

Harrison, J. Frank. (1983) *The Modern State: An Anarchist Analysis*. Montreal: Black Rose Books.

Hartmann, T. (2010) *Unequal Protection: How Corporations Became "People" – and You Can Fight Back*. San Francisco, CA: Berrett-Koehler.

Hassim, S. (2006) *Women's Organizations and Democracy in South Africa: Contesting Authority*. Durban, South Africa: University of Kwa Zulu Natal Press.

Hathaway, O. A. (2002) "Do human rights treaties make a difference?" *The Yale Law Journal* 111: 1935–2042.

Hays, G. and Hornick, R. (1990) "No end in sight: politicians hurl blame as the $500 billion S&L crisis races out of control." *Time* (August 13): 50–2.

Hedges, C. (2012) "A victory for all of us." *Truthdig*. Available from: <http:// www.truthdig.com/report/item/a_victory_for_all_of_us_20120518/>; June 1, 2013.

Hedges, C. (2013) "Locking out the voices of dissent." *Truthdig*. Available from: <http://www.truthdig.com/report/item/locking_out_the_voices_of_dis sent_20130714/>; July 16, 2013.

References

Hedges, C., and Sacco, J. (2012) *Days of Destruction Days of Revolt*. New York: Nation Books.

Hertel, S. and Libal, K. (2011) *Human Rights in the United States: Beyond Exceptionalism*. Cambridge: Cambridge University Press.

Hiskes, Richard P. (2008) *The Human Right to a Green Future: Environmental Rights and Intergenerational Justice*. Cambridge: Cambridge University Press.

Hodai, B. (2010) "Corporate con game: how the private prison industry helped shape Arizona's anti immigrant law." *In These Times*. Available from: <http://www.inthesetimes.com/article/6084/corporate_con_game>; August 20, 2012.

Hooks, G. (1990) "The rise of the Pentagon and US state building: the defense program as industrial policy." *American Journal of Sociology* 96: 358–404.

Hooks, G. (1991) *Forging the Military-Industrial Complex: World War II's Battle of the Potomac*. Urbana, Illinois: University of Illinois Press.

Horne, G. (2008) *The End of Empires: African Americans and India*. Philadelphia, PA: Temple University Press.

Howell, L. (2013) "Global risks 2013 [8th edition]." *World Economic Forum*. Available from: <http://www3.weforum.org/docs/WEF_GlobalRisks_Report_2013.pdf>; August 15, 2013.

Human Rights Watch. (2011) *World Report 2011, Country Summary: United States*. Available from: <http://www.hrw.org/sites/default/files/related_material/United%20States.pdf>; July 15, 2013.

Ignatieff, M. (ed.). (2009) *American Exceptionalism and Human Rights*. Princeton, NJ: Princeton University Press.

Hynes, M. (2012) "Sociology, health data, and health equity: one state agency as a site of social change." *Current Sociology* 60 (March): 161–77.

Immergluck, D. (2004) *Credit to the Community: Community Reinvestment and Fair Lending Policy in the United States*. Armonk, NY: M.E. Sharpe, Inc.

Intergovernmental Panel on Climate Change (IPCC). (2013) *Fifth Assessment Report [AR5], Climate Change 2013: The Physical Science Basis*. Available from: <http://www.ipcc.ch/report/ar5/wg1/#.UkyYYhYoqAE>; September 20, 2013.

In the Public Interest. (2013) "Criminal: how lockup quotas and 'low-crime taxes' guarantee profits for private prison corporations." Available from: <http://www.inthepublicinterest.org/article/criminal-how-lockup-quotas-and-low-crime-taxes-guarantee-profits-private-prison-corporations>; August 15, 2013.

International Human Rights and Conflict Resolution Clinic (Stanford Law School) and Global Justice Clinic (NYU School of Law). (2012) *Living under Drones: Death, Injury, and Trauma to Civilians from U.S. Drone Practices in Pakistan*. Available from: <http://www.livingunderdrones.org/wp-content/uploads/2013/10/Stanford-NYU-Living-Under-Drones.pdf>; July 15, 2013.

References

Ishay, M. R. (2008) *The History of Human Rights: From Ancient Times to the Globalization Era*. Berkeley, CA: University of California Press.

Jackson, M. I. (2008) *Model City Blues: Urban Space and Organized Resistance in New Haven*. Philadelphia, PA: Temple University Press.

Jeltsen, M. (2013) "John Lewis on Voting Rights Act: Supreme Court 'put a dagger in the heart' of the law." Available from: <http://www. huffingtonpost. com /2013/06/25/john-lewis-voting-rights-act_n_3496783.html>; June 26, 2013.

Jenkins, C. and Perrow, C. (1977) "Insurgency of the powerless: farmworkers' movements (1946–1972)." *American Sociological Review* 42: 249–68.

Jenkins, J. C. and Brents, B. G. (1989) "Social protest, hegemonic competition, and social reforms." *American Sociological Review* 54: 891–909.

Jessop, B. (1990) *State Theory: Putting the Capitalist State in its Place*. University Park, PA: Pennsylvania State University Press.

Johnstone, D. (2014) "Ukraine and Yugoslavia: when will Americans come to their senses?" *Counterpunch*. Available from: <http://www.counterpunch. org/2014/03/21/ukraine-and-yugoslavia/>; June 10, 2013.

Jones, P. (1999) "Human rights, group rights, and peoples' rights." *Human Rights Quarterly* 21(1): 80–107.

Katzenstein, M. (1995) "Discursive politics and feminist activism in the Catholic Church." In M. M. Ferree and P. Y. Martin (eds), *Feminist Organizations: Harvest of the New Women's Movement*. Philadelphia, PA: Temple University Press, pp. 35–52.

Kaufman, R. (2011) "State and local commissions as sites for domestic human rights intervention." In S. Hertel and K. Libal (eds), *Human Rights in the United States: Beyond Exceptionalism*. New York: Cambridge University Press, pp. 89–112.

Kelley, R. D. G. (1993) "We are not what we seem: rethinking black working class opposition in the Jim Crow South." *Journal of American History* 80: 75–112.

Kelley, R. D. G. (1994) *Race Rebels: Culture, Politics, and the Black Working Class*. New York: The Free Press.

Keys, Tracey and Thomas Malnight. (2013) "Corporate clout: the influence of the world's economic entities." *Global Trends*. Available from: <http:// www.globaltrends.com/images/stories/corporate%20clout%20the%20worl ds%20100%20largest%20economic%20entities.pdf>; August 25, 2013.

Kibria, Nazli. (2011) *Muslims in Motion: Islam and National Identity in the Bangladeshi Diaspora*. New Brunswick, NJ: Rutgers University Press.

Klandermans, B. (1984) "Mobilization and participation: social-psychological expansion of resource mobilization theory." *American Sociological Review* 49: 583–600.

Klandermans, B. (1988) "The formation and mobilization of consensus." *International Social Movement Research*, vol. 1, ed. Bert Klandermans, Hanspeter Kriesi, and Sidney G. Tarrow. Greenwich, CT: JAI Press.

References

Klein, N. (2000) *No Logo: Taking Aim at the Brand Bullies*. New York: Taylor and Francis.

Klein, N. (2010) *Fences and Windows: Dispatches from the Front Lines of the Globalization Debate*. Toronto, Canada: Vintage.

Klein, N. (2013) "Naomi Klein: how science is telling us all to revolt." *New Statesman*. Available from: <http://www.newstatesman.com/2013/10 /science-says-revolt>; October 29, 2013.

Knuckey, S., Glenn, K., and MacLean, E. (2012) "Suppressing protest: human rights violations in the U.S. response to Occupy Wall Street." *Protest and Assembly Rights Project*. Available from: <http://hrp.law.harvard.edu /wp-content/uploads/2013/06/suppressing-protest-2.pdf>; August 1, 2013.

Koskenniemi, M. (1991), "The future of statehood." *Harvard International Law Journal* 32: 397–410.

Kotlowitz, A. (2009) "All boarded up." *New York Times Sunday Magazine*, March 8, 28–35.

Kravets, D. (2013) "Cops can track cellphones without warrants, appeals court rules." *Wired*. Available from: <http://www.wired.com/threatlevel/2013/07 /warrantless-cell-tracking/>; August 30, 2013.

Krivo, L. and Kaufman, R. (2004) "Housing and wealth inequality: racial-ethnic differences in home equity in the United States." *Demography* 41: 585–605.

Krugman, P. (2012) *End This Depression Now!* New York: WW Norton & Co.

Kumar, R. (1997) *The History of Doing: An Illustrated Account of Movements for Women's Rights and Feminism in India 1800–1990*. New Delhi, India: Zubaan Books.

Landman, T. (2002) "Comparative politics and human rights." *Human Rights Quarterly* 24: 890–923.

Lauren, P. (1998) *The Evolution of International Human Rights*. Philadelphia, PA: Temple University Press.

Lauren, P. G. (2011) *The Evolution of International Human Rights: Visions Seen*. Philadelphia, PA: University of Pennsylvania Press.

Lawson, S. (1997) *Running for Freedom: Civil Rights and Black Politics in America Since 1941*. Boston, MA: McGraw Hill Press.

Lee, M. (2013) "Twice the trouble when couple lose jobs." *The Hartford Courant*, May 19. Available from: <http://www.mercurynews.com/business /ci_23270924/twice-trouble-when-couples-lose-jobs>; September 5, 2013.

Lenin, V. I. (1976) *The State and Revolution*. Peking, China: Foreign Languages Press.

Leonard, D. and Quely, K. (2014) "The American middle class is no longer the world's richest." *New York Times*, Available from: <http://www.nytimes. com/2014/04/23/upshot/the-american-middle-class-is-no-longer-the-worlds-richest.html?_r=0>; April 22, 2014.

Leopold, L. (2013) "The rich have gained $5.6 trillion in the 'recovery,' while the rest of us have lost $669 billion." Available from: <www.huffingtonpost.

com/ les-leopold/the-rich-have-gained-56-t_b_3237528.html>; September 5, 2013.

Levine, R. (1988) *Class Struggle and the New Deal: Industrial Labor, Industrial Capital and the State.* Lawrence, KS: University of Kansas Press.

Lewis, A. (2003) *Race in the School Yard: Negotiating the Color Line in Schools and Communities.* New Brunswick, NJ: Rutgers University Press.

Liptak, A. (2010) "Justices, 5–4, reject corporate spending limit." *The New York Times.* Available from: <http://www.nytimes.com/2010/01/22/us/politics/22scotus.html?pagewanted=1&_r=1>; August 15, 2013.

Liptak, A. (2013) "Supreme Court invalidates key part of Voting Rights Act." *The New York Times.* Available from: <http://www.nytimes.com/2013/06/26/us/supreme-court-ruling.html?_r=1&>; August 15, 2013.

Liptak, A. (2014) "Court backs Michigan on affirmative action." *New York Times.* Available from: <http://www.nytimes.com/2014/04/23/us/supreme-court-michigan-affirmative-action-ban.html>; April 22, 2014.

Lord, R. (2005) *American Nightmare: Predatory Lending and the American Dream.* Monroe, ME: Common Courage Press.

Lugar, S. (2000) *Corporate Power: American Democracy and the Automobile Industry.* New York: Cambridge University Press.

Lutz, A. (2012) "These 6 corporations control 90% of the media in America." *Business Insider.* Available from: <http://www.businessinsider.com/these-6-corporations-control-90-of-the-media-in-america-2012-6>; August 15, 2013.

Lynd, S. (2010) *From Here to There: The Staughton Lynd Reader,* ed. A. Grubacic. Oakland, CA: PM Press.

McAdam, D. (1983) "Tactical innovation and the pace of insurgency." *American Sociological Review* 48: 735–54.

McAdam D. (1997) "Conceptual and Theoretical Issues." In D. McAdam and D. Snow (1997), *Social Movements: Readings on their Emergence, Mobilization, and Dynamics.* Los Angeles, CA: Roxbury Publishing Company, pp. xviii–xxvi.

McAdam, D. and Snow, D. (1997) *Social Movements: Readings on their Emergence, Mobilization, and Dynamics.* Los Angeles, CA: Roxbury Publishing Company.

MacAdam, D., McCarthy, J. D., and Zald, M. N. (eds). (1996) *Comparative Perspectives in Social Movements: Political Opportunities, Mobilizing Structures, and Cultural Framings.* New York: Cambridge University Press, pp. 23–40.

Macalister, T. (2012) "BP's $25bn annual profit sees confidence and dividends soar." *Guardian.* Available from: <http://www.theguardian.com/business/2012/feb/07/bp-announces-25bn-annual-profit>; August 15, 2013.

McCarter, J. (2013) "Oregon becomes the 16th state to call for amendment overturning Citizens United." *Daily Kos.* Available from: <http://www.daily

References

kos.com/story/2013/07/02/1220717/-Oregon-becomes-16th-state-to-call-for-amendment-overturning-Citizens-nbsp-United#>; August 15, 2013.

McCarthy, J. and Zald, M. (1976) "Resource mobilization and social movements: a partial theory." *American Journal of Sociology* 82: 1212–41.

McConnell v. *Federal Election Commission*, 540 U.S. 93 (2003).

McCorquodale, R. and Fairbrother, R. (1999) "Globalization and human rights." *Human Rights Quarterly* 21: 735–66.

McNally, D. (2006) *Another World is Possible: Globalization and Anti-capitalism*. Winnipeg: Arbeiter Ring.

McNally, David. (2010) *Global Slump: The Economics and Politics of Crisis and Resistance*. Winnipeg, Canada: Fernwood Publishing.

Mandel, E. (1975) *Late Capitalism*. London: New Left Books.

Mandela, N. (1964) "Nelson Mandela's statement from the dock at the opening of the defense case in the Rivonia Trial." Available from: <http://www.anc.org.za/show.php?id=3430>; June 1, 2013.

Manza, J. and Uggen, C. (2008). *Locked Out: Felon Disenfranchisement and American Democracy*. Oxford: Oxford University Press.

Market Watch. (2008). Available from: <http://articles.marketwatch.com/2008-12-31/research/30779215_1_dow-gains-stock-market-dow-jones-indus trial-average>; September 5, 2013.

Marshall, G. (2013) "Global power project, part 1: exposing the transnational capitalist class." *Truthout*. Available from: <http://www.truth-out.org/news/item/16965-global-power-project-part-1-exposing-the-transnational-capital ist-class>; August 15, 2013.

Massey, D. and Denton, N. (1993) *American Apartheid*. Cambridge, MA: Harvard University Press.

Max-Neef, M. and Smith, P. B. (2011) *Economics Unmasked: From Power and Greed to Compassion and the Common Good*. Totnes, UK: Green Books.

Mayer, J. (2013) "What's the matter with metadata?" *The New Yorker Magazine*. Available from: <http://www.newyorker.com/online/blogs/newsdesk/2013/06/verizon-nsa-metadata-surveillance-problem.html>; June 7, 2013.

Meier, A. and Ruddick, E. (1973) "*CORE: A Study of the Civil Rights Movement, 1942–1968.*" New York: Oxford University Press.

Melluci, A. (1989) *Nomads of the Present: Social Movements and Individual Needs in Contemporary Society*. London: Hutchinson Press.

Mettress, C. (2002) *The Lynching of Emmett Till: A Documentary Narrative*, The American South series. Charlottesville, VA: University of Virginia Press.

Miliband, R. (1969) *The State in Capitalist Society*. New York: Basic Books.

Miliband, R. (1983) *Class Power and State Power*. London: Verso.

Mintz, B. and Schwartz, M. (1985) *The Power Structure of American Business*. Chicago, IL: University of Chicago Press.

References

Mitter, S. and Rowbotham, S. (eds). (1994) *Dignity and Daily Bread: New Forms of Economic Organization Among Poor Women*. London: Routledge.

Mkandawire, T. and Soludo, C. (2003) *African Voices on Structural Adjustment: A Companion to Our Continent, Our Future*. Dakar, Senegal: CODESERIA.

Moe, K. (2013) "Timeline of the climate movement: how direct action took center stage." *YES! Magazine*. Available from: <http://www.yesmagazine.org/planet/timeline-of-climate-movement-how-direct-action-took-center-stage>; October 1, 2013.

Moghadam, V. (2005) *Globalizing Women: Transnational Feminist Networks*. Baltimore, MD: Johns Hopkins Press.

Molloff, J. (2012) "HR 347 'Trespass Bill' criminalizes protest." *Huffington Post*. Available from: <http://www.huffingtonpost.com/jeanine-molloff/trespass-bill_b_1328205.html>; August 15, 2013.

Monshipouri, M., Welch, C., and Kennedy, E. (2003) "Multinational corporations and the ethics of global responsibility: problems and possibilities." *Human Rights Quarterly* 25: 965–89.

Morris, A. (1984) *The Origins of the Civil Rights Movement: Black Communities Organizing for Change*. New York: Free Press.

Morris, A. and Mueller, C. (1992) *Frontiers of Social Movement Theory*. New Haven, CT: Yale University Press.

Morris, L. (2006) "Sociology and rights: an emergent field." In L. Morris (ed.), *Rights: Sociological Perspectives*. New York: Knopf, pp. 1–17.

Moyn, S. (2010) *The Last Utopia: Human Rights in History*. Cambridge, MA: Belknap Press.

Mueller, C. (1994) "Conflict networks and origins of women's liberation." In E. Larana, H. Johnston, and J. Gusfield (eds), *New Social Movements: From Ideology to Identity*. Philadelphia, PA: Temple University Press, pp. 234–63.

Muzaffar, C. (2013) "Trans Pacific Partnership is a threat to national sovereignty." *Counterpunch*. Available from: <http://www.counterpunch.org/2013/07/10/trans-pacific-partnership-tpp-threat-to-national-sovereignty/>; August 15, 2013.

Nace, T. (2005) *Gangs of America: The Rise of Corporate Power and the Disabling of Democracy*. San Francisco, CA: Berrett-Koehler.

Naples, N. and Desai, M. (eds). (2002) *Women's Activism and Globalization: Linking Local Struggles and Transnational Politics*. New York: Routledge.

Narayan, A., Purkayastha, B., and Banerji, S. (2011) "Constructing virtual, transnational identities on the web: the case of Hindu student groups in the U.S. and UK." *Journal of Intercultural Studies* 32: 495–517.

National Commission on the BP Deepwater Horizon Oil Spill and Offshore Drilling Report (2010) "The use of surface and subsea dispersants during the BP Deepwater Horizon Spill." Available from: <http://media.mcclatchydc.com/smedia/2010/10/06/18/_Staff_Report_No._4.source.prod_affiliate.91.pdf>; August 15, 2013.

References

National Community Reinvestment Coalition (2007) *Income is No Shield: Against Racial Differences in Lending: A Comparison of High-Cost Lending in America's Metropolitan Areas.* Available from: <www.ncrc. org>; September 5, 2013.

Nerdwallet. (2012) "NerdWallet study: top companies paid 9% U.S. tax rate. Analysis based on data from SEC filings in 2011." Available from: <http://www.nerdwallet.com/blog/markets/2012/corporate-taxes-only-9-percent/#. UCLRyRx3bn1>; August 8, 2012.

Neubeck, K. J. (2006) *When Welfare Disappears: The Case for Economic Human Rights.* New York: Routledge.

Neubeck, K. J. and Cazenave, N. (2001) *Welfare Racism: Playing the Race Card Against America's Poor.* New York: Routledge.

Neumeister, L. (2012) "Federal judge: terror law violates 1st Amendment." *Associated Press.* Available from: <http://news.yahoo.com/federal-judge-terror-law-violates-1st-amendment-233222966.html>; June 1, 2013.

Newman, R. (2012) "The Romney and Obama tax fantasy plans." *US News and World Report.* Available from: <http://www.usnews.com/news/blogs/rick-newman/2012/08/03/the-romney-and-obama-fantasy-tax-plans/>; August 8, 2012.

New York Times (1989) "Saving units' junk bonds." July 19, D17.

Oakley, D. and Burchfield, K. (2009) "Out of the projects, still in the hood: the spatial constraints on public housing residents' relocation in Chicago." *Journal of Urban Affairs* 31: 589–614.

Obama for America. (2008) "The change we need in Washington: stop wasteful spending and curb influence of special interests so government can tackle our great challenges [press release]." Available from: <http://obama.3cdn.net/00 80cc578614b42284_2a0mvyxpz.pdf>; June 1, 2013.

Oberschall, A. (1973) *Social Conflict and Social Movements.* Englewood Cliffs, NJ: Prentice Hall.

Olsen, J. (2012) "ALEC feels the heat from anti-corporate campaigns." *Waging Nonviolence* website. Available from: <http://wagingnonviolence.org /2012/08/alec-feels-the-heat-from-anti-corporate-campaigns/>; August 8, 2012.

Opp, K. D. and Roehl, W. (1990) "Repression, micromobilization, and political protest." *Social Forces* 69: 521–47.

OXFAM. (2013) "The cost of inequality: how wealth and income extremes hurt us all [published media briefing]." Available from: <http://www.oxfa m.org/sites/www.oxfam.org/files/cost-of-inequality-oxfam-mb180113.pdf>; August 15, 2013.

Pannekoek, A. (2003) *Workers' Councils.* Oakland, CA: AK Press.

Parenti, M. (2010) *Democracy for the Few.* Boston, MA: Wadsworth.

Parenti, C. (2011) *Tropic of Chaos: Climate Change and the New Geography of Violence.* New York: Nation Books.

References

Parikh, B. (2001) *Gandhi: A Short Introduction*. Sterling Publishing Company, New York.

Parrenas, R. S. (2001) *Servants of Globalization: Women, Migration, and Domestic Work*. Stanford, CA: Stanford University Press.

Pearce, T. (2001) "Human rights and sociology: some observations from Africa." *Social Problems* 48: 48–56.

Peck, J. (2010) *Ideal Illusions*. New York: William Holt and Company.

Peck, J. (2011) *Ideal Illusions: How the US Government Co-opted Human Rights*. New York: Metropolitan Books.

Pew Charitable Trust. (2013) "Big racial divide over Zimmerman verdict: whites say too much focus on race, blacks disagree." Available from: <http://www.people-press.org/2013/07/22/big-racial-divide-over-zimmerman-verdict/>; July 30, 2013.

Pilger, J. (2013) "There's a new fascism on the rise, and the NSA leaks show us what it looks like." *Alternet*. Available from: <http://www.alternet.org/media/understanding-latest-leaks-understanding-rise-new-fascism>; June 23, 2013.

Pilkington, E. (2013) "Edward Snowden's digital 'misuse' has created problems, says Ban Ki-Moon." *Guardian*. Available from: <http://www.guardian.co.uk/world/2013/jul/03/edward-snowden-digital-misuse-ban-ki-moon>; July 8, 2013.

Piven, F. F. (2008) "Can power from below change the world?" *American Sociological Review* 73: 1–14.

Piven, Frances Fox and Cloward, Richard. (1979) *Poor People's Movements: Why They Succeed, How They Fail*. New York: Vintage Books.

Plummer, K. (2006) "Rights work: constructing lesbian, gay, and sexual rights in modern times." In L. Morris (ed.), *Rights: Sociological Perspectives*. New York: Routledge, pp. 152–67.

Poitras, L. (2013) "Miranda detention: blatant attack on press freedom." *Der Spiegel Online*. Available from: <http://www.spiegel.de/international/world/laura-poitras-on-british-attacks-on-press-freedom-and-the-nsa-affair-a-918592.html>; August 30, 2013.

Potter, W. (2011) *Green is the New Red: An Insider's Account of a Social Movement Under Siege*. San Francisco, CA: City Lights Books.

Poulantzas, N. (1969) "The problem of the capitalist state." *New Left Review* 58 (November/December): 67–78.

Poulantzas, N. (1978) *State, Power, and Socialism*. London: Verso.

Prashad, V. (2007) *The Darker Nations: A People's History of the Third World*. New York: New Press.

Prechel, H. (1990) "Steel and the state," *American Sociological Review* 55: 634–47.

Prechel, H. (2000) *Big Business and the State*. Albany, NY: State University of New York Press.

References

Price, Wayne. (2007) *The Abolition of the State: Anarchist and Marxist Perspectives.* Bloomington, IN: AuthorHouse.

Protess, B. and Silver-Greenberg, J. (2012) "HSBC to pay $1.92 billion to settle charges of money laundering." *Dealbook, The New York Times.* Available from: <http://dealbook.nytimes.com/2012/12/10/hsbc-said-to-near-1-9-billion-settlement-over-money-laundering/?_r=0>; August 15, 2013.

Pudrovska, T. and Ferree, M. M. (2004) "Global activism in 'virtual space': the European women's lobby in the network of transnational women's NGOs on the web." *Social Politics: International Studies in Gender, State and Society* 11: 117–43.

Purkayastha, B. (2005) *Negotiating Ethnicity: Second-generation South Asian Americans Traverse a Transnational World.* New Brunswick, NJ: Rutgers University Press.

Purkayastha, B. (2012) *Human Rights: Voices of World's Young Activists.* London and Kolkata: Frontpage Publications.

Purkayastha, A., Purkayastha, B., and Waring, C. (2011) "From international platforms to local yards: standing up for the elimination of racial discrimination in the United States." In W. Armaline, D. Glasberg, and B. Purkayastha (eds), *Human Rights in Our Backyard: Injustice and Resistance in the United States.* Philadelphia, PA: University of Pennsylvania Press, pp. 175–88.

Pyke, A. (2013a) "Detroit becomes largest city to declare bankruptcy." *Think Progress.* Available from: <http://thinkprogress.org/economy/2013/07/18/2326141/detroit-becomes-largest-city-to-declare-bankruptcy/>; August 15, 2013.

Pyke, A. (2013b) "Alabama bankruptcy deal calls attention to Wall Street abuses." *Think Progress.* Available from: <http://thinkprogress.org/economy/2013/06/05/2106441/alabama-bankruptcy-deal-calls-renewed-attention-to-wall-street-abuses/>; August 15, 2013.

Quadagno, J. (1984) "Welfare capitalism and the Social Security Act of 1935." *American Sociological Review* 49: 632–47.

Quadagno, Jill. (1992) "Social movements and state transformation: labor unions and racial conflict in the war on poverty." *American Sociological Review* 57: 616–34.

Quadagno, J. and Meyer, M. H. (1989) "Organized labor, state structures, and social policy development: a case study of old age assistance in Ohio, 1916–1940." *Social Problems* 36: 181–96.

Randerson, J. (2006) "World's richest 1% own 40% of all wealth, UN report discovers." *Guardian.* Available from: <http://www.theguardian.com/money/2006/dec/06/business.internationalnews>; August 15, 2013.

Reich, R. (2013) "The three biggest lies about why corporate taxes should be lowered." *RobertReich.org.* Available from: <http://robertreich.org/post/57431623768>; August 15, 2013.

References

Risse, T., Ropp, S., and Sikkink, K. (eds). (1999) *The Power of Human Rights: International Norms and Domestic Change.* Cambridge: Cambridge University Press.

Robertson, A. (2013) "New slide from leaked PRISM presentation promotes directly collecting data from servers." *The Verge.* Available from: <http://www. theverge.com/2013/6/8/4410358/leaked-slide-from-prism-presentation-supp orts-directly-collecting-data>; June 8, 2013.

Robinson, W. (2001) "Social theory and globalization: the rise of a transnational state." *Theory and Society* 30: 157–200.

Robinson, W. (2004) *A Theory of Global Capitalism: Production, Class, and the State in a Transnational World.* Baltimore, MD: Johns Hopkins University Press.

Robinson, G. and Robinson, T. (2005) "Korematsu and beyond: Japanese Americans and the origins of strict scrutiny." *Law and Contemporary Problems* 68: 29–56.

Rohricht, A. (2013a) "Secrecy, drones, prisons, and kill lists." *CounterPunch.* Available from: <http://www.counterpunch.org/2013/05/15/secrecy-drones -prisons-and-kill-lists/>; June 1, 2013.

Rohricht, A. (2013b) "What Dzokhar Tsarnaev and Bradley Manning have in common." *Counterpunch.* Available from: <http://www.counterpunch. org/2013/04/24/what-dzokhar-tsarnaev-has-to-do-with-bradley-manning/>; June 1, 2013.

Rosales, F. A. (1996) *Chicano: A History of Mexican American Civil Rights Movement.* Houston, TX: Arte Publico Press.

Rowbotham, Swasti and Sheila Mitter. (1993) *Dignity and Daily Bread.* New York: Routledge.

Said, E. (1978) *Orientalism.* New York: Vintage Books.

Sanders, B. (2013) "Democracy is for people amendment." *Website: Bernie Sanders, US Senator for VT.* Available from: <http://www.sanders. senate.gov/newsroom/recent-business/democracy-is-for-people-amendment >; August 15, 2013.

Santa Clara County v. *Southern Pacific Railroad Co.*, 118 U.S. 394 (1886).

Sassen, S. (1994) *Cities in a World Economy.* Thousand Oaks, CA: Pine Forge.

Sassen, S. (1996) *Losing Control? Sovereignty in an Age of Globalization.* New York: Columbia University Press.

Schaeffer, R. (2003) *Understanding Globalization.* Lanham, MD: Rowman and Littlefield.

Scahill, J. (2013) *Dirty Wars: The World is a Battlefield.* New York: Nation Books.

Schellnhuber, H. (2012) *Turn Down the Heat – Why a 4 C Warmer World Must Be Avoided.* The World Bank (published report).

References

Scheuermann, C. (2013) "Guardian editor: 'British more complacent' about surveillance." *Der Spiegel Online*. Available from: <http://www. spiegel.de/international/world/interview-with-guardian-editor-rusbridger-on-snowden-information-a-918059.html>; August 30, 2013.

Schmitter. P. C. (1974) "Still the century of corporatism?" *Review of Politics* 36: 85–127.

Schwartz, A. (1998) "Banking lending to minority and low-income households and neighborhoods: do community reinvestment agreements make a difference?" *Journal of Urban Affairs* 20: 269–301.

Schwartz, A. (2000) "The past and future of community reinvestment agreements." *Housing Facts and Findings* 2: 3–7.

Scott, J. (1985) *Weapons of the Weak: Everyday Forms of Peasant Resistance*. New Haven, CT: Yale University Press.

Segura, D. and Zavella, P. (2007) *Women and Migration in the U.S.-Mexico-Borderlands: A Reader*. Durham, NC: Duke University Press.

Seidenberg, S. (2008) "Homing in on foreclosure: lawyers are finding aggressive defenses against foreclosure actions. And courts are listening as never before." *The American Bar Association Journal* (July). Available from: <http://abajournal.com/magazine/homing_in_on_foreclosure/>; September 5, 2013.

Shannon, D. (2011) "Food Not Bombs: the right to eat." In W. T. Armaline, D. S. Glasberg, and B. Purkayastha (eds), *Human Rights in Our Own Back Yard: Injustice and Resistance in the United States*. Philadelphia, PA: University of Pennsylvania Press, pp. 49–56.

Shannon, D. and Asimakopoulos, J. (eds). (2012) *The Accumulation of Freedom: Writings on Anarchist Economics*. Oakland, CA: AK Press.

Shannon, D. and Rogue, J. (2009) "Refusing to wait: anarchism and intersectionality. *Anarkismo.*" Available from: <http://www.anarkismo.net /article/14923>; July 16, 2013.

Shiffman, J. and Cooke, K. (2013) "Exclusive: U.S. directs agents to cover up program used to investigate Americans." *Reuters*. Available from: <http:// www.reuters.com/article/2013/08/05/us-dea-sod-idUSBRE97409R2013 0805>; August 30, 2013.

Shiva, V. (2000) *Stolen Harvest: The Hijacking of the Global Food Supply*. Boston, MA: South End Press.

Shiva, V. (2001) *Water Wars*. Boston, MA: South End Press.

Shiva, V. (2008) *Soil Not Oil*. Boston, MA: South End Press.

Shlay, A. (1999) "Influencing the agents of urban structure: evaluating the effects of community reinvestment organizing on bank residential lending practices." *Urban Affairs Review* 35: 247–78.

Sjoberg, G., Gill, E. A., and Williams, N. (2001). "A sociology of human rights." *Social Problems* 48: 11–47.

References

Skahill, J. (2013) *Dirty Wars: The World is a Battlefield*. New York: Nation Books.

Skocpol, T. (1985) "Bringing the state back in: strategies of analysis in current research." In P. B. Evans, D. Rueschemeyer, and T. Skocpol (eds), *Bringing the State Back In*. Cambridge: Cambridge University Press, pp. 3–37.

Skocpol, T. (1992) *Protecting Soldiers and Mothers: The Political Origins of Social Policy in the United States*. Cambridge, MA: Harvard University Press.

Skocpol, T. and Ikenberry, J. (1983) "The political formation of the American welfare state in historical and comparative perspective." *Comparative Social Research* 6: 87–148.

Slater, A. (2012) "Voter ID laws: the republican ruse to disenfranchise 5 million Americans." *Guardian*. Available from: <http://www.theguardian.com /commentisfree/2012/aug/10/voter-id-laws-republican-ruse-disenfranchise>; August 15, 2013.

Smelser, N. (1962) *Theory of Collective Behavior*. New York: Free Press of Glencoe.

Smiley, T. and West, C. (2012) *The Rich and the Rest of Us*. New York: Smiley Books.

Smith, D. (2005) *Institutional Ethnography: A Sociology for People*. Walnut Creek, CA: AltaMira Press.

Smith, P. and Max-Neef, M. (2011) *Economics Unmasked: From Power and Greed to Compassion and the Common Good*. London: Green Books.

Snow, D. and Benford, R. (1988) "Ideology, frame resonance and participant mobilization." In B. Klandermans, H. Kreisi, and S. Tarrow (eds), *Structure to Action: Social Movement Participation Across Cultures*. Greenwich, CT: Jai Press.

Snow, D. and Oliver, P. (1995) "Social movements and collective behavior: social psychological dimensions and considerations." In K. Cook, G. Fine, and J. House (eds), *Sociological Perspectives in Social Psychology*. Boston, MA: Allyn and Bacon, pp. 571–99.

Snow, D., Zurcher, L, and Ekland-Olson, S. (1980) "Social networks and social movements: a microstructural approach to differential recruitment." *American Sociological Review* 45: 787–801.

Squires, G. (ed.). (1992) *From Redlining to Reinvestment: Community Responses to Urban Disinvestment*. Philadelphia, PA: Temple University Press.

Squires, G. (ed.). (2003) *Organizing Access to Capital: Advocacy and Democratization of Financial Institutions*. Philadelphia, PA: Temple University Press.

St John, P. (2013) "U.N. torture investigator seeks access to California prisons." *Los Angeles Times*. Available from: <http://articles.latimes.com/2013/ oct/18/local/la-me-ff-un-torture-investigator-seeks-access-to-california-pris ons-20131018>; October 20, 2013.

References

Stammers, N. (1999) "Social movements and the social construction of human rights." *Human Rights Quarterly* 21: 980–1008.

Stewart, K. (2013) "The right wing donors who fuel America's culture wars." *Guardian*. Available from: <http://www.theguardian.com/commentis free/2013/apr/23/rightwing-donors-fuel-america-culture-wars>; February 15, 2014.

Stiglitz, J. E. (2012) *The Price of Inequality: How Today's Divided Society Endangers Our Future*. New York: WW Norton & Co.

Stiglitz, J. (2013) "So-called free trade talks should be in the public, not corporate interests." *Guardian*. Available from: <http://www.theguardi an.com/business/economics-blog/2013/jul/05/free-trade-talks-public-corpo rate-interest>; August 15, 2013.

Strum, P. (2010) *Mendez vs. Westminister: School Desegregation and Mexican American Rights*. Lawrence, KS: University Press of Kansas.

Sturgis, S. (2013) "North Carolina turns back the clock on voting rights." Available from: <http://www.southernstudies.org/2013/07/naacp-links-pro posed-nc-voting-changes-to-historic.html>; July 27, 2013.

Swenson, P. A. (2002) *Capitalists Against Markets: The Making of Labor Markets and Welfare States in the United States and Sweden*. New York: Oxford University Press.

Taibbi, M. (2011) *Griftopia: A Story of Bankers, Politicians, and the Most Audacious Power Grab in American History*. New York: Spiegel & Grau.

Taibbi, M. (2013) "Everything is rigged: the biggest price-fixing scandal ever." *Rolling Stone* (April 25); Available from: <www.rollingstone.com /politics/news/everything-is-rigged-the-biggest-financial-scandal-ever.html>; September 15, 2013.

Tarrow, S. (1983) *Struggling to Reform: Social Movements and Policy Changes During Cycles of Protest*. Western Societies Occasional Paper. No 15. Ithaca, NY: Center for International Studies, Cornell University.

Tarrow, S. (1994) *Power in Movement: Social Movements, Collective Action and Politics*. New York: Cambridge University Press.

Taylor, V. and Whittier, N. (1992) "Collective identity in social movement communities: lesbian feminist mobilization." In A. Morris and C. M. Mueller (eds), *Frontiers in Social Movement Theory*. New Haven, CT: Yale University Press, pp. 104–30.

Temkin, K., Johnson, J., and Levy, D. (2002) *Subprime Markets, the Role of GSEs, and Risk-based Pricing*. Washington, DC: Urban Institute and the U.S. Department of Housing and Urban Development, Office of Policy Development and Research.

Thompson, G. (2012) "How students in San Jose raised the minimum wage." *The Nation*. Available from: <http://www.thenation.com/article/171510 /how-students-san-jose-raised-minimum-wage#>; August 15, 2013.

References

Tilly, C. (1978) *From Mobilization to Revolution*. New York: Random House.

Touraine, A. (1985) "An introduction to the study of social movements." *Social Research* 52: 749–87.

Travis, A., Osborne, L., and Davies, L. (2013) "World leaders seek answers on U.S. collection of communication data." *Guardian*. Available from: <http://www.guardian.co.uk/world/2013/jun/10/european-reaction-us-surveillance-revelations>; June 10, 2013.

Tsesis, A. (2008) *We Shall Overcome: The History of Civil Rights and Law*. New Haven, CT: Yale University Press.

Turner, B. S. (1993) "Outline of a theory of human rights." *Sociology* 27: 489–512.

Turner, B. S. (2006) *Vulnerability and Human Rights*. University Park, PA: Pennsylvania State University Press.

Turner, J. (2013) "'Take back the streets': repression and criminalization of protest around the world." *International Network of Civil Liberties Organizations [INCLO]*. Available from: <https://www.aclu.org/sites/default/ files/assets/global_protest_suppression_report_inclo.pdf>; October 4, 2013.

Turning Left. (2008) "Sheriff Tom Dart sees the faces of the evicted." Oct. 9. Available from: <http://www.turningleft.net/2008/10/sheriff-tom-dart-sees-the-faces-of-the-evicted/>; September 5, 2013.

Uggen, C. and Manza, J. (2002) "Democratic contraction? Political consequences of felon disenfranchisement in the United States." *American Sociological Review* 67(6): 777–803.

United Nations General Assembly resolution 217 A (III), December 10, 1948, p. 72. Available from: <http://www.ohchr.org/en/udhr/pages/introduction.aspx>; May 1, 2012.

Urie, R. (2013). "The NSA and that 1970's show." *Counterpunch*. Available from: <http://www.counterpunch.org/2013/07/05/the-nsa-and-that-1970s-show/>; August 1, 2013.

US Census Statistical Abstracts. (2008–13) Available from: <http://www.census.gov>; September 5, 2013.

US CERD report (2007) "Periodic report of the United States of America to the UN Committee on elimination of all types of racial discrimination." Available from: <www.state.gov/documents/organization/83517.pdf >; May 9, 2009.

US Congress: House of Representatives. (1979) Committee on Banking, Finance, and Urban Affairs, Subcommittee on Economic Stabilization. *The Chrysler Corporation Financial Situation*. 96th Congress, 1st Session. Washington, DC: Government Printing Office.

US Congress: House of Representatives. (1989) Committee on Banking, Finance, and Urban Affairs, Subcommittee on General Oversight and Investigations.

References

Junk Bonds: 1988 Status Report. 100th Congress, 2nd Session. Washington, DC: Government Printing Office.

US Congress: House of Representatives. (1989) Committee on Banking, Finance, and Urban Affairs, Subcommittee on General Oversight and Investigations. *Junk Bonds: 1988 Status Report.* 100th Congress, 2nd Session. Washington, DC: Government Printing Office.

US Congress: House of Representatives. (1990) Committee on Banking, Finance, and Urban Affairs, General Oversight and Investigations. *Financial Institution Reform, Recovery, and Enforcement Act of 1989, FIRREA, and its Impact on the Federal Home Loan Bank System.* 101st Congress, 2nd Session. Washington, DC: Government Printing Office.

US Department of Housing and Urban Development. (2000) "Unequal burden: Income and racial disparities in subprime lending in America." Available from: <http://www.huduser.org/publications/fairhsg/unequal.html>; October 31, 2006.

Useem, M. (1984) *The Inner Circle.* New York: Oxford University Press.

Valocchi, S. (1989) "The relative autonomy of the state and the origins of British welfare policy." *Sociological Forum* 4: 349–65.

Vitali, S., Glattfelder, J. B., and Battiston, S. (2011) "The network of global corporate control." *PLoS ONE,* (6)1. Available from: <http://www.plosone.org/article/info%3Adoi%2F10.1371%2Fjournal.pone.0025995>; August 20, 2013.

Wallach, L. (2012) "NAFTA on steroids." *The Nation.* Available from: <http://www.thenation.com/article/168627/nafta-steroids#>; August 15, 2013.

Waters, M. (1996) "Human rights and the universalization of interests: Towards a social constructivist approach." *Sociology* 30: 593–600.

Watkins, A., Landy, J., and Taylor, M. (2014) "CIA's use of harsh interrogation went beyond legal authority, Senate report says." *McClatchy DC.* Available from: <http://www.mcclatchydc.com/2014/04/11/224085/cias-use-of-harsh-interrogation.html>; April 12, 2014.

Weinstein, J. (1968) *The Corporate Ideal in the Liberal State, 1900–1918.* Boston, MA: Beacon Press.

Weiser, W. and Norden, L. (2012) "Voting law changes in 2012." *Brennan Center for Justice.* Available from: <http://www.brennancenter.org/sites/default/files/legacy/Democracy/VRE/Brennan_Voting_Law_V10.pdf>; August 1, 2013.

Wexler, S. (1993) *The Civil Rights Movement: An Eye Witness History.* New York: Facts on File.

White, J. (1990) *Black Leadership in America: From Booker T. Washington to Jesse Jackson.* London: Pearson.

Whitt, J. A. (1979) "Toward a class dialectic model of power: an empirical assessment of three competing models of political power." *American Sociological Review* 44: 81–100.

References

Whitt, J. A. (1982) *The Dialectics of Power: Urban Elites and Mass Transportation.* Princeton, NJ: Princeton University Press.

Wilson, C. A. (1996) *Racism: From Slavery to Advanced Capitalism.* New York: Sage.

Wilson, R. A. (1997) "Human rights culture and context: an introduction." In R. A. Wilson (ed.), *Human Rights, Culture, and Context: Anthropological Perspectives.* London: Pluto, pp. 1–27.

Wilson, R. A. (2001) *The Politics of Truth and Reconciliation in South Africa: Legitimizing the Post Apartheid State.* Cambridge: Cambridge University Press.

Wilson, R. A. (2006) Afterword to "Anthropology and human rights in a new key: the social life of human rights." *American Anthropologist* 108: 38–51.

Witte, E. E. (1972) "Organized labor and Social Security." In M. Derber and E. Young (eds), *Labor and the New Deal.* New York: DeCapo Press, pp. 241–74.

Woodiwiss, A. (2005) *Human Rights.* New York: Routledge.

Wright, E. O. (1978). *Class, Crisis, and the State.* London: Verso.

Zeitlin, M. and Ratcliff, R. E. (1975) "Research methods for the analysis of the internal structure of dominant classes: the case of landlords and capitalists in Chile." *Latin American Research Review* 10: 5–61.

Zeitlin, M., Ewen, L. A., and Ratcliff, R. E. (1974) "New princes for old? The large corporation and the capitalist class in Chile." *American Journal of Sociology* 80: 87–123.

Zinn, M. and Dill, B. (eds). (1984) *Women of Color in US Society.* Philadelphia, PA: Temple University Press.

Index

Index

Index

theories 26–46
see also business dominance
theory; instrumentalism;
state-centered structuralism
transnational state 132, 180 n.11
see also government; capitalist state
state-centered structuralism 38–40
Stonewall Riots 118, 179 n.4
structural adjustment programs 12, 47
Student Non-violent Coordinating
Committee 96, 98–9, 101–2,
108, 177
see also civil rights organizations
submerged resistance 96
subprime lending 57–9, 74
substantive rights 81, 87, 89, 175 n.2
surveillance program(s) 150, 156–8,
160

TARP *See* Troubled Asset Relief
Program
Tarrow, S. 85–6
Taylor Law 32
TCC *See* transnational capitalist class
TNC *See* transnational corporation
torture 1–2, 23, 151, 154
TPP *See* Trans-Pacific Partnership
transnational capitalist class 131
Trans-Pacific Partnership 133–4
"trickle-down economics" 21
Troubled Asset Relief Program 28,
33, 140

UDHR *See* Universal Declaration of
Human Rights

United Negro Improvement
Association 100
see also civil rights organizations
Universal Declaration of Human
Rights 5, 23, 91, 93–4, 105,
116–19, 176 n.7, 177 n.19, 179
n.3, 179–80 n.5
Universal Declaration Model 119,
179 n.5
UN Charter 118–19, 146
UN Security Council 123
US Federal Reserve Bank 21
US Human Rights Network 106
US Securities and Exchange
Commission 28–9
US Treasury Department 28

voter ID laws 140–1

war on women 141–2
Waring, C. 179 n.28
wealth disparity/inequality 38,
130–1
whistleblowers 158, 160–1
Woodiwiss A. 4
working class 21, 33, 41, 43, 176
n.12
World Bank 47, 63, 70, 132, 180
n.11
World Trade Organization 9, 47,
132–3, 135, 143, 163, 180 n.11
WTO *See* World Trade Organization

Zapatista movement 141, 180 n.6
Zero Dark Thirty 2